"An invaluable resource."

Bruce D. Perry, MD, PhD, *principal,*
The Neurosequential Network, Houston, Texas, USA

"Based on her vast clinical experience with abused and traumatized children, Kenney-Noziska has assembled an impressive group of top experts in the field to write the definitive guide to understanding the clinical needs of sexually abused children and how the therapeutic powers of play facilitate their healing. An essential resource for all play therapists to expand their depth of knowledge and practice and improve the care of sexually abused children!"

Sue C. Bratton, PhD, *LPC-S, RPT-S, professor*
emerita and director emerita, Center for Play Therapy,
University of North Texas, USA

"This book reads like a who's who of renowned play therapists whose extensive wisdom is collectively shared. This is an exquisite, much-needed, and thorough volume that extensively covers all the critical aspects of childhood sexual abuse treatment. Readers are taken on a journey from treatment needs, theoretical and ethical frameworks, to crucial self-care of the therapist, with all other areas imaginable in-between. This is an important, must-have book for your clinical toolbox given the ever-growing epidemic of childhood sexual abuse."

Athena A. Drewes, PsyD, MA, MS Ed, *founder and past president*
of the New York Association for Play Therapy and former director of the
Association for Play Therapy

"An excellent and much-needed volume. Victims of childhood sexual abuse experience both intense emotional and physical betrayal at the hands of those who sexually offend. Therapists can find themselves reacting by maintaining too much distance from the child and their pain for fear of reactivating the trauma of that betrayal. This text reminds therapists of the need to address these children's need for emotional closeness, physical safety and, most of all, to reestablish their ability to play and have fun."

Kevin O'Connor, PhD, *ABPP, RPT-S,*
board certified in clinical child and adolescent psychology and director
of the Academy for Development of Ecosystemic Play Therapy (ADEPT)

PLAY THERAPY AND CHILDHOOD SEXUAL ABUSE

Play Therapy and Childhood Sexual Abuse is a comprehensive guide for mental health clinicians and play therapists who work with the victims of childhood sexual abuse. Chapters cover seminal and historically significant models of play therapy, burgeoning practices, and much more.

Clinical case examples of each play therapy approach are included in the chapters. The contributing authors are established leaders in using play therapy with sexually abused children and adolescents. This is a vital guide for clinicians using play therapy to help young people heal.

Sueann Kenney-Noziska, MSW, LCSW, RPT-S, specializes in using play therapy in clinical practice with sexually abused children and adolescents. She is an esteemed clinician, author, presenter, and expert witness.

PLAY THERAPY AND CHILDHOOD SEXUAL ABUSE

A CLINICAL GUIDE TO PRACTICE

EDITED BY SUEANN KENNEY-NOZISKA

Routledge
Taylor & Francis Group

NEW YORK AND LONDON

Designed cover image: Getty Images

First published 2026
by Routledge
605 Third Avenue, New York, NY 10158

and by Routledge
4 Park Square, Milton Park, Abingdon, Oxon, OX14 4RN

Routledge is an imprint of the Taylor & Francis Group, an informa business

DOI: 10.4324/9781003451549

ISBN: 978-1-032-58644-1 (hbk)
ISBN: 978-1-032-58639-7 (pbk)
ISBN: 978-1-003-45154-9 (ebk)

Typeset in Galliard
by Apex CoVantage, LLC

To my three moms
Betty, Bonnie, and Jennifer
Strong women raise strong women.

Contents

FOREWORD

It is discordant that "Play" and "Childhood Sexual Abuse" should be in the same phrase; childhood sexual abuse (CSA) is a fundamentally destructive experience, while play is a primary driver of health and wellness throughout life. In childhood, sexual abuse – in its many "forms" – delays, distorts, devastates, and destroys physical, social, emotional, and cognitive growth. In contrast, play provides complex, multidimensional opportunities for curiosity and repetition, which lead to mastery in all domains of functioning. The permeating qualities of CSA are fear, unpredictability, confusion, and helplessness; permeating qualities of play are agency – choice, predictability, control, and pleasure. Play is rewarding, and often, outright fun. Sexual abuse exploits a power differential and distorts and ruptures relational connection; play provides repetitive, reciprocal relational interactions which build "connectivity." Sexual abuse can impair future capacity for forming and maintaining healthy relationships; play helps build the basic capacities that make future relational engagement easier and relational bonds more enduring. Play integrates; CSA disintegrates.

So, in order to make "Play" and "Childhood Sexual Abuse" harmonious in the same phrase, add "therapy." Play has unique, positive qualities that counter-balance the negative impacts of CSA; this makes the therapeutic use of play so sensible. Play therapies are uniquely powerful due to their capacity to provide developmentally sensitive and flexible reparative experiences, which are needed to address the complex needs of CSA survivors. Play therapy can provide targeted doses of therapeutic experience tailored to the unique needs of each child. The developmental flexibility and multi-system "activations" (i.e., physical, social, emotional, and cognitive) that are possible with play therapies are very hard to replicate with most of the other focused therapeutic modalities (e.g., pharmacotherapy and cognitive behavioral therapy). The range of play "therapies" presented in this book speaks to this flexibility.

Play has therapeutic qualities, and many of the healing experiences in individuals following trauma and adversity take place outside the context of formal "therapy." In fact, most of the healing following CSA is outside the context of therapy; most individuals who experience CSA never have any formal therapy, and while they carry the effects of those experiences, they often find their way to safe, stable, and healthy lives. Many of these healing individuals have found sport, music, dance, and a caring community as a primary source of belonging and "pleasure" – play and playfulness are part of that therapeutic journey. The value of formal therapy in this process is to enrich and "center"" therapeutic activities and experiences that can lead to a larger set of options for the healing child, youth, or adult. There is value in having a "Sherpa" – an experienced guide who can help carry the load on a difficult healing journey. That is where this book comes in.

Play Therapy and Childhood Sexual Abuse: A Clinical Guide to Practice, edited by Sueann Kenney-Noziska, is an invaluable resource for those therapeutic "Sherpas" seeking to deepen their understanding and refine their skills in using play therapy to address CSA. It offers a comprehensive exploration of the theoretical foundations, practical applications, and emerging models of play therapy, all grounded in the latest research and clinical expertise. The contributors to this volume bring a wealth of knowledge and experience, presenting evidence-based and research-informed strategies and creative interventions. Each author highlights the therapeutic relationship, focusing on the role of the therapist's presence, attunement, and cultural humility in creating a safe and trusting environment. There are many therapeutic "approaches" presented, but all of them seek to provide culturally responsive care that honors the individuality of each child and family.

Play Therapy and Childhood Sexual Abuse provides the reader with not only a wealth of knowledge but also a profound sense of hope. These authors remind us that even in the face of profound trauma, children possess an innate capacity for healing and growth. This alone makes this book a valuable addition to any therapist's library.

Bruce D. Perry, MD, PhD
Principal, The Neurosequential Network
Houston, Texas, USA; Professor (Adjunct),
School of Allied Health, Human Services and Sport
La Trobe University, Melbourne, Victoria, Australia

PREFACE

This text is intended to serve as an overview and guide for clinicians working with children and adolescents who have been impacted by childhood sexual abuse (CSA). Given that CSA is a worldwide epidemic, it is crucial that therapists working with victims are well-equipped with an understanding of the use of play therapy in treatment for children and adolescents who are victims of this abuse. When I was a novice clinician, a resource bringing together different theories of play therapy as well as information on the nuances of this work would have been invaluable. I am hopeful this text will meet this need.

Part I of the text, "An Overview of Childhood Sexual Abuse and Play Therapy," addresses frontline concepts regarding using play therapy when addressing the sequelae of CSA. These concepts will help clinicians understand the scope of the problem and the clinical needs of victims. Readers will also learn about the crucial concept of therapeutic presence and its essential role in play therapy with victims of CSA. The impact of traumatic events such as CSA on the developing brain and the role of the therapeutic powers of play in treatment are discussed.

Part II, "Applications of Seminal and Historically Significant Play Therapy Theories in Treating Childhood Sexual Abuse," explores clinical applications of seminal and historic play therapy theories in the treatment of CSA. These theories, which have been delineated by the Association for Play Therapy (APT), are presented in alphabetical order. Each theory's primary constructs are discussed, and each chapter includes a review of the literature supporting its approach with victims of CSA, a case example, limitations of the approach when working with victims of CSA, and key takeaways for the therapist.

Given that the field of play therapy is evolving, Part III of the text, "Applications of Burgeoning Models in Treating Childhood Sexual Abuse," covers the use of emerging approaches of play therapy that are used in treatment with victims of CSA. These models are presented in alphabetical order. Each chapter outlines the specific play therapy model's constructs as well as professional literature that supports its use with victims of CSA, a case example, limitations of the approach, and key takeaways for the clinician.

In the final section of the book, Part IV "Additional Considerations When Using Play Therapy With Sexually Abused Children and Adolescents," topics presented include culture and diversity, ethical considerations, self-care, and professional development. These chapters are intended to facilitate the development of well-rounded clinicians who are equipped to provide treatment to vulnerable, often marginalized, victims impacted by CSA. This section highlights the importance of possessing nuanced skills beyond knowledge of play therapy theories to provide quality care to victims of CSA.

Each chapter is written by well-known, established play therapists in the field. Their contributions to this text are invaluable. I am hopeful this text will serve as an important contribution to the field and assist therapists in providing the best possible treatment for those impacted by CSA.

About the Editor

Sueann Kenney-Noziska, MSW, LCSW, RPT-S, is a Licensed Clinical Social Worker and Registered Play Therapist Supervisor specializing in clinical practice with abused, maltreated, and traumatized children, adolescents, and their families. She has over 20 years of clinical experience, owns and operates her private practice, and is part of her community's multidisciplinary team (MDT) on child abuse. Sueann serves on the National Center for Missing and Exploited Children's Family Advocacy & Outreach Network and the Association for Play Therapy's Board of Directors. She is the former clinical director of Dona Ana County's Children's Advocacy Center (Las Cruces, NM). In addition, she has served as adjunct faculty at New Mexico State University (NMSU) and the University of California San Diego (UCSD).

Sueann is internationally recognized for her work, consistently presents at the major child abuse and maltreatment conferences throughout the United States, and has presented across the globe including places such as Japan, China, Jamaica, Estonia, and England. She has developed many trauma-informed interventions for clinical work with abused and traumatized children and adolescents, is a contributing author to multiple publications, and has testified as an expert witness in child abuse and trauma at both state and federal levels. Sueann serves on the International Society for the Prevention of Child Abuse and Neglect's (ISPCAN's) working group on child sexual victimization, exploitation, and trafficking, and participates in the American Professional Society on the Abuse of Children's (APSAC) children's mental health section group.

Sueann received her Bachelor of Science in psychology from the University of South Dakota (1993) and her Master of Social Work from San Diego State University (1998). She is independently licensed to provide clinical social work in New Mexico, California, and South Dakota.

CONTRIBUTORS

Kadesha Adelakun, LCSW, RPT-S™, PMH-C, The Journey Counseling Services, Kennesaw, Georgia. Kadesha Adelakun is a licensed clinical social worker (LCSW) in the states of Georgia, New Jersey, and Florida and a Registered Play Therapist–Supervisor™ (RPT-S™). She also holds a perinatal mental health-certification (PMH-C). She is the founder and owner of The Journey Counseling Services in Kennesaw, GA, and the vice president of the Georgia Association for Play Therapy (APT). She is also a cultural and racial diversity play therapy consultant and international speaker and trainer.

Jeffrey S. Ashby, PhD, RPT-S™, Georgia State University, Atlanta, Georgia. Jeffrey S. Ashby is a professor in the Department of Counseling and Psychological Services at Georgia State University. He is the director of the GSU Play Therapy Training Institute and the codirector of the Matheny Center for the Study of Stress, Trauma, and Resilience.

Ann Beckley-Forest, LCSW, RPT-S™, Playful EMDR, Buffalo, New York. Ann Beckley-Forest, LCSW, RPT-S™, has a private practice in Buffalo, New York, where she specializes in treating trauma in younger children using a combination of play therapy and EMDR, and she writes and teaches about this integrated model as cofounder of Playful EMDR.

Felicia Carroll, LMFT and RPT-S™, West Coast Institute for Gestalt Therapy with Children and Adolescents, LLC, Private Practice, Solvang, California. Felica Carroll is in private practice in California. She is the founder-director of the West Coast Institute for Gestalt Therapy with Children and Adolescents, LLC. She is an international trainer and writer on Gestalt Therapy with children. Early in her career, she practiced for four years in a community agency focused on the treatment of child sexual abuse trauma.

Angela M. Cavett, PhD, LP, RPT-S™, Chrysalis Behavioral Health Service and Training, Fargo, North Dakota. Dr Angela Cavett is clinical director, licensed psychologist, and RPT-S™ at Chrysalis Behavioral Health Services and Training Center. She is a sought-after speaker and author and provides supervision in play therapy. She is certified in Theraplay and TF-CBT. She developed the Integrative Attachment Informed Model (IAIM).

H. M. Cowart, MS, NCC, Georgia State University, Atlanta, Georgia. H. M. Cowart is a doctoral student in counseling psychology at Georgia State University. Hannah's research and clinical focuses include stress, trauma, veteran mental health, rural mental health, and issues related to sexual, gender, and relationally diverse populations.

David A. Crenshaw, PhD, ABPP, RPT-S™, retired chief of clinical services, Children's Home of Poughkeepsie, Poughkeepsie, New York. David A. Crenshaw, PhD, ABPP. RPT-S™ is the retired chief of clinical services of the Children's Home of Poughkeepsie. He is a Board-certified clinical psychologist and author. His latest book, *Play Therapy: Theory, Research and Practice* (Guilford, 2025), is coedited with Anne Stewart and Dee Ray. He has published widely in peer-reviewed journals on child abuse and trauma, resilience, and child and adolescent psychotherapy.

Richard L. Gaskill, EdD, LCPC, RPT-S™, Wichita State University, Wichita, Kansas. Dr. Richard L. Gaskill retired from community mental health after 47. He has taught at Wichita State University for 30 years. He was a Child Trauma Academy fellow, is in the Wichita State University Hall of Fame, and was awarded the Lifetime Achievement Award from APT. He has published and lectured regarding the neuroscience of trauma and play therapy in the USA, Canada, and Australia.

Eliana Gil, PhD, LMFT, RPT-S™, ATR, senior clinical consultant and cofounder, Gil Institute for Trauma Recovery and Education, Fairfax, Virginia. Eliana Gil, PhD, LMFT, is a founder/partner and senior clinical director of Gil Institute for Trauma Recovery and Education in Fairfax, VA. She has worked in the field of child abuse prevention and treatment since 1973 and has written chapters and books on these subjects. She has also provided training on the use of play therapy and other expressive therapies for helping children process traumatic experiences. Dr Gil provides training nationally and internationally.

Daire Gilmartin, Psychol., Ps.S.I., BA (Hons), Grad. Dip., MSc., DPsych. <u>Oak Tree Therapy, Raheny, Dublin 5, Ireland.</u> Daire Gilmartin is a chartered counseling psychologist, a doctor of psychotherapy, and a certified filial therapist-supervisor-instructor from Dublin, Ireland. Daire has over 20 years of clinical experience working with adults and children who have suffered maltreatment and abuse. His experience includes work in specialist child sexual abuse service; alternative care services; and counseling services for adults who experienced childhood abuse. He is a founding board member of the International Institute for Filial Therapy Professional Education (IIFTPE).

Paris Goodyear-Brown, LCSW, RPT-S™, Creator of TraumaPlay™; Executive Director, TraumaPlay Institute; Clinical Director, Nurture House, Franklin, Tennessee. Paris Goodyear-Brown, LCSW, RPT-S™, is the creator of TraumaPlay™, the executive director of the TraumaPlay Institute, the clinical director of Nurture House, and a guest lecturer with Vanderbilt University. She is a TED Talk speaker, an internationally renowned presenter, a master clinician, and a prolific writer. Her latest books include *Trauma and Play Therapy*, *Parents as Partners in Child Therapy*, *Polyvagal Power in the Playroom*, and *Big Behaviors in Small Containers*.

Linda E. Homeyer, PhD, LPC-S, RPT-S™, RST-C/T, Texas State University, Canyon Lake, Texas. Dr Linda E. Homeyer is a distinguished professor emerita at Texas State University and director emerita with the APT. She serves as APT's representative on the board of directors of the International Consortium for Play Therapy Associations. She is also editor of the World Journal for Sand Therapy Practice. Linda publishes extensively on play therapy and sand therapy, including books, chapters, and journal articles. She continues to teach nationally and internationally.

Hannah Pellegrino Jarrett, MA, EdS, Secure Child & Virginia Attachment Center, Charlottesville, Virginia. Hannah Pellegrino Jarrett is a resident in counseling at the Secure Child & Virginia Attachment Center in Charlottesville, VA. She received an MA and an EdS degree in clinical mental health counseling from James Madison University. Hannah has coauthored book chapters and presented on applications of attachment theory in play therapy, nature-based play therapy interventions, and working with child refugees. Her clinical interests include attachment theory, interpersonal neurobiology, play therapy, and working with multi-stressed children and families.

Sueann Kenney-Noziska, MSW, LCSW, RPT-S™, private practice, Las Cruces, New Mexico. Sueann Kenney-Noziska is an esteemed, internationally recognized clinician, author, and presenter who is well known for her work in the child abuse field. She maintains a private practice and is an expert witness at the state and federal levels. Sueann serves on her community's multidisciplinary team (MDT) on child abuse and the APT's board of directors.

Elizabeth Konrath, licensed professional counselor (LPC), RPT-S™, Healing Together, PLLC, Boulder, Colorado. Elizabeth is a certified Theraplay® therapist and a Registered Play Therapist™. She spent five years in community mental health before moving into private practice. Elizabeth specializes in working with children, adolescents, and families whose lives are affected by physical abuse, sexual abuse, family violence, neglect, bullying, and attachment issues. Elizabeth values the importance of working with the whole family system to heal from trauma, improve mental wellness, and adjust to changes in the family dynamic.

Terry Kottman, PhD, LMHC, NCC, RPT-S™, League of Extraordinary Adlerian Play Therapists, Cedar Falls, Iowa. Terry Kottman developed the Adlerian play therapy. She founded the League of Extraordinary Adlerian Play Therapists in 2018. She is coauthor of *Doing Play Therapy: From Building the Relationship to Facilitating Change* and *Partners in Play: An Adlerian Approach to Play Therapy*, and co-author of *Play Therapy: Basics and Beyond.*

J.P. Lilly, MSW, LCSW (deceased), Sierra Counseling Associates, Provo, Utah. John Paul "Chief" Lilly, the founder of Bikers Against Child Abuse (BACA), passed away in June 2024. JP was a renowned therapist, specializing in Jungian play therapy, and taught at Brigham Young University (BYU). He is the recipient of the Lifetime Achievement Award from APT and was a treasured colleague and friend who left an enduring mark on the field.

Marshall Lyles, LMFT-S, LPC-S, RPT-S™, The Workshop, Austin, Texas. Marshall Lyles, LMFT-S, LPC-S, RPT-S™, EMDRIA-approved consultant, has over 20 years of practice in marriage and family therapy and expressive/play therapies. Drawing on lessons learned from working with attachment trauma in a variety of settings, Marshall regularly writes on sandtray therapy and other expressive modalities and teaches around the globe.

Amber-Lea Martinez, PhD, LPC-Associate, University of North Texas, Lewisville, Texas. Dr Amber-Lea Martinez is a counselor and counselor educator based in Lewisville, Texas. Her clinical and research interests include play therapy, interpersonal trauma, and attachment disruptions. Amber-Lea specializes in play therapy with foster and adoptive families and currently volunteers for A Home Within, a national nonprofit organization that provides free counseling services to individuals who have experienced time in the foster care system.

Annie J. Monaco, LCSW, RPT-S™, Playful EMDR, Buffalo, New York. Annie J. Monaco, LCSW, RPT-S™, specializes in work with highly dissociative children and teens and offers consultation and training in EMDR, supported by play therapy and dissociation theory. She is a cofounder of Playful EMDR and author of several chapters related to this work.

Julie Blundon Nash, PhD, RPT-S™, Riverside Psychological Associates, LLC, Chester, Connecticut. Dr. Julie Blundon Nash is the owner of Riverside Psychological Associates, LLC. She is the author of *Nature-based Play Therapy: A prescriptive approach to integrating the therapeutic powers of nature and play* (Routledge, 2023) and various publications related to play therapy. Dr Nash provides continuing education training on play therapy and is on the board of directors for the APT.

Michelle M. Pliske, DSW, LCSW, RPT-S™, Pacific University, Forest Grove, Oregon. Dr Michelle M. Pliske, DSW, LCSW, RPT S™, is a leading authority in clinical social work, trauma-informed care, and play therapy. A tenured associate professor at Pacific University and Clinical Director of the Firefly Institute, she has over a decade of experience as an educator and clinician, specializing in behavioral health treatment for children and families. She is a published researcher with expertise in adverse childhood experiences and relational-cultural theory.

Dee C. Ray, PhD, LPC-S, RPT-S™, EmpathyWell, Highland Village, Texas. Dee C. Ray, PhD, LPC-S, NCC, RPT-S™, is co-owner of the counseling practice, EmpathyWell, in Highland Village, TX, where she facilitates play therapy, training, consultation, and supervision.

Dr Ray is regents emeritus professor in the counseling program and director emeritus of the Center for Play Therapy at the University of North Texas. Dr Ray has published over 150 articles, chapters, and books in the field of play therapy, specializing in child-centered play therapy research.

Bridgette Mitchell Sanders, PsyD, LCSW, RPT-S™, California State University, Los Angeles, California. Dr Bridgette Sanders is a professor in the School of Social Work at California State University, Los Angeles. She is a licensed clinician and RPT-S™ with more than 25 years of experience supporting children, adolescents, and families impacted by trauma and adverse childhood experiences. Her scholarly and clinical work integrates play therapy, neurobiological principles, and trauma-informed approaches to promote healing and resilience.

Janine Shelby, PhD, RPT-S™, University of California, Los Angeles, California State University, Long Beach, California. Janine Shelby, PhD, is an associate clinical professor at UCLA and a forensic psychology expert. She is also the founder and former director of the Child Trauma Clinic at Harbor-UCLA. From 2017 to 2018, Dr Shelby was the Drake Guest Professor and distinguished fellow at Kobe College in Japan. She was honored to receive the 2021 Sarah J. Haley Clinical Excellence Award from the International Society for Traumatic Stress Studies (ISTSS).

Sarah D. Stauffer, PhD, LPC, NCC, NCSC, RPT-S™, Psychologue-Psychothérapeute FSP, Art-thérapeute APSAT, clinical director, Espace de Soutien et de Prévention – Abus Sexuels (Association ESPAS), and private practice, Lausanne, Vaud, Switzerland. Sarah D. Stauffer, PhD, LPC, NCC, NCSC, RPT-S™, Psychologist-Psychotherapist FSP, is clinical director for the Association ESPAS, a nonprofit clinic that helps individuals and families facing sexual abuse. She counsels clients of all ages in a private practice in Lausanne, Switzerland. She has practiced and taught play therapy and has edited peer-reviewed publications for 25 years. She is coeditor of *Disenfranchised grief: Examining social, cultural, and relational impacts.*

Anne Stewart, PhD, RPT-S™, James Madison University, Harrisonburg, Virginia. Anne Stewart, PhD, is a professor emerita of graduate psychology at James Madison University and a playful practitioner of play therapy across the lifespan. Anne has coauthored a variety of books, book chapters, and articles on attachment, crisis intervention, play and family therapy, resilience, interprofessional collaboration, and supervision. She served as chair of the APT board of directors and founded the Virginia APT.

Bonnie L. Stice, MA, LPC, University of North Texas, Denton, Texas. Bonnie L. Stice, MA, is finishing a PhD in counseling at the University of North Texas. She holds an LPC license in the state of Texas. She is passionate about uplifting unheard voices, in particular through research on intimate labor, relational-cultural theory, and cultural humility.

Jessica Stone, PhD, RPT-S™, Virtual Sandtray App, Fruita, Colorado. Jessica Stone, PhD, RPT-S™, specializes in digital tools for mental health, including the innovative Virtual Sandtray App®©. Dr Stone is the past chief psychology officer for AscendantVR, is a member of various boards, and serves as an affiliate of the East Carolina University College of Education Neurocognition Science Laboratory.

Erica Tatum-Sheade, LCSW, RPT, CAdPT, CDWF, Integrated Mental Health Associates, Scottsdale, Arizona. Erica Tatum-Sheade, DSW, LCSW, RPT-S™, is an LCSW, RPT-S™, and co-owner of Integrated Mental Health Associates in Arizona. She is the author of *Layla Goes to Therapy* and the creator of the G.E.M.S.® and Rooted® empowerment programs. Her professional work integrates Adlerian play therapy, multicultural responsiveness, and empowerment-based approaches in clinical practice and supervision.

Kim Vander Dussen, PsyD, RPT-S™, The Chicago School | Anaheim, Anaheim, California. Dr Kim Vander Dussen, PsyD, RPT-S™, is a full professor at The Chicago School of Professional Psychology in Anaheim and coordinator of the child and adolescent psychology major area of study. A licensed psychologist in private practice in Placentia, she specializes in trauma, attachment, and neurodivergent youth. She is certified in EMDR, the neurosequential model of therapeutics, and circle of security parenting, and serves on the board of directors for the APT.

Risë VanFleet, PhD, Lic Psych, RPT-S™, FT-I, CDBC, CAEBI, Family Enhancement & Play Therapy Center, Inc., Boiling Springs, Pennsylvania. Risë VanFleet, PhD, RPT-S™, FT-I, CDBC, CAEBI, is a psychologist, credentialed play and filial therapist/supervisor, and certified animal ethologist/behaviorist with nearly 50 years of experience in play therapy and filial therapy. She is also the cofounder of the field of Animal Assisted Play Therapy®. She has trained thousands of professionals worldwide and is the recipient of over 20 national and international awards for her workshops and writing.

Erica Wassenaar, LMHC, NCC, RPT-S™, CAdPT-A, Touchstone Counseling, League of Extraordinary Adlerian Play Therapists, Sheldon, Iowa. Erica Wassenaar holds a master's degree in clinical mental health counseling from Wayne State College. She specializes in play therapy, more specifically Adlerian play therapy. She also holds a level-II certification in AutPlay Therapy, which is play therapy specifically for children with autism spectrum disorder. She is also trained in traumatic incident reduction, critical incident stress management. EMDR. She owns a private practice and is a member of the APT and Iowa Association of Play Therapy. Erica is also a member of the NWIA Crisis Intervention Stress Management Team, in which she leads debriefing for area first responders and law enforcement.

Holly Willard, MSW, LCSW, RPT-S™, Grandview Family Counseling, Bountiful, UT. Holly Willard, LCSW, RPT-S™, is the owner and clinical director of Grandview Family Counseling, a private practice in Utah. She has over 25 years of experience in various clinical settings, including school counseling, residential care, foster care, outpatient clinics, and private practice. Holly is an adjunct professor at Utah Valley University and certified in TF-CBT and EMDR. She is an RPT-S™ and presents nationally on play therapy topics.

FIGURES

PART I

AN OVERVIEW OF CHILDHOOD SEXUAL ABUSE AND PLAY THERAPY

CHAPTER 1
CHILDHOOD SEXUAL ABUSE
UNDERSTANDING A WORLDWIDE EPIDEMIC

Sueann Kenney-Noziska

It is difficult to know where to begin when exploring the global epidemic of childhood sexual abuse (CSA). Despite the advances in our world, we continue to fail our children, youth, and adolescents when it comes to protecting them from sexual harm. CSA transcends all cultural influences and impacts every community in the world. Arguably, it is one of the most significant issues affecting our youth. CSA is a broad victimization encompassing contact (i.e., fondling of the genitalia, oral copulation, penetration) and noncontact offenses (i.e., voyeurism, online sexual exploitation) perpetrated on our children and adolescents. According to the World Health Organization (WHO, 1999), CSA is an infringement on a child's rights to health and protection and the most devastating, cruel, and tragic of all forms of child abuse and neglect (1999).

Per the Centers for Disease Control and Prevention (CDC) and for this chapter, CSA is defined as:

> *Involvement of a child (person less than 18 years old) in sexual activity that violates the laws or social taboos of society and that he/ she does not fully comprehend does not consent to, or is unable to give informed consent to, or is not developmentally prepared for and cannot give consent to.*
>
> (Centers for Disease Control and Prevention
> [CDC], 2022, p. 15)

Approximately one in four girls and one in 13 boys in the United States experience child sexual abuse (CDC, 2022). Although CSA can be perpetrated in intra- and extrafamilial contexts, 91% of CSA occurs at the hands of someone the victim and the victim's family know and trust

DOI: 10.4324/9781003451549-2

(CDC, 2022). Given the prevalence of CSA, most play therapists will encounter clients who have experienced CSA. Therefore, play therapists must recognize that treatment for this population requires specialized training, multidisciplinary work, and ongoing professional development.

The Impact of Childhood Sexual Abuse: *"It Is Unimaginable Heartbreak"*

The deleterious short- and long-term impact of CSA is well-documented in the peer-reviewed literature. The Adverse Childhood Experiences (ACEs) study (Felitti et al., 1998) provides the foundation for understanding the negative impact of adversities, such as CSA, on victims throughout the life span and across domains. Among others, this includes psychological functioning, social functioning, relational functioning, physical health, and life expectancy. In other words, even after sexual abuse has stopped, the impact remains.

Most mental health problems and multiple adverse social conditions can be linked to CSA (Conte &Vaughan-Eden, 2018). According to the peer-reviewed literature, there is an association between sexual abuse and depression, anxiety, posttraumatic stress disorder (PTSD), eating disorders, internalizing symptoms, externalizing problems, sexual revictimization, regressed behaviors, suicide attempts, and substance abuse (Benuto & O'Donohue, 2015; Chen et al., 2010; Conte & Vaughan-Eden, 2018; Fletcher, 2021; Lalor & McElvaney, 2010; Odacı & Türkkan, 2023; Trask et al., 2011). Associations between CSA and the aforementioned adverse outcomes are multifaceted and complex. CSA is a nonspecific risk factor that, in correlation with other variables, can create pathways for psychiatric disorders, substance abuse, eating disorders, and various other struggles (Kenney-Noziska, 2020).

Although notorious for poor outcomes, victims of CSA are a heterogeneous population. Not all victims of CSA experience difficulties that require clinical intervention. Resiliency, protective factors, and cultural influences are essential variables to consider when conceptualizing cases of sexual abuse (Sanjeevi et al., 2018). According to Domhardt et al. (2015), protective factors with the best empirical support for better outcomes for victims of CSA include education, interpersonal and emotional competence, control beliefs, active coping, optimism, social attachment, external attribution of blame, and most importantly, support from the family and the broader social environment.

The Betrayal of Childhood Sexual Abuse: "I Will Never Trust Anyone Again"

The betrayal inherent in CSA adds insult to injury for victims, substantially interferes with healing, and complicates treatment. Acknowledging betrayal, one of the four traumagenic dynamics inherent in sexual abuse is paramount in understanding sexual abuse and its impact on victims (Finkelhor & Brown, 1985). In a recent review of treatment issues for victims of CSA, Odacı and Türkkan (2023) refer to this as the "trauma of betrayal." CSA by a family member typically results in a greater sense of betrayal. Loss of primary attachment figures due to the betrayal of CSA may be the most damaging psychological trauma victims of CSA sustain (Weihmann, 2022).

Betrayal is primarily conceptualized as the betrayal experienced by the victim at the hands of a sexual perpetrator who destroys trust through manipulation, deceit, and enticement. However, secondary betrayal can occur from nonoffending caregivers and other adults who fail to believe, support, and protect the victim after the sexual abuse is disclosed or discovered. If the primary caregiver does not believe the victim and is unwilling to protect them, the victim experiences the greatest betrayal.

Feelings related to the betrayal inherent in CSA are a heavy burden for victims (Odacı & Türkkan, 2023). Betrayal results in depression, anger, reduced trust, and increased vulnerability to future abuse (Cantón-Cortés et al., 2012; Finkelhor & Browne, 1985). Victims may experience secondary betrayal by the child welfare and criminal justice systems. Societal shaming and blaming beliefs can be additional sources of betrayal.

The Sexual Grooming Process: *Hiding in Plain Sight*

(Note: This section focuses on in-person sexual grooming. It does not address online sexual grooming.)

The process of sexual grooming is an integral dynamic in CSA (Winters et al., 2022). Gaining access to the victim, decreasing the likelihood of discovery, and increasing the possibility of future sexual victimization are the overarching goals of grooming. Sexual grooming is complex, subtle, and mimics everyday adult/child interactions (i.e., buying gifts, playing child-like games, taking the victim on outings, and special privileges) (Bennett & O'Donohue, 2014). Subsequently, it is easier to recognize sexual grooming retrospectively versus prospectively (Bennett & O'Donohue, 2014; Winters et al., 2020, 2022). Those who perpetrate sexual abuse on children, youth, and adolescents use typical adult/child behaviors to allow them to hide in plain sight. Their behaviors are easily justified and dismissed as normative if an astute caregiver or a protective adult observes them.

There are four broad categories of sexual grooming: (1) grooming the child, (2) grooming the self, (3) grooming the family, and (4) grooming the community. Winters et al. (2020) define sexual grooming as the multilayered, deceptive process used to facilitate sexual contact while simultaneously avoiding detection. Sexual grooming involves selecting, gaining access to, and isolating the victim as well as developing trust with the victim and essential others (i.e., caregivers, guardians, community, and youth-serving institutions). As part of sexual grooming, offenders desensitize the victim to sexual content and physical contact. Grooming also includes post-abuse maintenance strategies by the offender to facilitate future sexual abuse and prevent disclosure.

Sexual grooming often leaves victims believing that the sexual victimization is, in some way, their fault and that they were "complicit." Clinicians may hear these distortions through victims' statements such as "I did not say no," "I did not tell sooner," I touched them too," and "I let them do this to me." Offenders often engage in post-abuse maintenance grooming by using victim blaming to imply that the victim is a consensual partner (i.e., "You will get in trouble if people find out what *we* are doing" and I am only doing this because you want me to").

Understanding Disclosures of Childhood Sexual Abuse: *"Nothing Was Ever the Same After That"*

CSA is cloaked in secrecy. Its insidious onset at the hands of a trusted individual renders victims helpless and unable to disclose their victimization readily. In the field of CSA, it is widely accepted that most disclosures are delayed (Alaggia et al., 2016; Manay & Collin-Vézina, 2021; Townsend, 2016). Many victims do not disclose CSA until adulthood or fail to disclose it at all. Victims wonder if to tell, when to tell, whom to tell, and what to tell. Adult survivors retrospectively report disclosure of sexual abuse as a lifelong process anchored in the involvement of attentive, attuned others marked with deciding whether to tell, delay, re-try, turn toward others, or disclose (Brattfjell & Flåm, 2019).

Disclosure of sexual abuse is a courageous endeavor impacted by a complex interplay of individual, familial, contextual, and cultural factors (Alaggia et al., 2016). A social-ecological, person-in-environment conceptualization has helped us understand that disclosures of sexual abuse are a process whereby victims test adults and reveal sexual victimization with hints. Disclosure is an ongoing process that typically occurs in the context of a relationship and a dialogue. Disclosure is iterative and interactive instead of being a single, discreet event.

Identifying factors facilitating or inhibiting disclosure is essential in understanding the disclosure process. Age and gender are important facilitators in CSA disclosures. More specifically, we tend to get more disclosures from females as they age into adulthood (Alaggia et al., 2016). Disclosure has a lifelong course and is different at various ages and stages. Results from a systematic review regarding recipients of disclosures of CSA indicate that younger children tend to disclose to their parents. In contrast, older children and adolescents typically disclose to their peers rather than family members (Manay & Collin-Vézina, 2021).

For some victims, disclosing sexual abuse is disastrous and is responded to with shock, denial, disbelief, blaming, and failure to protect. Disclosing CSA is very risky. It can come at the cost of losing loved ones, being called a liar, entering the foster care system, and testifying in criminal proceedings. Victims have reported instances where the response to their disclosure was more traumatizing than the sexual abuse itself.

Victim Blaming: Silencing Victims and Perpetuating Childhood Sexual Abuse

Myths, misperceptions, and false beliefs about CSA are widespread and play a pivotal role in how society understands and responds to the sexual victimization of our youth. A result of these phenomena is victim blaming. Victim blaming is any statement or question that shifts responsibility for sexual victimization off of the abuser and onto the victim. Victim blaming is primarily based on rape myth acceptance. These myths imply that the victim is somehow to blame or responsible for all or part of their victimization. Examples include questions or statements about what the victim was wearing, why the victim did not fight back, why the victim did not disclose right away, and why the victim did not say "no" or stop the sexual abuse.

Victim blaming exonerates perpetrators and minimizes the sex crime they have perpetrated. It creates a justice gap whereby those who commit

CSA are not held culpable. In many ways, victim blaming places the victim "on trial" and shifts the burden of guilt onto the child or adolescent.

Victim blaming can occur at the individual, societal, or cultural level (Ryan, 2019). The media's portrayal of CSA is pivotal in perpetuating rape myths and blaming victims. This includes providing inaccurate information and misleading language when portraying CSA in the media. Victim blaming silences generations of victims who fear the secondary victimization of being blamed for what happened to them. Victim blaming can lead to self-blame and creates a significant barrier to disclosure (Alaggia et al., 2016).

Healing and Recovery From Childhood Sexual Abuse: From Victim to Survivor to Thriver

When clients enter treatment, they enter as the victim of a crime. They are not automatically "survivors" or "thrivers." Arguably, there are many moving parts to healing and progressing from victim to survivor to thriver. There is evidence that psychotherapeutic treatments benefit victims of CSA (Odacı & Türkkan, 2023). Advances in trauma treatment have helped us refine what is currently accepted as best practice in terms of treatment.

A recent systematic review of psychosocial interventions for CSA indicated that cognitive behavioral approaches with a trauma focus appear to be the most effective for addressing the impact and symptoms resulting from CSA (McTavish et al., 2021). This same review additionally indicates that optimal treatment results are experienced when nonoffending caregivers are involved with treatment (McTavish et al., 2021). The National Child Traumatic Stress Network (2024) identifies core components of trauma treatment as a guide for play therapists and clinicians working with victims of CSA. In addition, the components contained in the Trauma-Focused Cognitive Behavioral Therapy (TF-CBT) protocol (Cohen et al., 2006, 2017) can also serve as treatment targets.

From a trauma-informed lens, play therapy theories may be integrated into trauma-focused protocols. Play therapy is developmentally sensitive and supported by neuroscientific findings related to trauma's impact on the brain. Trauma is stored implicitly as fragments in the right hemisphere of the brain. Broca's region, the area of the brain that encodes language, is bypassed during trauma. This is why victims of CSA often struggle to express their experiences verbally. Play therapy provides a means to access and reprocess these nonlinguistic traumatically stored memories.

In addition to neuroscientifically sound treatment, CSA treatment must be relationally based. The therapeutic relationship provides a corrective experience for victims through connection, growth, and healing. The relationship is beneficial for the high betrayal trauma experienced by many victims of CSA (Gómez et al., 2016; Odacı & Türkkan, 2023). A potential explicit limitation of a short-term treatment protocol is that the betrayal trauma and relational damage of CSA are not mitigated in a mere 25 sessions. Given the relational trauma of CSA and the chronicity of most sexual victimization, manualized protocols may inadvertently minimize the relational healing essential for victims of CSA.

Conclusion

CSA is a nonspecific risk factor that, in correlation with other variables, can create pathways for psychiatric disorders, substance abuse, eating disorders, and various other struggles (Kenney-Noziska, 2019). Well-trained clinicians and informed citizens are the best defense for combating CSA. Play therapists and other clinicians working with victims of CSA need specialized, ongoing training. Clinical interventions should be tailored to the client's developmental level, emphasize relational healing, and be primarily trauma-focused to mitigate the effects of CSA successfully.

Considerations for Practice: Key Takeaways

- CSA transcends all cultural barriers and impacts every community in the world.
- There is a myriad of short- and long-term adverse outcomes associated with experiencing CSA. These outcomes impact multiple domains of functioning across the lifespan.
- CSA involves betrayal and relational trauma which may cause the most significant distress.
- Offenders set up children and adolescents through sexual grooming which includes desensitization to increasingly more intrusive sexual content and contact.
- Disclosures of CSA are often delayed and involve a process that unfolds over time, typically in the context of a relationship and dialogue. Disclosure is not a single, discreet event.

- Although cognitive behavioral approaches with a trauma focus have the most support for being effective in treating the sequelae of CSA, they may not address the relational trauma victims of CSA experience.
- Play therapy approaches are developmentally sensitive and aligned with neuroscientific findings regarding the impact of trauma on the brain and body.

References

Alaggia, R., Collin-Vezina, D., & Lateef, R. (2016). Facilitators and barriers to child sexual abuse (CSA) disclosures: A research update (2000–2016). *Trauma, Violence, and Abuse, 20*(2), 260–283. https://doi.org/10.1177/1524838017697312

Bennett, N., & O'Donohue, W. (2014). The construct of grooming in child sexual abuse: Conceptual and measurement issues. *Journal of Child Sexual Abuse, 23*(8), 957–976. https://doi.org/10.1080/10538712.2014.960632

Benuto, L. E., & O'Donohue, W. (2015). Treatment of sexually abused children: A review and synthesis of recent meta-analyses. *Children and Youth Services Review, 56,* 52–56. https://doi.org/10.1016/j.childyouth.2015.06.009

Brattfjell, M. L., & Flåm, A. M. (2019). "They were the ones that saw me and listened." From child sexual abuse to disclosure: Adults' recalls of the process towards final disclosure. *Child Abuse and Neglect, 89,* 225–236.

Cantón-Cortés, D., Cortés, M. R., & Cantón, J. (2012). The role of traumagenic dynamics on the psychological adjustment of survivors of child sexual abuse. *European Journal of Developmental Psychology, 9*(6), 665–680.

Centers for Disease Control and Prevention. (2022). *Preventing child sexual abuse.* U.S. Department of Health and Human Services. CDC. https://www.cdc.gov/violenceprevention/childsexualabuse/fastfact.html

Chen, L. P., Murad, M. H., Paras, M. L., Colbenson, K. M., Sattler, A. L., Goranson, E. N., Elamin, M. B., Seime, R. J., Shinozaki, G., Prkop, L. J., & Zirakzadeh, A. (2010). Impact of child sexual abuse and lifetime diagnosis of psychiatric disorders: Systematic review and meta-analysis. *Mayo Clinical Proceeding, 85*(7), 618–629.

Cohen, J. A., Mannarino, A. P., & Deblinger, E. (2006). *Treating trauma and traumatic grief in children and adolescents.* Guilford Press.

Cohen, J. A., Mannarino, A. P., & Deblinger, E. (2017). *Treating trauma and traumatic grief in children and adolescents* (2nd ed.). Guilford Press.

Conte, J. R., & Vaughan-Eden, V. (2018). Child sexual abuse. In J. B. Klika & J. R. Conte (Eds.), *The APSAC handbook on children maltreatment* (4th ed., pp. 95–110). Sage Publication.

Domhardt, M., Münzer, A., Fegert, J. M., & Goldbeck L. (2015). Resilience in survivors of child sexual abuse: A systematic review of the literature. *Trauma, Violence and Abuse, 16*(4), 476–493.

Felitti, V. J., Anda, R. F., Nordenberg, D., Williamson, D. F., Spitz, A. M., Edwards, V., Koss, M. P., & Marks, J. S. (1998). Relationship of childhood abuse and household dysfunction to many of the leading causes of death in adults: The adverse childhood experiences (ACE) study. *American Journal of Preventative Medicine*, *14*(4), 245–258. https://doi.org/10.1016/s0749-3797(98)00017-8

Finkelhor, D., & Browne, A. (1985). The traumatic impact of child sexual abuse: A conceptualization. *American Journal of Orthopsychiatry*, *55*(4), 530–541. https://doi.org/10.1111/j.1939-0025.1985.tb02703.x

Fletcher, K. (2021). A systematic review of the relationship between child sexual abuse and substance use issues. *Journal of Child Sexual Abuse*, *30*(3), 258–277. https://doi.org/10.1080/10538712.2020.1801937

Gómez, J. M., Lewis, J. K., Noll, L. K., Smidt, A. M., & Birrell, P. J. (2016). Shifting the focus: Nonpathologizing approaches to healing from betrayal trauma through an emphasis on relational care. *Journal of Trauma Dissociation*, *17*(2), 165–185. https://doi.org/10.1080/15299732.2016.1103104

Kenney-Noziska, S. (2019). Therapeutic games for sexually abused children. In J. Stone & C. E. Schaefer (Eds.), *Game play: Therapeutic use of games with children and adolescents* (pp. 239–254). John Wiley & Sons.

Lalor, K., & McElvaney, R. (2010). Child sexual abuse, links to later sexual exploitation/high risk sexual behavior, and prevention/treatment programmes. *Trauma, Violence, and Abuse*, *11*(4), 159–177. https://doi.org/10.1177/1524838010378299

Manay, N., & Collin-Vézina, D. (2021). Recipients of children's and adolescents' disclosures of childhood sexual abuse: A systematic review. *Child Abuse and Neglect*, *116*(1). https://doi.org/10.1016/j.chiabu.2019.104192

McTavish, J. R., Santesso, N., Amin, A., Reijnders, M., Ali, M. U., Fitzpatrick-Lewis, D., & MacMillan, H. L. (2021). Psychosocial interventions for responding to child sexual abuse: A systematic review. *Child Abuse and Neglect*, *116*(1), 1–11. https://doi.org/10.1016/j.chiabu.2019.104203

National Child Traumatic Stress Network. (2024, January 1). *Core components of trauma-informed interventions*. http://www.nctsn.org/resources/topics/treatments-that-work/promising-practices

Odacı, H., & Türkkan, T. (2023). Treatment issues while addressing child sexual abuse: A review. *Psikiyatride Güncel Yaklaşımlar – Current Approaches in Psychiatry*, *15*(3), 534–547.

Ryan, K. M. (2019). Rape mythology and victim blaming as a social construct. In W. T. O'Donohue & P. A. Schewe (Eds.), *Handbook of sexual assault and sexual assault prevention* (pp. 151–174). Springer. https://doi.org/10.1007/978-3-030-23645-8_9

Sanjeevi, J., Houlihan, D., Bergstrom, K. A., Langley, M. M., & Judkins, J. (2018). A review of child sexual abuse: Impact, risk, and resilience in the context of culture. *Journal of Child Sexual Abuse*, *27*(6), 622–641.

Townsend, C. (2016). Child sexual abuse disclosure: What practitioners need to know. *Darkness to Light*. https://www.d2l.org/wp-content/uploads/2016/10/ChildSexualAbuseDisclosurePaper_20160217_v.1.pdf

Trask, E., Walsh, K., & DiLillo, D. (2011). Treatment effects for common outcomes of child sexual abuse: A current meta-analysis. *Aggression and Violent Behavior*, *16*(1), 6–19. https://doi.org/10.1016%2Fj.avb.2010.10.001

Weihmann, R. (2022). Symptomatology of reconstitution of trauma in adults with a history of childhood sexual abuse. An approach from the perspective of SONapp application. *International Journal of Advanced Studies in Sexology, 4*(1), 31–40. https://doi.org/10.46388/ijass.2022.4.3

Winters, G. M., Jeglic, E. L., & Kaylor, L. E. (2020). Validation of the sexual grooming model of child sexual abusers. *Journal of Child Sexual Abuse, 29*(7), 855–875.

Winters, G. M., Kaylor, L. E., & Jeglic, E. L. (2022). Toward a universal definition of child sexual grooming. *Deviant Behavior, 43*(8), 926–938.

World Health Organization. (1999). *Report of the consultation on child abuse prevention.* Author.

Chapter 2
Childhood Maltreatment, Trauma, and the Developing Brain
Algorithms for Effective Play Therapy

Richard L. Gaskill and Bridgette Mitchell Sanders

Adults generally believe children should be protected, yet maltreatment is staggeringly high dating to antiquity (deMause, 1974). The National Center for Victims of Crime (n.d.) reports 1 in 5 girls and 1 in 20 boys in the United States have suffered sexual victimization, while the Centers for Disease Control and Prevention (2023) reports 1 in 7 children in the United States experienced abuse or neglect, including 1,750 deaths, in 2020. Such experiences increase the probability of childhood and adult physical and psychiatric morbidity (Downey & Crummy, 2022). van der Kolk (2007) observed that only a third of our children are asymptomatic by adulthood, creating our most significant public health challenge.

Traumatology clearly reveals the deleterious impact of trauma on brain architecture, disrupting cognition, language, emotional regulatory and inhibitory capabilities, behavioral, relational and social capacities, sensory registration and integration capacities, as well as motor and physiological functioning of the autonomic nervous system (Hambrick et al., 2019). Hambrick et al. linked life stressors in the first two months of life with sensory integration and self-regulatory difficulties, while stressors during childhood were associated with relational issues later in life. Hambrick et al. further documented cognitive difficulties arising from stressors during infancy and childhood. Clearly, functional problems in specific brain regions are linked to stressors during that region's active development. Last, traumatic experiences have been irrefutably associated with nearly all psychiatric diagnoses and brain-mediated capabilities (Devi et al., 2019; Johnson, 2018), suggesting virtually all physical and emotional maladies are caused or worsened by traumatic exposure.

DOI: 10.4324/9781003451549-3

Lacking this knowledge, early play therapists developed an enormous array of theories, techniques, methods, and models to treat traumatized children, in an earnest effort to help (De Bellis, 2001). Possessing limited knowledge of neurobiological symptomatology, early practitioners struggled to determine which therapy, implemented how often, for how long, and under what conditions could provide effective treatment (Barkham et al., 2021). These laudable efforts produced less than optimal outcomes as treatment methods impacting immature neural development were poorly understood (Frimodig, 2023).

Today, neuroscience is expanding treatment capabilities far beyond early efforts. Helpful neurodevelopmental algorithms are evolving and improving outcomes. These algorithms employ brain region-specific treatment methods (often specific play therapy techniques) to enhance outcomes (Barfield et al., 2011; Gaskill & Brown, 2016).

Principles of Neurodevelopmental Algorithms

Principle 1: Hierarchical Brain Organization

Brain development begins in utero, following a predictable order, with lower regions before upper regions (Perry, 2006). From utero through age 2, the brainstem and diencephalon develop basic life support and survival functions, but below consciousness. Stimuli arising outside or inside the body are processed, integrated, and responded to through innate or previously experienced patterns of sensory input. Sensory activity entering the low brain is processed independently, before higher centers integrate the stimuli (limbic or cortex), demonstrating the autonomy of low brain sensory functions. Children displaying low brain dysregulation must establish state regulation before higher-level treatment is initiated (Gaskill & Perry, 2017).

Complex and conscious brain functions (language, conceptual thought, problem solving, self-awareness, morality, emotional awareness and regulation, relational attachment, play, and experience of reward) are progressively mediated through cortical and limbic structures from age 1 through teens (Perry, 2006). Ultimately, higher-order structures form interconnected neural networks, communicating and interacting within and between structures, creating sophisticated, complex representations of the world. Symptomatology involving higher-level functions suggests traumatic experiences during limbic and cortical development.

Recognizing the origin and brain location of trauma symptomatology is crucial to selecting and sequencing effective treatments.

Any perception of danger initiates the threat response system in the low brain before higher-level awareness (Gaskill & Perry, 2017). Once experienced, similar stimuli will automatically trigger low brain alarm responses. The absence of consciousness potentiates the reactionary response. The threshold for involuntary threat responses has been "set," resulting in future predictable alarm responses, with scant cortical control. Cognitions and behaviors will be consistent with low brain arousal patterns (Gaskill & Perry, 2017). Reactive, pre-cortical response patterns quickly derail cognitively based play therapy interventions, since responses are unconscious, making them less responsive to words, thoughts, or relational agents of change. Transference or countertransference complications are also possible since they operate unconsciously. Treatment success depends on repeated opportunities for healthy experiences to modify false associations and overgeneralizations. Creation of healthy low brain architecture must precede emotional, expressive, or cognitive play therapy interventions (Kearney & Lanius, 2022). Symptoms and deficits must be ameliorated through the same brain regions mediating symptomatology (brainstem and diencephalon) (Gaskill &Perry, 2017).

Algorithm 1: Play therapy must begin at the lowest disorganized brain region.

Principle 2: The Brain Is "Use Dependent," Organizing Through Experience

The "use dependent" brain is an evolutionary survival ability allowing the brain to adapt to the environment, organizing and changing through experiences (Perry, 2006). Functional capacities of the brain are dependent upon appropriately timed and patterned signals stimulating neural systems mediating various functions. For example, normal motor organization requires opportunities to crawl, stand, walk, and run. Normal social-emotional development requires attentive, attuned caregiving and numerous relational opportunities during childhood (Perry, 2006). Healthy neural networks depend upon the pattern, frequency, and timing of key experiences during development. Consistent, predictable, nurturing, and enriched experiences enhance the child's neurobiological capabilities, developing healthy, regulated, and integrated neural systems, optimizing self-regulation and executive functioning (Kestly, 2014; Porges, 2011).

When the developing brain adapts to repeated/patterned exposure from antagonistic experiences, the resulting architecture may disrupt healthy brain development, resulting in poorly regulated and impulsive behavior (Kestly, 2014; Perry, 2009; Porges, 2011; Rogers, 2022). For instance, persistent activation of the child's stress response system creates use-dependent alterations in those systems leading to sensitized, overly reactive, and dysfunctional stress response networks. Neuroimaging reveals increased activation of subcortical regions during highly emotional and arousal states, coupled with significant blood flow reduction in the frontal lobe (van der Kolk, 2006). The combination of an overly sensitized, hyper-reactive stress response system and a shut-down, under-developed cortex, results in globally dysregulated, impulsive behavior displaying unpredictable patterns of hyper-responsiveness, withdrawal, or an erratic mixture of conflicting responses (Gaskill & Perry, 2014; Rogers, 2022; van der Kolk, 2014). It is imperative that clinicians select interventions that influence, activate, and target the impacted neural networks that mediate the trauma symptomatology, otherwise treatment will be less effective or completely fail (Perry, 2006).

Algorithm 2: Reorganizing experiences must be targeted and repetitive

Principle 3: Brain Regions Are Sensitive to Specific Experiences During Specific Developmental Periods

The origin of the stress response system is the lower brain, which in turn impacts the upper brain structures. Poorly organized and regulated lower brain structures result in inadequate organization and regulation of upper brain regions as well (Perry, 2006). Anxiety and hypervigilance typically degrade academic, therapeutic, and social-emotional functioning, explaining why traumatized children are notoriously mercurial in their movement along the arousal continuum. Hence, low brain dysfunction renders cognitive behavioral, insight-oriented, and affect-based interventions less effective until healthy lower brain functions are restored (Kearney & Lanius, 2022; Kamp et al., 2023). Children cannot heal until a felt sense of safety and regulation is established. Felt safety and regulation (low brain functions) are the first and most influential therapeutic steps in establishing healthy state regulation. Successful treatment is built on the healthy regulatory capacity of the brainstem and diencephalon. As state regulation improves, traditional therapies become increasingly effective, demonstrating the importance of neurodevelopmental sequencing of interventions. Healing traumatic wounds progresses from the bottom up, just as developmental abilities progress sequentially from foundational skills to advanced abilities (Kearney & Lanius, 2022; van de Kamp et al., 2023).

Since somatosensory experiences influence both autonomic arousal and the primordial experience of self, encouraging re-connection with felt bodily experiences of movement and touch within a safe, positive relationship can reorganize adverse multisensory experiences and attachment disruptions, promoting desirable upstream regulation of arousal and affect modulation (Kearney & Lanius, 2022; van der Kolk & Buczynski, 2015). Traumatized children are noted to respond well to play-based approaches, using vestibular and somatosensory feedback when accompanied by positive affective interpersonal relationships. Kearney and Lanius (2022) asserted that play-based movement therapies help restore intrinsic capacities for orienting to others, enriching the capacity for positive affective responding, and restoring the primal need to experience relational connections through somatic sensory experience. Traditional childhood games such as Peek-a-Boo, Hide and Seek, Ring Around the Rosie, and Tag promote reorganization of brainstem-level sensory and affective circuitry.

Perry and Dobson (2013) and Gaskill and Perry (2014, 2017) outlined repetitive, patterned neurodevelopmental activities for dysregulated brain regions. Primary brainstem goals are regulation, primary attachment, and a flexible stress response system promoting resilience. Outcome optimization requires repeated, patterned, and rhythmic auditory, tactile, and motor sensory input with attuned and responsive caregiving, optimally during the first year of life. In the second year of life, the diencephalon develops rapidly with primary goals of sensory integration, motor control, relational flexibility, and attunement with others. Optimizing experiences include complex rhythmic movement, simple narrative, and emotional and physical warmth with a responsive caregiver. From years one through four, the limbic system develops with the primary goal of emotional regulation and emotive qualities of empathy, affiliation, and tolerance. Optimizing experiences such as complex movement, simple narrative, and social experiences, including parallel play, dramatic play, as well as preforming and creative arts, are enormously beneficial (Perry, 2006). Traditional play therapy interventions become optimally impactful at this point. The final focus of neural development addressed by Perry is cortical, actively developing from age 2 through adulthood. The final goals, according to Perry, are abstract reasoning, creativity, respect, and empathy for others, as well as moral conceptualization, complex conversation, social interactions, exploratory play, and a sense of safety and security. Therapeutic experiences include storytelling, dramatic arts, formal education, and traditional insight-oriented or cognitive behavioral therapies. Play therapy interventions must be matched to the brain region exhibiting pathology for optimal results.

Algorithm 3: Does the play therapy activity incorporate the somatosensory elements unique to the disorganized brain region(s)?

Principle 4: Social Mastery Grows in the Child's Comfort Zone (Safety/Security)

Successful execution of all principles and algorithms relies on a final principle. Children must feel safe to develop and thrive. No matter how well-intended, therapeutic interventions cannot succeed unless the child feels safe and secure with the play therapist (Panksepp & Biven, 2012). This principle is foundational for healthy, social, and emotional growth. When the brain wires in response to pathological caregiving, chaotic environments, or traumatic experiences, healthy development and social engagement are impaired. Not only is the child's ability to coregulate and self-regulate impaired, but faulty neuroception also distorts the child's ability to accurately sense the intentions of others, through incorrectly reading facial cues and body language (Porges, 2011). Instead of being calmed and coregulated by a caregiver, the child may misinterpret another's voice, facial expression, or approach as dangerous or threatening, reacting inappropriately, producing mistrust, and creating a pervasive perception that the world is unsafe (Porges, 2011). Porges further added, children cannot play successfully without healthy neuroception.

Clearly, children depend on repetitive experiences of warmth, attunement, and safety. Healthy neuroception permits children to interact with their environment freely, without fear, allowing our endocrine system to release oxytocin (the bonding hormone), dopamine, and neural growth hormones, stimulating brain development. Children experience optimal social, emotional, cognitive, psychological, and neurological growth when immersed in familiar, safe, predictable, routine, and nurturing environments (Panksepp & Biven, 2012). Play therapists must prioritize activities which are perceived by the child as safe and calming of their hyper-reactive stress response system to create the neuroception of safety. In the context of a safe relationship, play therapy experiences become neurobiologically reinforcing and healing. Thinking therapies don't accomplish this.

As the child becomes more comfortable with their play therapist, a sense of safety grows, and the child becomes open to reciprocal engagement, increasing the play therapist's opportunity to act as the child's co-regulator, encouraging uncoupling of previously wired negative associations. Through repetition, new and healthier neural connections form, become stronger, and facilitate neural reorganization. This process allows a child to develop healthier neuroception and decrease emotional and behavioral reactivity. As the child's sense of safety grows, they experience social engagement and become increasingly open to therapeutic engagement, emotional bonding, and social and emotional growth.

Algorithm 4: Does the child feel safe?

Conclusion

For over 100 years, play therapy has progressed through numerous theoretical models and processes. Many proved helpful and some attained evidence-based status. Unfortunately, until now, there have been few scientifically verifiable principles set forth that satisfactorily explain how or why these varied methods worked or provided guidance regarding adapting and improving treatment methods. Historically, this has been detrimental to the advancement of play therapy as a science-based treatment modality and intern slowing its acceptance as a significant health care treatment modality. Fortunately, over the past 30 years, neuroscience has steadily contributed vast knowledge regarding brain development, social/emotional influences impacting neurodevelopment, and the effect of trauma on neurodevelopment. Today, we understand children with histories of traumatization present complex social, emotional, biological, and behavioral challenges resulting from overly sensitized and disorganized neural networks.

Further, we understand that the human brain is extremely immature at birth and remains malleable to both positive and negative experiences for many years. Research informs us that a child's social, emotional, physical, and play experiences have a profound impact on brain development and ultimately the child's global functional capacity. Such studies have produced neurodevelopmental principles which can guide play therapy treatment design for maltreated children. Four foundational developmental principles were reviewed and offered as treatment algorithms to improve treatment outcomes.

The first principle discussed was the sequential development of the brain, lower regions before higher regions, indicating bottom-up therapeutic designs. This informs play therapists that trauma strongly affects developing brain regions, suggesting bottom-up therapy designs are more likely to be beneficial. The first algorithm directs play therapists to target lower disorganized brain regions first. The second principle emphasized the use-dependent nature of the brain. Neural connections frequently used become permanent, those not used atrophy. Since trauma creates entrenched problematic neural connections, new healthy connections need multiple repetitions over time to become the default neural network. The second algorithm emphasized creation and stimulation of healthy neural connections until they become permanent. The third principle focused on specific types of stimulation for specific brain regions. The algorithm becomes: Does the play therapy activity utilize the unique somatosensory modalities that influence the targeted, disorganized brain region? The final principle advised that social mastery grows in the child's comfort zone. The algorithm is simple: Does the child feel safe in the playroom with the therapist?

A growing body of evidence suggests using these basic principles to guide treatment planning and play therapy methods improves therapeutic outcomes (Evans et al., 2023). As play therapy enters its second century, practitioners must become aware of the neurobiological principles influencing child development, trauma symptomatology, relational factors, and resulting treatment algorithms if we hope to help the children we serve.

References

Barfield, S., Gaskill, R., Dobson, C., & Perry, B. (2011). Neurosequential model of therapeutics in a therapeutic preschool: Implications for work with children with complex neuropsychiatric problems. *International Journal of Play Therapy*, 21(1), 30–44. https://psycnet.apa.org/doi/10.1037/a0025955

Barkham, M., Lutz, W., & Castonguay, L. (2021). *Bergin and Garfield's handbook of psychotherapy and behavior change* (7th ed.). John Wiley & Sons.

Centers for Disease Control and Prevention. (2023). *Fast facts: Preventing child abuse and neglect.* https://www.cdc.gov/violenceprevention/childabuseandneglect/fast-fact.html

De Bellis, M. D. (2001). Developmental traumatology: The psychobiological development of maltreated children and its implications for research, treatment, and policy. *Development and Psychopathology, 13*(3), 539–564. https://doi.org/10.1017/s0954579401003078

deMause, L. (1974). *The history of childhood.* Jason Aronson.

Devi, F., Shahwan, S., Teh, W. L., Sambasivam, R., Zhang, Y. J., Lau, Y. W., Ong, S. H., Fung, D., Gupta, B., Chong, A., & Subramaniam, M. (2019). The prevalence of childhood trauma in psychiatric outpatients. *Annals of General Psychiatry, 18,* Article 15. https://doi.org/10.1186/s12991-019-0239-1

Downey, C., & Crummy, A. (2022). The impact of childhood trauma on children's wellbeing and adult behavior. *European Journal of Trauma & Dissociation, 6*(1), Article 100237.

Evans, K. E., Bender, A. E., Rolock, N., Hambrick, E. P., Bai, R., White, K., Diamant-Wlison, R., & Baily, K. A. (2023). Exploring adherence to client treatment recommendations in the Neurosequential Model of Therapeutics. *Sage: Research on Social Work Practice,* 1–12. https://doi.org/10.1177/10497315231160588

Frimodig, B. (2023). *Heuristics: Definition, examples, and how they work.* https://www.simplepsychology.org/what-is-a-heuristic.html

Gaskill, R., & Brown, J. (2016, June 8–10). *NMT guided school based mental health collaborative* [Conference session]. Proceedings of the 2nd International Neurosequential Model Symposium, Child Trauma Academy and Hull Services.

Gaskill, R., & Perry, B. (2014). The neurobiological power of play: Using the neurosequential model of therapeutics to guide play in healing process. In C. Malchoidi & D. Crenshaw (Eds.), *Creative arts and play therapy for attachment problems* (pp. 178–194). Guilford Press.

Gaskill, R. L., & Perry, B. D. (2017). A neurosequential therapeutics approach to guided play, play therapy, and activities for children who won't talk. In C. A. Malchiodi & D. A. Crenshaw (Eds.), *What to do when children clam up in psychotherapy: Interventions to facilitate communication* (pp. 38–68). Guilford Press.

Hambrick, E. P., Brawner, T. W., & Perry, B. D. (2019). Timing of early-life stress and the development of brain related capacities. *Frontiers in Behavioral Neuroscience, 13,* Article 183. https://doi.org/10.3389/fnbeh.2019.00183

Johnson, M. E. (2018). The effects of traumatic experiences on academic relationships and expectations in justice-involved children. *Psychology in the Schools, 55*(3), 240–249.

Kearney, B. E., & Lanius, R. A. (2022). The brain-body disconnect: A somatic sensory basis of trauma-related disorders. *Frontiers in Neuroscience, 16,* Article 1015749. https://doi.org/10.3389/fnins.2022.1015749

Kestly, T. A. (2014). *The interpersonal neurobiology of play: Brain-building interventions for emotional well-being.* W.W. Norton.

National Center for Victims of Crime. (n.d.). *Child sexual abuse statistics.* https://victimsofcrime.org/child-sexual-abuse-statistics/

Panksepp, J., & Biven, L. (2012). *The archaeology of mind: Neuroevolutionary origins of human emotions.* W. W. Norton.

Perry, B. D. (2006). Applying principles of neural development to clinical work with maltreated and traumatized children. In N. B. Webb (Ed.), *Working with traumatized youth in child welfare* (pp. 27–52). Guildford Press.

Perry, B. D. (2009). Examining child maltreatment through a neurodevelopmental lens: Clinical applications of the neurosequential model of therapeutics. *Journal of Loss and Trauma, 14,* 240–255. https://doi.org/10.1080/15325020903004350

Perry, B. D., & Dobson, C. (2013). Application of the neurosequential model (NMT) in maltreated children. In J. Ford & C. Courtois (Eds.), *Treating complex traumatic stress disorders in children and adolescents* (pp. 249–260). Guilford Press.

Porges, S. W. (2011). *The polyvagal theory: Neurophysiological foundations of emotions, attachment, communication, and self-regulation.* W. W. Norton.

Rogers, A. T. (2022). *Human behavior in the social environment: Perspectives on development and the life course* (6th ed.). Routledge.

van de Kamp, M. M., Scheffers, M., Emck, C., Fokker, T. J., Hatzmann, J., Cuijpers, P., & Beek, P. J. (2023). Body- and movement-oriented interventions for posttraumatic stress disorder: An updated systematic review and meta-analysis. *Journal of Traumatic Stress, 36*(5), 835–848. https://doi.org/10.1002/jts.22465

van der Kolk, B. (2014). *The body keeps score: Brain, mind, and body in the healing of trauma.* Viking Press.

van der Kolk, B., & Buczynski, R. (2015). *Four concrete steps for working with trauma.* National Institute for the Clinical Application of Behavioral Medicine. https://docslib.org/download/12893731/four-concrete-steps-for-working-with-trauma-with-bessel-van-der-kolk-md-and-ruth-buczynski-phd

van der Kolk, B. A. (2006). Clinical implications of neuroscience research in PTSD. *Annals of the New York Academy of Sciences, 1071*(1), 277–293.

van der Kolk, B. A. (2007). The developmental impact of childhood trauma. In L. J. Kirmayer, R. Lemelson, & M. Barad (Eds.), *Understanding trauma: Integrating biological, clinical, and cultural perspectives* (pp. 224–241). Cambridge University Press. https://doi.org/10.1017/CBO9780511500008.016

CHAPTER 3
CLINICAL NEEDS OF SEXUALLY ABUSED CHILDREN AND ADOLESCENTS

Holly Willard

Childhood sexual abuse (CSA) presents a complex and widespread challenge that play therapists frequently encounter. Understanding CSA's deep impact on affected youth and their families is crucial for providing effective, trauma-informed play therapy (Kenney-Noziska, 2022). This modality leverages creative and expressive techniques crucial for healing from CSA. Effective CSA treatment involves a comprehensive, multidisciplinary approach integrating the client's support system. Play therapy is key in promoting self-expression, processing trauma, teaching indirectly, enabling emotional catharsis, reducing fears, and fostering positive emotions, essential in the healing journey (Carey, 2010; Malchiodi, 2005; The National Child Traumatic Stress Network [NCTSN], 2023; National Institute of Mental Health [NIMH], 2023).

Literature Review of the Impact of CSA

The effects of CSA are extensive, causing short- and long-term emotional, physical, and behavioral regulation issues. Short-term effects include emotional reactions like shock, fear, and depression, physical symptoms such as pain or injuries, and behavioral dysregulation like aggression and regression. Long-term impacts include depression, posttraumatic stress disorder (PTSD), substance abuse, chronic disease, and relational and sexual dysfunction. Additionally, clients may experience sexual reactivity.

DOI: I0.4324/978I003451549-4

Core Components of Trauma Treatment

The National Child Traumatic Stress Network (National Child Trau-matic Stress Network [NCTSN], 2024) describes the core components of trauma treatment as follows:

- Conducting a trauma-informed assessment
- Psychoeducation
- Teaching and reinforcing healthy coping skills
- Actively involving parents or caregivers
- Cultivating skills for emotional regulation
- Facilitating the child's ability to process trauma
- Safety and stabilization
- Promoting connection and supportive relationships
- Using a strengths-based perspective.

One treatment approach for CSA that is widely accepted and well-studied is trauma-focused cognitive behavioral therapy (TF-CBT) (Thielemann et al., 2022). TF-CBT integration with play therapy is beneficial because play therapy serves as an effective medium through which TF-CBT can be delivered. In TF-CBT, "PRACTICE" is the acronym that outlines the protocol's key components. These components include Psychoed-ucation, Relaxation techniques, Affective modulation skills, Cognitive coping and processing, Trauma narrative, In vivo mastery of trauma reminders, Conjoint child-parent sessions, and Enhancing future safety and development. The integration of TF-CBT and play therapy enables therapists to provide developmentally comprehensive, trauma-informed care tailored to the unique needs of each child.

Treatment Needs of Sexually Abused Children and Adolescents

Treatment needs for victims of CSA are multifaceted and must be tai-lored to address the unique impact of the abuse on each client. Treat-ment should be customized, recognizing specific needs and suitability of different interventions based on developmental and psychological levels. These treatment goals aim to minimize the short- and long-term nega-tive effects of CSA and prevent future revictimization. While treatment needs vary, play therapists should utilize NCTSN's core components of trauma treatment as a guide for treatment of CSA.

TF-CBT (PRACTICE) Model and Play Therapy

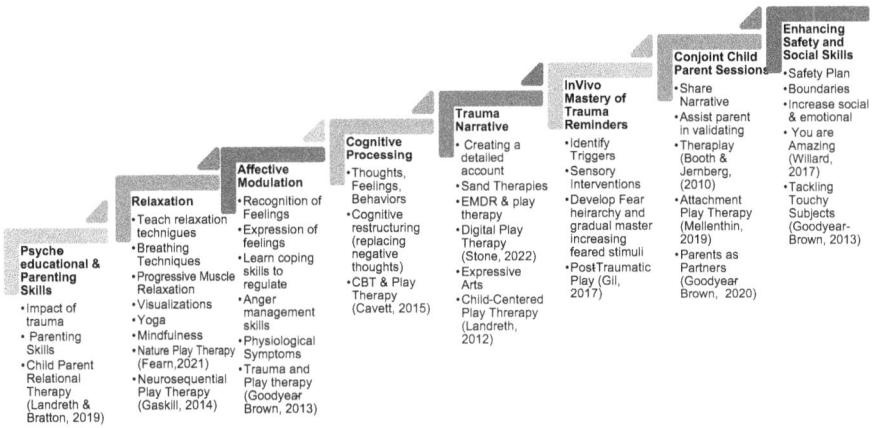

Psyche educational & Parenting Skills	Relaxation	Affective Modulation	Cognitive Processing	Trauma Narrative	Trauma Reminders	InVivo Mastery of Trauma	Conjoint Child Parent Sessions	Enhancing Safety and Social Skills
•Impact of trauma • Parenting Skills •Child Parent Relational Therapy (Landreth & Bratton, 2019)	•Teach relaxation technigues •Breathing Techniques •Progressive Muscle Relaxation •Visualizations •Yoga •Mindfulness •Nature Play Therapy (Fearn,2021) •Neurosequential Play Therapy (Gaskill, 2014)	•Recognition of Feelings •Expression of feelings •Learn coping skills to regulate •Anger management skills •Physiological Symptoms •Trauma and Play therapy (Goodyear Brown, 2013)	•Thoughts, Feelings, Behaviors •Cognitive restructuring (replacing negative thoughts) •CBT & Play Therapy (Cavett, 2015)	• Creating a detailed account •Sand Therapies •EMDR & play therapy •Digital Play Therapy (Stone, 2022) •Expressive Arts •Child-Centered Play Threrapy (Landreth, 2012)	•Identify Triggers •Sensory Interventions •Develop Fear heirarchy and gradual master increasing feared stimuli •PostTraumatic Play (Gil, 2017)	•Share Narrative •Assist parent in validating •Theraplay (Booth & Jernberg, 2010) •Attachment Play Therapy (Mellenthin, 2019) •Parents as Partners (Goodyear Brown, 2020)	•Safety Plan •Boundaries •Increase social & emotional • You are Amazing (Willard, 2017) •Tackling Touchy Subjects (Goodyear-Brown, 2013)

Figure 3.1 *Willard TF-CBT (PRACTICE) Model and Play Therapy.*

Conducting Trauma-Informed Assessments

Trauma-informed assessments, vital for treating sexual abuse, involve a detailed evaluation of the trauma's emotional, psychological, and physical effects. This approach, focusing on the trauma's impact on overall functioning, aids in accurate diagnosis and individualized treatment planning (McTavish et al., 2021). Play therapists require specialized training in trauma-informed care for CSA to meet each client's needs effectively.

Central to this process are screenings and evaluations using standardized measures such as the PTSD Checklist for DSM-5 (PCL-5) (Weathers et al., 2013). The PCL-5 is a valid instrument for assessing PTSD, is researched, and is widely used in clinical settings. Play therapists can use the PCL-5 as a screening tool for PTSD, diagnostic purposes, and to monitor symptom change over time. Additional measures which may be helpful during the assessment and treatment process include the UCLA PTSD Index (Steinberg et al., 2004), the Trauma Symptom Checklist for Young Children (TSCYC) (Briere, 2005), and the Trauma Symptom Checklist for Children (TSCC) (Briere, 1996).

Psychoeducation Regarding Trauma

Psychoeducation is key in the treatment of CSA as it educates both clients and caregivers about trauma's effects, validates children's feelings, and teaches effective parenting. Client's perceptions of CSA are crucial in their understanding of what they have experienced. Trauma is an overwhelming emotional assault leading to a loss of control and helplessness, potentially causing symptoms like nightmares, flashbacks, bedwetting, aggressiveness, and emotional dysregulation (Terr, 1991). van der Kolk (2014) notes that disassociation during trauma can influence the development of PTSD and underscores the profound impact of sexual trauma on children and adolescents.

Safety and Stabilization

Ensuring emotional and physical safety is crucial for victims of CSA. Play therapists should ensure clients' safety in various settings, including home and school, as well as address any physical health concerns. Safety plans, especially when involving contact with the perpetrator, should cover supervision, boundaries, and an understanding of safe touch (Kenney-Noziska, 2022). For clients with suicidal tendencies, plans incorporating coping strategies, support networks, trigger recognition, and emergency contacts are critical. Established early, these plans may also support the management of sexually reactive behaviors, help children and caregivers navigate actions misaligned with developmental norms, and safeguard the child's well-being.

Facilitating the Child's Ability to Process Trauma

Importance of Therapeutic Relationship

The therapeutic relationship is key in the healing process for sexual trauma survivors as it provides a safe space for exploring emotions and learning new relational skills (Stewart & Echterling, 2014; Kestly, 2014). It fosters trust, safety, and growth, helping clients reframe negative beliefs about self, others, and the world. Child-Centered Play Therapy (CCPT) highlights this bond, valuing children's self-healing capacity. CCPT empowers children by offering play and expressive materials, allowing autonomy in their healing, and supporting personal development (Landreth, 2012; Ray, 2021).

Trust

Establishing trust is crucial in therapy for CSA. Therapy should provide a consistent, safe, non-judgmental environment that fosters understanding and validation. Play therapists are pivotal in rebuilding trust through empathy, transparency, and unconditional positive regard. Additionally, it's important to restore self-trust and embodiment, as clients may struggle with feelings of betrayal by their bodies. Through therapeutic techniques, psychoeducation, and play, therapists work to rebuild self-trust and encourage healthy embodiment which combat victim-blaming and self-blame.

Consent

Consent is essential in therapy, especially for CSA victims who were denied it during their trauma. These clients may display various struggles including helplessness, anger, or defiance. These symptoms reflect their past lack of control. CCPT is particularly effective in targeting this area as it empowers children to lead sessions and make safe choices, thereby restoring their sense of agency and control. CCPT respects the importance of consent and caters to the specific needs of CSA survivors.

Narrative

Children and adolescents need developmentally appropriate therapy to narrate and process their sexual abuse to promote meaning-making and organize fragmented and distressing memories and cognitions. This helps integrate the sexual trauma coherently into their life story and diminish its impact and power. Therapists assist in correcting misconceptions, reducing blame and shame, and enhancing coping skills (Cavett, 2016). Revisiting the trauma narrative over time aids in gaining mastery over the memories and reducing the sexual trauma's emotional impact (Deblinger et al., 2011).

Cultivating Skills for Emotional Regulation

Recognizing and managing emotions are crucial in trauma therapy, given that CSA often evokes feelings of fear and shame. Identifying emotions and moving from avoidance to awareness is the first step in emotional regulation. This shift allows maladaptive coping mechanisms to be replaced with healthier strategies including mindfulness, enhancing control, and supporting self-efficacy. Emotional regulation is essential for processing trauma, building resilience, and improving relationships. The Neurosequential Play

Therapy model by Gaskill and Perry (2014) uses a "bottom-up" approach, starting from basic sensory brain functions with activities like music and dance. This foundational self-regulation prepares for advanced cognitive and emotional processing and differs from traditional "top-down" therapies which focus on cognitive and verbal expression.

Promoting Connection and Supportive Relationships

Actively Involving Caregivers and Family

Involving caregivers and family members in therapy is crucial for recovery from sexual abuse. It helps rebuild trust, enhances communication, and provides essential emotional support. The family's role includes understanding the child's experiences, responding to behavioral dysregulation changes, and facilitating resource access. Active family involvement and collaboration with professionals are key in addressing sexual abuse and go beyond emotional support. This involvement is vital in reducing the short- and long-term negative psychological impact of CSA, fostering resilience, and establishing a foundation for healthier relationships. Family support is a critical component in the multidisciplinary treatment and recovery from CSA.

Collaboration

Interdisciplinary collaboration involves short- and long-term recovery planning with healthcare (physical and developmental needs), mental health (emotional healing), education (stable educational environment), and legal (protect the child's rights) professionals to address all aspects of the child's well-being. Particularly important in reconciliation and reunification cases, the focus remains on the victim's best interests that have been outlined by Kenney-Noziska (2022). This unified approach creates a cohesive support system, emphasizing fostering the recovery and growth, and facilitating collective responsibility in victim support and empowerment.

Strengths-Based Perspective

In trauma-informed therapy, a strength-based perspective highlights an individual's inherent capacities for healing and growth. This focuses on resilience and resourcefulness and reinforces that clients are more than their sexual trauma. It recognizes each client's internal strengths and coping skills while promoting empowerment, autonomy, and self-efficacy. Strength-based therapy leverages internal and external support, including family, community resources, and cultural practices, to build a positive self-identity and counteract negative self-perceptions. This method guides clients toward recovery by helping them explore strengths, rediscover interests, and set future goals for a holistic and empowering healing journey.

Posttraumatic Self

Therapy for children who have experienced CSA includes helping them define and understand their posttraumatic self and adapt to a "new normal." It involves creating a narrative that acknowledges trauma but focuses on resilience and recovery. More than just coping with trauma, this approach encourages growth and positive transformation. Therapists aid victims in integrating sexual trauma into their life stories in an empowering manner, aiming for thriving, not just surviving. This supports developing an identity that includes the CSA history in a manner that is not overwhelming and establishes the foundation for a resilient and fulfilling life.

Using the Therapeutic Powers of Play Therapy to Address Child Sexual Abuse

Therapeutic Powers of Play

Self-Expression

Utilizing play therapy with victims of CSA allows expression and processing emotions effectively. Play is a natural communication mode for children and adolescents. Through play, they can articulate thoughts and feelings in a third-person narrative, which is often easier than direct, verbal expression (Bennet & Eberts, 2013). This allows expression of complex experiences safely, provides space for dealing with intense emotions, and supports creatively processing their inner world (Gil, 2012).

Access to the Unconscious

CSA can affect how children and teens process and store memories, leading to unconscious storage. Trauma can fragment memories causing dissociation, flashbacks, and altered emotional responses. Play therapy is instrumental in accessing and externalizing these unconscious thoughts and feelings. It enables children to use symbolism to indirectly engage with emotionally charged memories and fosters a safe environment for addressing complex emotions tied to sexual abuse (Crenshaw & Tillman, 2014). Eliana Gil describes this process as follows:

> *By miniaturizing events that loom large in the child's mind or body, the child begins to face the intolerable by moving the toy objects, giving them a voice and becoming the change agents of the traumatic memory. The child moves from a passive stance of victim to the more active stance of someone who is in charge. Children can take miniaturized or symbolized scenes, and they can hold the power to make the necessary changes in the storyline.*
>
> (Gil, 2017, p. 17)

Indirect Teaching

Indirect teaching through metaphorical play is a key therapeutic strategy for treatment of CSA as it helps process emotions and experiences. Using metaphors and symbols in play, children and adolescents explore complex feelings and situations in a less intimidating manner facilitating insight and meaning-making. Incorporating stories enhances this process. Victims resonate with characters and scenarios that mirror their experiences, supporting emotional and cognitive development. In play therapy, this therapeutic power of play is creative and imaginative, boosts increased problem-solving and supports resilience. It is adaptable across various ages and developmental stages and provides a versatile tool to understanding trauma and the world around them.

Catharsis

Play therapy effectively facilitates catharsis, the release of intense emotions. This is crucial for therapeutic transformation. It allows children to discharge strong negative emotions such as anger or sadness, improves emotional awareness, and contributes to psychological growth (Schaefer & Drewes, 2014). Large motor play, such as running or dancing, is beneficial for victims who have experienced CSA as it aids in physical tension release and symptom alleviation. These activities empower children, foster control, and support a positive body image. Additionally, play therapy enhances positive emotions that are essential for overall well-being (Kottman, 2014). These activities create a nurturing environment, reinforce positive emotions, and support health. Catharsis through play therapy develops a positive emotional landscape in therapeutic settings.

Counterconditioning Fears

Counterconditioning fears involves reducing and ultimately eradicating fearful or anxious responses to certain stimuli by teaching clients alternative, positive responses such as relaxation or engaging in playful activities. This technique is especially effective and crucial in treating CSA where trauma often manifests as fears, triggers, and anxiety. Counterconditioning modifies these traumatic responses and replaces fear or anxiety with more positive and manageable reactions, thereby altering their emotional reactivity to trauma-related triggers (Van Hollander, 2014).

Stress Management and Stress Inoculation

Play therapy is essential for managing stress, especially for children who have experienced CSA. It activates positive emotions and self-soothing behaviors and regulates responses to foster social connections and endorphin production. This therapeutic power reduces arousal and improves self-regulation, which is essential for mental and physical health. This is important given that stress impacts the victim's neurobiology and physiology (Bemis, 2014). As described by Cavett (2014), play-based stress inoculation uses simulated challenging scenarios in play to assist individuals in familiarizing and reducing fear. This method enables practicing coping skills in a safe setting, counteracting anxiety, and empowering control over stressors to improve real-life stress management.

Social Competence

Social competence comprises conversational ability, empathy, reciprocity, and cooperation (Gaskill, 2014). Role-playing in social contexts is crucial for its enhancement. According to Nash (2014), interactive peer relationships are key to boosting social competence. Various play activities aid in this development including rough and tumble play, playful yet non-aggressive activities, and sociodramatic play involving social fantasies. This helps victims explore different roles and scenarios to improve social skills. Gameplay encompassing cooperative, competitive, or rule-based active play is vital for the social competencies of victims of CSA (Kenney-Noziska, 2021). These play forms are enjoyable and essential for developing social skills needed for effective interpersonal interactions and relationships.

Conclusion

CSA can lead to short- and long-term issues such as mental health problems, substance abuse, and chronic disease. This underscores the importance of early intervention and treatment. Tailored treatment for CSA survivors should include trauma-informed play therapy, an emphasis on self-identity, consent issues, narrative therapy, counterconditioning fears, stress management, and social competence enhancement. Play therapy enables children to express and process trauma-related emotions and experiences. It facilitates access to the unconscious through symbolism and metaphorical play. This provides the opportunity for indirect teaching through a trauma-informed lens. Additionally, play therapy supports catharsis, nurtures positive emotions, facilitates the management of stress, and improves social skills. Trauma-informed play therapy serves an important role in the holistic healing and development of victims of CSA.

Considerations for Practice: Key Takeaways

- Understanding the prevalence and impact of CSA is essential for play therapists.
- Specialized training in trauma-focused therapy specific to sexual abuse is necessary for effective treatment.
- Therapists working with victims of CSA need a thorough understanding of trauma-informed care principles and must remain current with relevant peer-reviewed literature.
- Recognizing the varied manifestations of CSA is crucial and requires play therapists to tailor treatment to each client's unique needs.

References

Bemis, K. S. (2014). Stress management. In C. E. Schaefer & A. A. Drewes (Eds.), *The therapeutic powers of play* (pp. 143–154). Wiley.

Bennet, M. M., & Eberts, S. (2013). Self-expression. In C. E. Schaefer & A. A. Drewes (Eds.), *The therapeutic powers of play: 20 core agents of change* (pp. 11–23). Wiley.

Briere, J. (1996). *Trauma Symptom Checklist for Children (TSCC): Professional manual.* Psychological Assessment Resources.

Briere, J. (2005). *Trauma Symptom Checklist for Young Children (TSCYC): Professional manual.* Psychological Assessment Resources.

Carey, L. (2010). A response to review of expressive and creative arts methods for trauma survivors. *Journal of Child & Adolescent Trauma, 3*(3), 243–244.

Cavett, A. M. (2014). Stress inoculation. In C. E. Schaefer & A. A. Drewes (Eds.), *The therapeutic powers of play* (pp. 131–142). Wiley.

Cavett, A. M. (2016). Playful trauma-focused cognitive-behavioral therapy for school-age children. In A. A. Drewes & C. E. Schaefer (Eds.), *Play therapy in middle childhood* (pp. 53–75). American Psychological Association. https://doi.org/10.1037/14776-004

Crenshaw, D., & Tillman, K. (2014). Access to the unconscious. In C. E. Schaefer & A. A. Drewes (Eds.), *The therapeutic powers of play* (pp. 25–38). Wiley.

Deblinger, E., Mannarino, A. P., Cohen, J. A., Runyon, M., & Steer, R. (2011). Trauma-focused cognitive behavioral therapy for children: Impact of the trauma narrative and treatment length. *Depression and Anxiety, 28,* 67–75.

Gaskill, R. L. (2014). Empathy. In C. E. Schaefer & A. A. Drewes (Eds.), *The therapeutic powers of play* (pp. 195–210). Wiley.

Gaskill, R. L., & Perry, B. D. (2014). The neurological power of play: Using the neurosequential model of therapeutics to guide play in the healing process. In C. Malchiodi & D. Crenshaw (Eds.), *Creative arts and play therapy for attachment problems* (pp.178–191). Guilford Press.

Gil, E. (2012). Trauma-focused integrated play therapy (TF-IPT). In P. Goodyear-Brown (Ed.), *Handbook of child sexual abuse: Identification, assessment, and treatment* (pp. 251–278). John Wiley & Sons.

Gil, E. (2017). *Posttraumatic play in children: What clinicians need to know.* Guilford Press.

Goodyear-Brown, P. (2013). *Tackling touchy subjects.* Self-published.

Kenney-Noziska, S. (2021). Therapeutic games for sexually abused children. In J. Stone & C. E. Shaefer (Eds.), *Game play: Therapeutic use of games with children and adolescents* (pp. 239–254). John Wiley & Sons.

Kenney-Noziska, S. (2022). Play therapy group work with sexually abused children. In J. Stone, R. J. Grant, & C. Mellenthin (Eds.), *Implementing play therapy with groups: Contemporary issues in practice* (pp.196–207). Routledge.

Kestly, T. (2014). *The interpersonal neurobiology of play: Brain-building interventions for emotional well-being.* W.W. Norton.

Kottman, T. (2014). Positive emotions. In C. E. Schaefer & A. A. Drewes (Eds.), *The therapeutic powers of play* (pp. 103–120). Wiley.

Landreth, G. L. (2012). *Play therapy: The art of the relationship.* Routledge.

Malchiodi, C. (2005). Using art activities to support trauma recovery in children. *Trauma & Loss: Research & Interventions, 5*(1), 8–11.

McTavish, J. R., Santesso, N., Amin, A., Reijnders, M., Ali, M. U., Fitzpatrick-Lewis, D., & MacMillan, H. L. (2021). Psychosocial interventions for responding to child sexual abuse: A systematic review. *Child Abuse and Neglect, 116,* 104203. https://doi.org/10.1016/j.chiabu.2019.104203

Nash, J. B. (2014). Social competence. In C. E. Schaefer & A. A. Drewes (Eds.), *The therapeutic powers of play* (pp. 185–195). Wiley.

National Child Traumatic Stress Network (NCTSN). (2023). *Creating, supporting, and sustaining trauma-informed schools: A systems framework.* SAMHSA. https://www.samhsa.gov/sites/default/files/programs_campaigns/childrens_mental_health/nctsi-creating-supporting-sustaining-trauma-informed-schools-a-systems-framework.pdf

National Child Traumatic Stress Network (NCTSN). (2024). *Core components of trauma-informed interventions.* https://www.nctsn.org/treatments-and-practices/trauma-treatments/overview

National Institute of Mental Health. (2023). Helping children and adolescents cope with traumatic events. *NIH.* https://www.nimh.nih.gov/

Ray, D. C. (2021). *Advanced play therapy: Essential conditions, knowledge, and skills for child practice.* Routledge.

Schaefer, C. E., & Drewes, A. A. (2014). *The therapeutic powers of play: 20 core agents of change.* Wiley.

Steinberg, A. M., Brymer, M. J., Decker, K. B., & Pynoos, R. S. (2004). The University of California at Los Angeles post-traumatic stress disorder reaction index. *Current Psychiatry Reports, 6,* 96–100. https://doi.org/10.1007/s11920-004-0048-2

Stewart, A. L., & Echterling, L. G. (2014). Therapeutic relationship. In C. E. Schaefer & A. A. Drewes (Eds.), *The therapeutic powers of play* (pp. 157–170). Wiley.

Terr, L. (1991). Childhood traumas: An outline and overview. *American Journal of Psychiatry, 148*(1), 10–20. https://doi.org/10.1176/ajp.148.1.10

Thielemann, J. F. B., Kasparik, B., König, J., Unterhitzenberger, J., & Rosner, R. (2022). A systematic review and meta-analysis of trauma-focused cognitive behavioral therapy for children and adolescents. *Child Abuse & Neglect, 134,* Article 105899. https://doi.org/10.1016/j.chiabu.2022.105899

van der Kolk, B. A. (2014). *The body keeps the score: Brain, mind, and body in the healing of trauma.* Viking.

Van Hollander, T. (2014). Counterconditioning fears. In C. E. Schaefer & A. A. Drewes (Eds.), *The therapeutic powers of play* (pp. 121–130). Wiley.

Weathers, F. W., Litz, B. T., Keane, T. M., Palmieri, P. A., Marx, B. P., & Schnurr, P. P. (2013). *The PTSD Checklist for DSM-5 (PCL-5).* U.S. Department of Veterans Affairs. www.ptsd.va.gov.

CHAPTER 4

THERAPEUTIC PRESENCE IN PLAY THERAPY WITH SEXUALLY ABUSED CHILDREN AND ADOLESCENTS

David A. Crenshaw

Introduction

I invite readers to indulge in fantasy as we often do in play therapy and imagine a castle where the collective wisdom of play therapy is housed; the key to enter the castle could be imagined as "therapeutic presence." Free association with therapeutic presence elicits, at minimum, the following qualities of a therapist: welcoming, receptive, warm, open, non-judgmental, safe, genuine, empathic, and accepting. Geller (2013) delineated the components of therapeutic presence as (a) attunement with oneself, (b) being unguarded, (c) open and receptive to what is emotionally relevant at this moment in time; (d) an expanded sense of awareness, spaciousness, and perception; and (e) clear intention of fully being with clients to facilitate a healing process. Expanding on the concept of therapeutic attunement, Geller et al. (2010) explained that the therapist's attunement is to a multidimensional internal world that includes not just the verbalizations of the client but also the client's somatic expressions, as well as the therapist's physiological responses at the moment. The total effect of therapeutic presence is to create a therapeutic space, including the relationship with the therapist, that is safe and enables the individual to freely express what needs to be said (Porges, 2021; Geller & Porges, 2014; Crenshaw & Kenney-Noziska, 2014). Safety is essential to all therapy clients, but to sexually abused children and adolescents, it is crucial for them to unburden and share their secrets, which may be mired in shame.

DOI: 10.4324/9781003451549-5

Rooted in Humanistic Psychology

Child-centered play therapy, and notably the writings of Virginia Axline (1986), and Garry Landreth (2023), has paid the most attention to therapeutic presence in play therapy and humanistic psychologists' writings, including Clark Moustakas (1975). The person-centered theory of Carl Rogers (1980) is the theoretical basis of child-centered play therapy. Late in his career, Rogers saw therapeutic presence as an integrative and overarching concept. Rogers is quoted by Baldwin (2000): "I am inclined to think that in my writing I have stressed too much the three basic conditions (congruence, unconditional positive regard, and empathic understanding). Perhaps something around the edges of these conditions is the most important element of therapy, which I am very clearly and present in" (Baldwin, 2000, p. 30).

The ability of the therapist to be fully present, to listen deeply, and to hear the child's thoughts, feelings, and perceptions was critical to what Moustakas (1997) called *relationship play therapy*. In relationship play therapy, the therapist's presence was considered the key. Moustakis explained, "Perhaps the most important attribute of the play therapist is his or her *presence* (italics in the original) as a human being, a person committed to being with a child, listening, and hearing the child's perceptions, thoughts, feelings, and meanings. Through empathy, compassion, and intuitive sensing, the therapist discerns the rhythms of the child, recognizes, accepts, and values the child's ways, and reinforces the child's potential of authentic expressions of self" (Moustakas, 1997, pp. 9–10).

Carl Rogers (1980), a humanistic psychology colleague of Moustakis, proposed a similar concept of *deep hearing,* which he viewed to be such a powerful experience that every time he was able to listen in such an in-depth and full-hearted way, it enriched the life not only of the speaker but also of the listener. Rogers asserted that deep listening required such engaged presence that what was heard was not only what was said but also what was unsaid. Moustakas (1975), in the book *Who Will Listen?*, further developed the concept of presence and fully engaged hearing.

Facility Dogs and Therapeutic Presence

Facility dogs are best known for their work in comforting child witnesses when they testify in criminal or family court trials against their alleged abuser. While comforting child witnesses in the courtroom is their most publicized benefit, Facility dogs are excellent, and arguably better than human therapists, in providing a therapeutic presence in the therapy room or office space. Facility dogs provide three significant contributions to play therapy sessions with young children. The child experiences calmness, safety, and trust when a facility dog enters the room (Crenshaw & Stella, 2021). Any child will benefit when these three conditions are established in the play therapy space but sexually abused children, and adolescents will significantly benefit. It is astonishing that even if the child does not engage with the dog (sleeping under a chair or table), they feel calmer, safer, and more trusting than when the dog is not present.

The work of Stephen Porges (2021) teaches us to appreciate safety as a cornerstone of therapy, and this is a point of great emphasis when working with sexually abused children who have no grounds to feel safe, calm, or trusting. The author's clinical experience with facility dogs dates back to 2011. Clinical experience reveals that the more severe the abuse history, the quicker the child or adolescent bonds with the facility dog.

Facility dogs receive the same extensive training that service dogs receive. However, unlike service dogs who are assigned to a single individual, such as a disabled person or a combat veteran with PTSD, they are assigned to an agency, a program, or a facility where they provide services to multiple individuals depending on need, thus, the name facility dog. In addition to the extensive training by professionals who are accredited by Assistance Dogs International (ADI), typically, these special dogs are bred for a calm temperament, which contributes to their ability to stay calm even under stressful conditions (e.g., in a courtroom during a criminal trial).

It is important to distinguish facility dogs, which are considered working dogs, from therapy dogs, which also do good work but whose training and role are more limited. In a residential program where the author has served as Chief of Clinical Services for the past 13 years, we currently have three Facility Dogs (two Golden Retrievers, Ace and Marshall, and one Black Labrador Retriever, Elvis) who work a full-time schedule. However, we also have therapy dogs from various local organizations that bring dogs once or twice a month to visit and play with our children. Our children love the experience of interacting with the therapy dogs, but they are available for an hour or two once or twice a month. The Facility Dogs, in contrast, are here during the hours that clinical services are offered each day. These working dogs are available to interact with a dysregulated child who needs calming, to be present during a therapy session, or to sit with a child during an intake session, which can be a highly stressful or anxious time. The dogs help the visiting youth regulate their hyperaroused physiological systems by their internal calmness (an example of coregulation). A tense youth barely able to communicate meets the dog and starts petting the dog and playing with the dog. Suddenly, a new youth is in the room: a more relaxed, receptive, and communicative child who can engage more with the staff, interviewing them. When a youth visits a new program and a potential placement is at stake, the presence of a friendly dog is often experienced as welcoming and offers "a touch of home," as children frequently tell us. Facility dogs are available to go to court if a youth is required to testify or meet with prosecutors in preparation for court testimony. Recently, one of our Facility dogs accompanied a child when meeting their biological relatives for the first time to help reduce their anxiety.

How Does This Relate to Play Therapy With Sexually Abused Children and Adolescents?

Establish Safety

Play therapists create safety in the therapy setting and relationship through therapeutic presence and sensitive attunement. Facility dogs have been especially helpful in establishing safety and trust (Caprioli & Crenshaw, 2015; Crenshaw et al., 2016). Careful reading of somatic cues indicating hyperarousal in the youthful client and then working with the client to reduce the overwhelming internal activation is important to creating and maintaining safety throughout therapy. Somatic attunement is a crucial skill needed to keep trauma therapy safe; it is vital with commercially sexually exploited children (CSEC).

For a child who has experienced sexual abuse, we expect to be tense and anxious, perhaps fearful, when meeting the play therapist for the first time. The play therapist's immediate challenge is making the child feel safe and comfortable. Playfulness is one of the powers of play (Schaefer & Drewes, 2014); just as playful actions with a Facility dog can shift the therapeutic context dramatically, so can playfulness with the human therapist. Playfulness is disarming, enabling the child to moderate rigid defenses such as avoidance or detachment to create a more meaningful bond with their play therapist. The play therapist, especially with sexually abused children, conveys a welcoming and friendly demeanor that further creates a context of safety and acceptance. Experienced play therapists recognize the need not to overreach since friendliness to an extreme can be threatening to a child or an adolescent who has been groomed for exploitation. Part of the training of Facility dogs cultivates a sense of attunement. These dogs do not rush up to a child but rather allow the child to approach them when they feel comfortable and safe.

Building Trust

Observations of the interactions between our Facility dogs and the adolescents in our program for commercially sexually exploited youth over the past 12 years reveal the ease with which the youth bond with our dogs. The key is the frequent explanation of these youths, "I know the dog will not hurt me." van der Kolk (2014) observed that when the degree of abuse is of an unthinkable degree, children may not be able to derive comfort from human beings. He notes in that event, "Dogs, horses and even dolphins offer less complicated companionship while providing the necessary sense of safety" (p. 80).

The play therapist begins building trust by proving over and over again to be a reliable, sincere, and committed person with the utmost concern for the child's needs. The play therapist is patient and sensitive to the needs of the child who has experienced sexual exploitation, to test the trustworthiness of the therapist repeatedly. The play therapist, because of the prior betrayals and experiences of exploitation, views mistrust as adaptive and protective and should be honored as a necessary survival response. The child or adolescent must know that the therapist will persevere and not give up on them. A portion of the sexually traumatized youth also experience attachment trauma in early life, and these significant disruptions in primary attachments require a therapeutic relationship that can offer an emotionally corrective experience. The attachment problems will likely surface in the therapeutic relationship as the process deepens and offers a cogent opportunity for therapeutic correction and healing.

Facilitating Calmness

The Facility dogs are bred and trained to remain calm under all conditions. The dog's internal calm facilitates calmness and self-regulation within the child. It is challenging for play therapists to maintain the same level of internal calm regardless of conditions, but the closer they can come to this aspirational goal, the more effective they will be in coregulating the child's or adolescent's affect, which is a central tenet of polyvagal theory (Porges, 2021).

How Can Human Therapists Cultivate Therapeutic Presence in Treating Clients Who Have Been Sexually Abused?

Cultivating a playful, welcoming, and friendly presence can be essential when meeting a child for the first time and building a therapeutic relationship. Other disciplines essential for working with children who bring to the playroom a history of abuse, especially sexual abuse, include establishing clear boundaries, creating safety, and a presence of authenticity and genuineness. The latter is paramount to adolescent clients who sense quickly when these qualities are absent or compromised.

A natural healing quality that Facility dogs are known for is their unconditional acceptance of a child. The dogs doing this healing work in our program do not seem to care about what divides us in human society, such as race, gender, class, nationality, or sexual preferences. Implicit bias is not observed in the interactions between dogs and children. Play therapists strive for unconditional positive regard in their interactions with children but are not exempt from implicit bias. Developing the discipline of self-awareness through self-monitoring, supervision, and consultation with colleagues is imperative to weed out unconscious bias of any form. This, again, is an aspirational goal that requires consistent attention and practice. Our "blind spots" will be particularly detrimental in therapy with those who have been exploited sexually. Frequently, the youth in our program for commercially sexually trafficked, whose exploitation is extreme and unthinkable, tell us that one of the things they love the most about the Facility dogs is that they will not judge them. Hopefully, youth who have suffered this form of "intimate wounding" (Crenshaw & Caprioli, 2018) can say the same about their human therapists.

Conclusion

Therapeutic presence creates a non-judgmental, fully accepting, open, friendly, and receptive space that is essential for safety. The need for safety is punctuated for those youths who have a history of sexual exploitation or commercially driven sex trafficking. When trust has been shattered to unthinkable degrees, special measures in play therapy are called for to meet the goal of safety for the child in the therapy space. This goal of therapy has always been viewed as basic and fundamental, but it has received special emphasis with the rise in prominence in the past decade of polyvagal theory. In fact, Stephen Porges, developer of polyvagal theory, has recently stated that "safety is the therapy" (Porges, 2022, personal communication). Such emphasis is particularly appropriate when stigma and judgmental attitudes create additional complications in the healing process, as often is the case when wounding involves sexual exploitation.

Considerations for Practice: Key Takeaways

- The writings of humanistic psychologists such as Axline (1986), Landreth (2023), and Moustakas (1997) lay a strong theoretical base for therapeutic presence as a healing force in play therapy.
- Although therapeutic presence is multi-contextual, one of its most central features is safety in therapy, a context essential for a child who has suffered sexual abuse.
- Human therapists can learn valuable lessons from Facility Dogs who by nature of their training and breeding are able to establish a calm, safe, and trusting space for therapy with a child.
- Sensitive attunement is one of the critical ingredients that both human therapists and Facility Dogs require to establish therapeutic presence. It can be argued that highly trained dogs do this more naturally than human therapists.
- In creating safe space via therapeutic presence, careful attention must be given to any rupture.

References

Axline, V. M. (1986). *Dibs in search of self: The renowned, deeply moving story of an emotionally lost child who found his way back.* Ballantine Books.

Baldwin, M. (2000). Interview with Carl Rogers on using self in therapy. In M. Baldwin (Ed.), *The use of self in therapy* (2nd ed., pp. 29–38). Haworth Press.

Caprioli, S., & Crenshaw, D. A. (2015). The culture of silencing child victims of sexual abuse: Implications for child witnesses in court. *Journal of Humanistic Psychology, 55*, 1–20.

Crenshaw, D. A., & Caprioli, S. (2018). The nature of intimate wounding and the "Shadow Abuser." *Journal of Humanistic Psychology, 64*(5), 1–17.

Crenshaw, D. A., & Kenney-Noziska, S. (2014). Therapeutic presence in play therapy. *International Journal of Play Therapy, 23*(1), 31–43.

Crenshaw, D. A., Stella, L., O'Neill-Stephens, E., & Walsen, C. (2016). Developmentally and trauma-sensitive courtrooms. *Journal of Humanistic Psychology, 59*(6), 779–795.

Geller, S. M. (2013). Therapeutic presence: An essential way of being. In M. Cooper, P. F. Schmid, M. O'Hara, & A. C. Bohart (Eds.), *The handbook of person-centred psychotherapy and counselling* (2nd ed., pp. 209–222). Palgrave.

Geller, S. M., Greenburg, L. S., & Watson, J. C. (2010). Therapist and client perceptions of therapeutic presence: The development of a measure. *Psychotherapy Research, 20,* 599–610. https://doi.org/10.1080/10503307.2010.495957

Geller, S. M., & Porges, S. W. (2014). Therapeutic presence: Neurophysiological mechanisms mediating feeling safe in therapeutic relationships. *Journal of Psychotherapy Integration, 24*(3), 178–192. https://doi.org/10.1037/a0037511

Landreth, G. L. (2023). *Play therapy: The art of relationship* (4th ed.). Routledge.

Moustakas, C. (1975). *Who will listen? Children and parents in therapy.* Ballantine Books.

Moustakas, C. (1997). *Relationship play therapy.* Jason Aronson.

Porges, S. W. (2021). *Polyvagal safety: Attachment, communication, and self-regulation.* W.W. Norton.

Rogers, C. R. (1980). *A way of being.* Houghton Mifflin.

Schaefer, C. E., & Drewes, A. A. (Eds.). (2014). *The therapeutic powers of play: 20 core agents of change* (2nd ed.). Wiley.

van der Kolk, B. (2014). *The body keeps the score: Brain, mind, and body in healing trauma.* Viking Press.

CHAPTER 5

THE THERAPEUTIC POWERS OF PLAY WHEN WORKING WITH SEXUALLY ABUSED CHILDREN

Sarah D. Stauffer and Michelle M. Pliske

Sexual abuse is a potentially traumatic experience at any age. For children, it may affect cognitive, physical, social, sexual, and relationship development by skewing developmental norms and preventing the attainment of developmental milestones (Colarusso, 2010), and not allowing for healthy boundaries to be established in many aspects of the person's life, whether academic, personal, or professional. The lived experience of intimate boundary violations can cause its survivors to be suspicious and wary of others. Trust becomes a scarce commodity that demands the highest price, a suspension of the confirmed belief that the world is a dangerous place and that terrible consequences can befall the unwitting and the unwilling. Violations of this nature are difficult to overcome and repair, despite whether justice is served and amends are made by their perpetrators – or not; the latter is more often the case.

To attenuate the myriad effects that sexual abuse may provoke so that a survivor may integrate the experience into their life story without further sequelae or intrusion, the survivor must be taken seriously in their allegations and when describing their consequences, treated with care and respect, and be met where they are developmentally. Sexual abuse creates unspeakable truths by the nature of the shame and guilt that perpetrators induce. For preverbal children, words may have been underdeveloped, circumscribed, or cut altogether by psychological trauma, rendering them unavailable for describing their experience. Words are not the means by which young children will gain mastery over their experience or themselves. For older children, adolescents, and even adults, words are often wholeheartedly inadequate for encapsulating the hurt and mistrust they may wear as a shield or wield as a weapon to protect themselves from further harm.

DOI: 10.4324/9781003451549-6

Therefore, using mediated means of self-expression through play therapy and the creative arts may help child sexual abuse survivors activate therapeutic powers of play (TPOP) on their own or benefit from those leveraged prescriptively by the therapist (cf. Kaduson et al., 2020). Play therapy expertly draws upon metaphor and symbolism by the very nature that toys and objects can stand for words with images which holds powerful meaning. A metaphor embodies thought and places that thought in the living context (Haen, 2020) held in the right hemisphere of the brain where implicit memory, abstract concepts and emotion reside (McGilchrist, 2009). Traumatic experiences are not easily captured by the left hemisphere's penchant for analysis and narrative. Trauma – often overwhelming and defying neat categorization – is more naturally held in the right hemisphere's domain, which is attuned to the holistic, embodied, and contextual aspects of experience. Relying too heavily on left-hemisphere processing can lead to a fragmented, overly rationalized version of what was experienced, potentially leaving the deeper, nonverbal emotional and unintegrated bodily components of the trauma untreated (Badenoch, 2017; McGilchrist, 2009). For genuine healing, it becomes essential to engage the right hemisphere's capacity to process and integrate the raw, lived reality of trauma, reconnecting it with a sense of meaning and wholeness. Recognizing natural emergence and/or spurring TPOP activation provides play therapists with the opportunity to help survivors integrate trauma content and support them in meaning making and posttraumatic growth.

Although TPOP are inherent to play therapy, many of these are also agents of therapeutic change that exist in other forms of therapy (e.g., Antichi & Giannini, 2023; Kazdin, 2009) and in non-therapeutic play as well (e.g., Pliske et al., 2021). When activated in play therapy by the child or the play therapist, TPOP help child clients to learn, heal, and restart their growth and development, because the psychological trauma resulting from sexual abuse may have severed "the normally integrated functions" of physiological arousal, emotion, cognition, and memory from one another (Herman, 2022, p. 34).

Schaefer and Drewes (2014) described 20 *therapeutic powers of play* as core agents of change categorized into four domains: communication, fostering emotional wellness, enhancing social relationships, and increasing personal strengths (see Figure 5.1). Schaefer and Drewes (2014) firmly believed that play therapists could and should use a combination of theoretical orientations in play therapy. The TPOP described in their

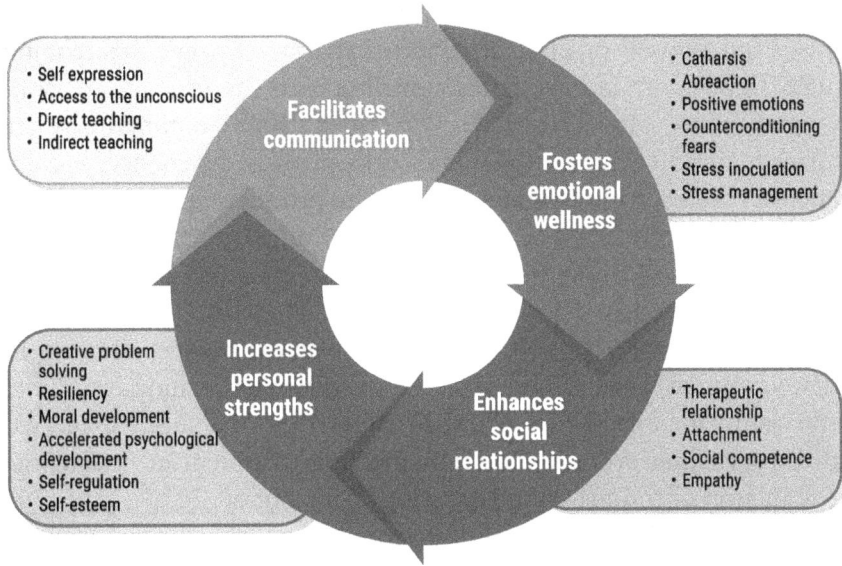

Figure 5.1 *Therapeutic Powers of Play.*

writings may be germane to one or more, and they may be used *pre-scriptively*, in a way tailored specifically to the individual needs of the client engaged in play therapy (e.g., Kaduson et al., 2020; Schaefer et al., 2016).

"Starting with the therapeutic powers of play lays a solid foundation and provides a learning progression onto which therapists then may overlay seminally or historically significant theories or add techniques" (Peabody & Schaefer, 2019, p. 6). For example, Stauffer (2021) described employing specific TPOP using Adlerian and psychological trauma theories in case studies of two child survivors of sexual abuse. She designed a structured superhero play therapy intervention to use with each boy to leverage self-expression, provide each with access to the unconscious, cultivate resiliency, practice self-regulation, and allow for abreaction and catharsis through drawing, writing, and movement. These TPOP and the play therapy processes in which they were used helped the boys to pass through toxic traumatic play (Gil, 2017) and to restart their development feeling more encouraged, empowered, and hopeful than before, according to the children prior to terminating therapy and their parents, two years after the last session was held.

Traumatic encounters of child sexual abuse shift the child's thought processes and perception of the world toward one of uncertainty, confusion, and threat. O'Connor differentiates therapeutic change processes from powers of play, believing that "the two are different but equally important, and the latter contributes to the former" (personal communication, May 17, 2023). O'Connor (2023) outlined care and treatment around three central frameworks: process, experience, and outcome. According to O'Connor (2023), the process requires play therapists to use interpretation of the case context or play to build awareness, supporting the selection or understanding of the emergence of therapeutic change agents required for recovery. The child's understanding of the problem will change through their play experience, allowing for renewed empowerment. The outcome of treatment includes resolution of the traumatic experience(s) and an integration of emotional and narrative storytelling processes, thereby meeting treatment goal outcomes for reduction of trauma symptomatology (O'Connor, 2023).

Although O'Connor's position diverged from Schaefer and Drewes's (2014) on the point of whether the therapeutic processes resulted from the play itself (K. O'Connor, personal communication, May 17, 2023), the current authors argue that play therapists should seek further education about play itself, and about how they can recognize the natural emergence of core agents of change initiated by the client in play therapy or how they can intentionally introduce these through implementing more or less structured interventions to help children overcome their difficulties and meet therapeutic goals. Through clinical case vignettes, the authors illustrate how the natural emergence or intentional introduction of TPOP may serve as change agents in trauma treatment for child sexual abuse.

Allie: Intentional Introduction of TPOP

Second grade had started off well for Allie (pseudonym), who was thriving in the classroom and within peer networks throughout the school, according to her teacher and parents. The school counselor reported concern about a month after winter break ended, stating Allie had grown inattentive during class, was moody, appeared fatigued, and was struggling in peer relationships during lunchtime and at recess. Allie's parents had taken her to a mental health provider in the community, but the clinician reporting to her parents considered Allie uncooperative and stated she was simply too young for talk-listen outpatient treatment to be effective. The outpatient provider suggested Allie seek support from the school counselor to assist with academic success and social skills. Her school counselor specifically recommended play therapy as a treatment approach.

Considering Allie had struggled previously with communication in therapy, her play therapist created an intentional introduction of the self-expression TPOP during treatment planning. Play provides children with the opportunity to access emotions and express those emotions into thoughts, making sense of their experiences (Morrison Bennett & Eberts, 2014). Nash (2021) described a procedure for intentionally selecting interventions or techniques in play therapy incorporating TPOP into the framework (see Figures 5.2 and 5.3). According to Nash, providers consider the context of the problem, characteristics of the child, and their theoretical orientation, then they develop a hypothesis to support the intentional activation of one or more TPOP to support the intervention. Allie required a play technique for self-expression, one which did not rely heavily on words to communicate emotion. Providing Allie with a vocabulary through images, toys, and other expressive arts materials, the play therapist could better support Allie's therapy.

Allie was drawn to the sandtray materials in play therapy. Sandtray can translate implicit memories or emotions into a concrete form through rich metaphors, with the play therapist reading the visual images created by the child to guide the therapeutic process (Homeyer & Lyles, 2022). Allie's sandtray depicted a scene of chaos, confusion, and fear. She added a present in the middle of her tray surrounded by layers of fencing. Near the present, she added a larger-than-life ear. Allie carefully selected and held a small horse in her hands. She stroked the horse gently with her finger and rocked side to side near the tray. Allie looked around the room and found a rocket ship with a removable door. She placed her horse inside the rocket ship, placing that rocket as far away from the ear as possible. She continued to add miniatures, carefully and precisely in the tray. When the tray was complete, the play therapist wondered aloud what the title of the tray would be if it had one. Allie whispered the one-word response of "feelings."

Allie had demonstrated clear therapeutic rapport and safety within the environment following several sessions designed to support the relationship. The horse and the ear stood out to the play therapist. Allie was presented with a directive sandtray prompt intentionally activating the TPOP for self-expression which would help both the provider and Allie gain a better understanding of the problem. Allie was asked to create

1 Presenting Problem

2 Hypothesis/ Theory

3 Play Characteristic

4 Therapeutic Power

5 Desired Outcome

6 Choose Technique

1 Shows fear of medical procedure (blood draw)

2 Developed fear from trauma (cognitive behavioral)

3 Non-literal, inner control, active Involvement

4 Abreaction

5 Reduce fear of medical procedure (ability to tolerate blood draw)

6 Release play therapy intervention

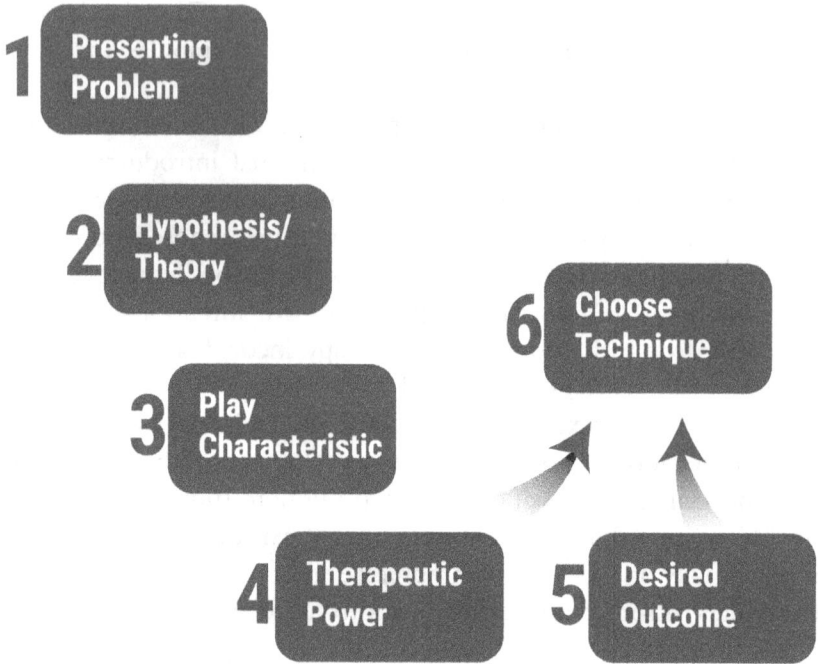

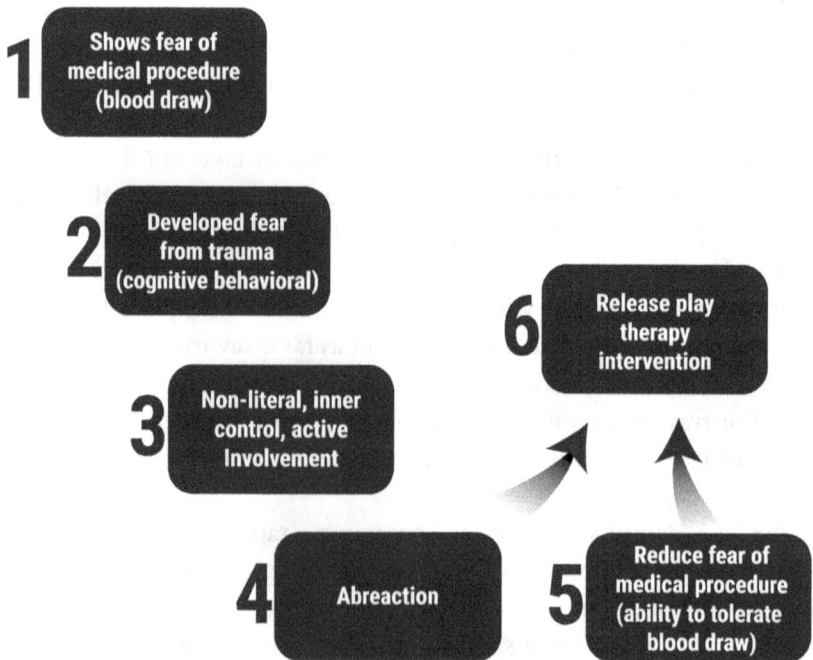

Figure 5.2 *and* 5.3 *Models for Treatment and Session Planning With Therapeutic Powers of Play.*

a story about the horse and the ear. Allie's story in the sand revealed a small horse who waited at night listening to the sounds which inevitably brought fear, pain, and confusion. A large tiger entered her room at night hissing terrible things in her ear before he joined her in bed. Allie's story was of a detailed sexual abuse experience, woven within the tapestry of lies being told to her. Allie was fearful her mother would no longer love her, she would be forced to live with another family if everyone knew what she had been forced to do, and that her younger sister would experience the same fate she endured at night if she spoke her truth. Allie carefully added the present from her original tray and a small Christmas tree, which later was understood as the timeframe for the onset of the sexual abuse. Together, through Allie's clear and consistent disclosures, Allie's mother and the forensic interview team were able to corroborate her symptom onset with the uncle's move-in date into the family's home. This session marked the beginning of a therapeutic process for trauma treatment and eventual recovery. Allie was able to identify her uncle as her abuse perpetrator and utilized the play materials to access self-expression for her storytelling, grounded in metaphor, to give voice to an uncomfortable truth in her family system.

Jared: Natural Emergence of TPOP

After a mid-February school holiday, Jared (pseudonym), a 9-year-old boy, disclosed the sexual abuse he had been experiencing at his father's hands and the threats to hurt him or his mother used to maintain his silence. Jared showed ambivalence toward his father, clearly stating that he no longer wanted to see his father during scheduled visits, which had been in place since his parents' divorce over six years prior, but also not wanting him to go to prison following his sexual abuse disclosure. His mother held full physical and legal custody of him, after a child protective services (CPS) investigation limited paternal authority following sexual abuse suspicions on Jared when he was 3 years old; the investigation was inconclusive, but the mother was awarded full custody and parental visitation was ordered for the father. Jared had seen a child psychiatrist at that time, but the therapy did not last very long.

Since this recent disclosure, Jared had been suffering from nighttime enuresis, headaches, and stomach aches. He had angry outbursts, began speaking to classmates and to his mother using profanity and sexual language that was inappropriate for his age, and showed a new curiosity to see his mother nude, which she found disconcerting. From a very early age, Jared had perturbed sleep cycles, often having trouble falling asleep. As he described it: "It's like there's a turbine in my head." He was also prescribed and was taking medication for attention deficit and hyperactivity disorder (ADHD).

His use of explicit language (profanity and sexual terms), as well as angry outbursts made it difficult for Jared to make and maintain friendships, though he explained, "I can't help it. [Those impulses are] stronger than I am." Jared found it difficult to communicate with words, citing math, art, and gym classes as his favorites. After taking several sessions to complete a kinetic family drawing (KFD; Sims, 1974) as part of play therapy assessment (cf. Stauffer, 2019), Jared activated the TPOP of self-expression, catharsis, positive emotions, stress management, creative problem solving, resiliency, self-regulation, self-esteem, attachment, and social competence largely through drawing comic strips outside of session that he would bring to session to share and continue completing, and by using the sand tray and the bop bag.

The play therapist offered empathetic witnessing to the traumatic content drawn or created in sand worlds (e.g., anger, violence, injustice, death, destruction, and the end of the world), noticing too, through tracking and encouragement, when a glimmer of hope appeared in the form of a friend that could help, a superhero that could intervene, or a creative way the main character in his comic strip would outsmart the bad guys. Over time, Jared's descriptions of his drawings went from "not that great" and "I can't really do it" to the play therapist observing the confidence he began to display when drawing, not erasing as much, completing panels with greater creativity, care, and ease. He entered states in session wherein ideas, solutions, and emotional self-regulation flowed naturally and more effortlessly, allowing for the TPOP of positive emotions to emerge.

Jared found his voice through his own processes of creation and catharsis, whether it was through pushing a pencil across the page or punching the bop bag across the playroom. He became more self-affirmed and able to clearly state that he did not want to see his father again and that what his father did was not right or fair. Both Jared's teacher and mother reported that he was making friends at school, drawing with a few boys in his class at recess and during free time in class, and that his use of profanity and sexualized words had diminished drastically. He no longer showed curiosity about naked bodies, and was able to fall asleep more quickly at night, especially after having created something in the playroom to put above his door "for protection." When therapy termination was recommended, he advocated to have three more sessions to be able to complete some drawings he wanted to finish, and to make one more creation out of clay – a 3D form of the protagonist in his comic strips to take with him. Jared activated TPOP resources to overcome social difficulties, emotional regulation issues, and relational barriers, finishing play therapy after the three additional sessions.

Limitations

Thirty years ago, Schaefer argued that the TPOP represented the basic mechanisms of change in play therapy and that by understanding these, play therapy could be more effective for clients engaged in this process. Over 20 years ago, Schaefer and Drewes (2014) expanded the initial list of 14 TPOP to 20, and the authors continued to argue that TPOP were grounded in a clear conceptualized framework. O'Connor (2023) cautioned play therapists not to "conflate the functions/powers of play with the functions/powers of therapy" lest they run the risk of "minimizing the importance of each on its own," as well as using a "cookbook approach" to designing interventions based on TPOP (Slide 13).

Play therapists risk limiting themselves and their therapies by not thinking deeply and critically about how they recognize or leverage the emergence of TPOP in and across their sessions. According to Peabody and Schaefer (2019), "training in the therapeutic powers of play creates an understanding of why and how play creates therapeutic change" (p. 5). Without such training or attention to these details, a play therapist may not realize that they do not just use toys; in fact, they create an environment to engage the TPOP core agents of change, promoting adaptive behaviors and strengthening therapeutic outcomes. This is where healing begins – through purposeful, evidence-based play.

Conclusion

The therapeutic powers of play (TPOP) offer profound avenues for healing and growth for sexually abused children. Through play therapy and creative arts, survivors can transcend the limitations of verbal expression, accessing the deeper, nonverbal realms where trauma resides. By engaging in metaphorical and symbolic play, facilitated by skilled play therapists, clients can integrate their traumatic experiences into a narrative, fostering resilience and restoring developmental trajectories. As Schaefer and Drewes (2014) interpreted, the diverse therapeutic powers of play are pivotal in guiding this transformative journey. Through these agents of change, children like Allie and Jared can reclaim agency over their experiences, find their voice through self-expression, and begin a path toward healing and renewed hope. Harnessing the intrinsic capacities of play, therapists empower their clients to not only heal from trauma but also rediscover their innate strengths and possibilities for a brighter future. When guided by the TPOP, every miniature, every sandtray, and every story becomes more than play – it becomes a pathway to connection, growth, and healing. It's where the invisible work of the heart is made visible, and where the unspeakable finds a voice.

Considerations for Practice: Key Takeaways

- Play therapists may recognize when therapeutic powers of play naturally emerge in children's play therapy processes to enhance these benefits further.
- Play therapists treating sexually abused children may recognize clients' avoidance of traumatic material and actively plan activities or potentialize key moments in therapy to activate the therapeutic powers of play so clients may benefit from them.
- Being mindful of the therapeutic powers of play may help play therapists bridge the emotional content of traumatic material with storytelling to help children remain within their windows of tolerance, and (co-)regulate their emotions prior to ending a play therapy session.
- Therapeutic powers of play may be considered a function of therapy and not necessarily the result of play itself; however, change agents immersed in play can offer children transformational opportunities for therapeutic growth.

References

Antichi, L., & Giannini, M. (2023). An introduction to change in psychotherapy: Moderators, course of change, and change mechanisms. *Journal of Contemporary Psychotherapy*, 53(4), 315–323. https://doi.org/10.1007/s10879-023-09590-x

Badenoch, B. (2017). *Heart of trauma: Healing the embodied brain in the context of relationships*. W. W. Norton.

Colarusso, C. A. (2010). *The long shadow of sexual abuse: Developmental effects across the life cycle*. Jason Aronson.

Gil, E. (2017). *Posttraumatic play in children: What clinicians need to know.* Guilford Press.

Haen, C. (2020). The roles of metaphor and imagination in child trauma treatment. *Journal of Infant, Child and Adolescent Psychotherapy, 19*(1), 42–55. https://doi.org/10.1080/15289168.2020.1717171

Herman, J. L. (2022). *Trauma and recovery: The aftermath of violence – from domestic abuse to political terror* (4th ed.). Basic Books.

Homeyer, L. E., & Lyles, M. N. (2022). *Advanced sandtray therapy: Digging deeper into clinical practice.* Routledge.

Kaduson, H. G., Cangelosi, D., & Schaefer, C. E. (Eds.). (2020). *Prescriptive play therapy: Tailoring interventions for specific childhood problems.* Guilford Press.

Kazdin, A. E. (2009). Understanding how and why psychotherapy leads to change. *Psychotherapy Research, 19*(4–5), 418–428. https://doi.org/10.1080/10503300802448899

McGilchrist, I. (2009). *The master and his emissary: The divided brain and the making of the Western world.* Yale University Press.

Morrison Bennett, M., & Eberts, S. (2014). Self-expression. In C. E. Schaefer & A. A. Drewes (Eds.), *The therapeutic powers of play: 20 core agents of change* (pp. 11–24). Wiley.

Nash, J. (2021, December). Utilizing the therapeutic powers of play to create change. *Play Therapy, 16*(4), 26–29.

O'Connor, K. (2023, October 10–15). *Therapeutic change processes: An integrative approach to optimizing play therapy outcomes* [Workshop]. International Association for Play Therapy Annual Conference, Palm Springs, CA. https://www.a4pt.org/resource/resmgr/annual_conference/2023/2023_APT_Conference_Brochure.pdf

Peabody, M. A., & Schaefer, C. E. (2019, September). The therapeutic powers of play: The heart and soul of play therapy. *Play Therapy, 14*(3), 4–6.

Pliske, M. M., Werner, A., & Stauffer, S. D. (2021). Healing from adverse childhood experiences through therapeutic powers of play: "I can do it with my hands." *International Journal of Play Therapy, 30*(4), 244–258. https://doi.org/10.1037/pla0000166

Schaefer, C. E., & Drewes, A. A. (2014). *Therapeutic powers of play: 20 core agents of change* (2nd ed.). Wiley.

Schaefer, C. E., & Drewes, A. A. (2016). Prescriptive play therapy. In K. J. O'Connor, C. E. Schaefer, & L. D. Braverman (Eds.), *The handbook of play therapy* (2nd ed., pp. 227–240). John Wiley & Sons.

Sims, C. A. (1974). Kinetic Family Drawings and the family relations indicator. *Journal of Clinical Psychology, 30*(1), 87–88. https://doi.org/dtrjt6

Stauffer, S. D. (2019). Ethical use of drawings in play therapy: Considerations for assessment, practice, and supervision. *International Journal of Play Therapy, 28*(4), 183–194. https://doi.org/10.1037/pla0000106

Stauffer, S. D. (2021). Overcoming trauma stuckness in play therapy: A superhero intervention to the rescue. *International Journal of Play Therapy, 30*(1), 14–27. https://doi.org/10.1037/pla0000149

PART II

APPLICATIONS OF SEMINAL AND HISTORICALLY SIGNIFICANT PLAY THERAPY THEORIES IN TREATING CHILDHOOD SEXUAL ABUSE

CHAPTER 6
ADLERIAN PLAY THERAPY
FACILITATING THE CRUCIAL CS IN SEXUALLY ABUSED CHILDREN

Terry Kottman and Erica Wassenaar

Adlerian Play Therapy (AdPT) is one approach to working with sexually abused children. Rooted in Alfred Adler's Individual Psychology (1927/1954), AdPT presents a dynamic and holistic approach to addressing children's psychological needs. This therapeutic modality combines the fundamental tenets of Individual Psychology with the creative expression inherent in play.

Overview and Basic Tenets of Individual Psychology and Adlerian Play Therapy

Alfred Adler, a prominent figure in the field of psychology, developed a theoretical framework known as Individual Psychology (Adler, 1927/1954, 1931/1958, 1925/2011). The basic tenets of this theoretical orientation include the following ideas: (a) people should be viewed from a holistic perspective, (b) the basic motivation for behavior is the striving for belonging and significance, (c) all behavior is purposive and supports individuals' movement toward their life goals, (d) individuals are born with the capacity to learn to connect with other people and their community, (e) all people are striving to overcome their feelings of inferiority, and (f) reality is perceived subjectively.

Terry Kottman (Kottman & Meany-Walen, 2016, 2018) developed Adlerian play therapy (AdPT), which combined the basic concepts underlying Individual Psychology with play therapy practices. In AdPT, the therapist conceptualizes clients from an Adlerian perspective while strategically and systematically using a wide variety of directive and non-directive skills and techniques as vehicles for supporting clients changing patterns of thinking, feeling, behaving, and interacting.

DOI: 10.4324/9781003451549-8

There are four phases of AdPT: building an egalitarian relationship; exploring the client's lifestyle (their perceptions of/beliefs about self, others, and the world and the behavior flowing from these perceptions and beliefs); helping clients gain insight into their lifestyles, and reorienting/re-educating by helping the client generate alternative, appropriate behavior; teaching skills (such as relationship skills, communication skills, self-regulation, problem-solving, and so forth); and providing opportunities to practice skills (Kottman & Meany-Walen, 2016, 2018). Adlerian play therapists believe that children need to have others (sometimes professionals, like counselors and teachers, and sometimes other influential people like parents, grandparents, neighbors) provide guidance in the forms of information, structure, insight, alternative perspective, skills teaching practice, and so forth to help them grow and flourish (Kottman & Meany-Walen, 2016). In AdPT, the relationship is a collaborative partnership in which the therapist and client share power and responsibility; the relationship serves as the foundation for everything else that follows in the therapeutic process.

Adlerian play therapists combine nondirective interaction with directive intervention, depending on the phase of counseling and the needs of specific clients (Kottman & Meany-Walen, 2016). In the first phase of counseling, Adlerian play therapists may use a few directive techniques to build a relationship with clients, but they are usually more nondirective. During the second phase, they use observation of children in the playroom, combined with asking questions of children and other informants, and introducing strategically planned activities to explore children's lifestyles. In the third phase of therapy, the play therapist uses directive techniques along with metaphors and metacommunication to help children gain insight. The fourth phase is the most directive phase, wherein the play therapist uses structured activities and homework as a way to teach skills and help reorient and re-educate clients. Because some clients are more amenable to directive techniques than others, Adlerian play therapists tailor the degree of directiveness to the needs of clients.

The therapeutic goals of AdPT include working to foster an increased sense of belonging and significance; helping clients learn to deal with feelings of discouragement and inferiority in healthier ways; assisting clients in changing their self-defeating beliefs, attitudes, and behaviors to more positive ones; helping clients gain a sense of equality with others; and helping people begin to make positive contributions to society and other people (Kottman & Meany-Walen, 2016, 2018). For specific clients, individual therapeutic goals will be related to their presenting problems and the underlying dynamics of clients' interpersonal and intrapersonal struggles. Adlerian play therapists also work with parents/caregivers and (when appropriate) teachers. The process of parent/caregiver and/or teacher consultation is an integral component of AdPT. The consultation with parents/caregivers and/or teachers follows the same progression as play therapy with clients. Adlerian play therapists also work with families in family play therapy and groups of school children with their teachers, when appropriate.

Among the most important tools for conceptualizing and treatment planning in AdPT is the assessment and enhancement of children's mastery of the Crucial Cs – Courage, Connect, Capable, Count. Lew and Bettner (1996), based on research on resilient children, suggested that children who are successful in life have strong relationships with others, feel valued by others, and perceive that they have control over some of the facets of their lives.

- Courage means being willing to try things without a guarantee of success. It does not mean the absence of anxiety or fear. Courage means not letting those anxious or fearful feelings stop individuals from doing what they think is important.
- Connect has two elements: valuing connecting with other people and having the ability and skills to connect with others.
- Capable involves believing that individuals are proficient at some things they think are important. It entails "owning" their achievements, skills, and gifts.
- Count requires that individuals believe that they are valuable and loveable without having to earn these things. They believe they make a contribution to others and the world in some ways.

    (Kottman & Meany-Walen, 2016; Lew & Bettner, 1996)

Adlerian play therapists assess their child clients through discussions with parents and teachers, observation, and structured play activities during the second phase of therapy to determine whether the clients are strong on each of the Cs or if they are struggling with mastering that C. For children who are strong in a particular C, play therapists work during Phases 3 and 4 to help them capitalize on that C. For children who are struggling with a specific C, play therapists use encouragement, metacommunication, and structured play interventions to help them strengthen their mastery of that C. In consultation, play therapists support parents/caregivers and teachers in learning more ways to foster the Cs with which the children might be struggling.

Children who have been sexually abused may struggle with all four of the Crucial Cs. Sexually abused children are frequently fearful of new situations because of the abuse–they may lack Courage because they are worried that trying new things will risk their safety. Difficulties in the sociorelational realm may also lead to difficulty with Connecting with others. They may also believe that the only way to connect is through sexualized behavior. Oftentimes, sexually abused children lack the sense that they are Capable because their confidence has been eroded through the abuse. They may also experience cognitive dysfunction, which can undermine their belief that they are Capable. Children in this population also tend to believe that the only way they count is through sexualized behavior or pleasing others because their abusers have taught them that the only way they matter is through placating through sexual interaction.

It is important to remember that, as Adler said, "Meanings are not determined by situations, but we determine ourselves by the meanings we give to situations" (1931/1958, p. 14). This tenet of Individual Psychology prevents Adlerian play therapists from overgeneralizing and making the assumption that all children who have experienced sexual abuse struggle with all four of the Crucial Cs. This leads therapists to consider the impact of sexual abuse on specific children based on their unique perceptions and interpretations of their experiences.

Literature Review of the Application of AdPT With Victims of Child Sexual Abuse

Childhood sexual abuse is a serious public health issue. Children who have experienced sexual abuse tend to exhibit a plethora of symptoms, including low self-esteem, anxiety, depression, anger and aggression, dissociation, substance abuse, sociorelational difficulties, cognitive dysfunction, internalization and externalization of problems, sexualized behaviors, and posttraumatic symptoms among others (Gupta & Garg, 2020; Lo Iacono et al., 2021).

Research has shown AdPT to be beneficial when working with students who exhibit disruptive behaviors (Meany-Walen et al., 2012), maladaptive perfectionism and anxiety in children (Akay & Bratton, 2017; Akay-Sullivan et al., 2016), maladjustment to preschool (Izzaty et al.,

2016), and children with externalizing behaviors and poor social skills (Meany-Walen et al., 2015b; Meany-Walen & Teeling, 2016). One study has also found the benefit of utilizing group AdPT when working with children with off-task behaviors (Meany-Walen et al., 2015a).

However, there is a dearth of professional literature about the application of AdPT with victims of child sexual abuse. Snow et al. (1999) presented a case study that suggested AdPT was effective with a child who had experienced trauma, but the lack of a research design in the case study prevented it from being considered evidence of the efficacy of AdPT. Evans (2020) conducted a multiple-baseline single-subject design study to investigate the effects of AdPT on five traumatized children who demonstrated symptoms of posttraumatic stress disorder (PTSD). She found that, after 16 sessions of AdPT, trauma symptoms were significantly reduced in all five participants in the sample. She acknowledged that due to the research design causation could not be determined. However, because of the use of a multiple-baseline intervention, she believed it was highly unlikely that trauma symptom reduction was the result of coincidence or extraneous variables.

Greenwood and Eldredge (2022) suggested that AdPT is congruent with the four core assumptions in a trauma-informed counseling approach. The first of those assumptions is the *Realization* of trauma, meaning that counselors who work with traumatized children have a fundamental knowledge base about trauma and its impact on those who have experienced trauma (Substance Abuse and Mental Health Services Association [SAMHSA], 2014). This assumption is met in the first phase of AdPT, *Building the Relationship*, where trauma-informed play therapists understand how a child's experience with trauma has an impact on the child's ability to build a relationship with them.

The second core assumption in trauma-informed counseling is *Recognition*, wherein counselors recognize traumatic symptoms and recognize that the expression of trauma symptoms is often influenced by age, culture, gender identity, and specific settings of service delivery. In AdPT, therapists take these factors into consideration in the second phase of therapy, Exploring the Client's Lifestyle. Adlerian play therapists always consider how the child's developmental stage, familial, and environmental factors impact the expression of traumatic stress.

The third core assumption in trauma-informed counseling is *Responding*, which involves the counselor, agency, and overarching organization applying the fundamental principles of trauma-informed care. Adlerian play therapists are intentional in searching for specific interventions that are appropriate for specific clients in all the phases of therapy. In the third phase, *Helping the Client Gain Insight*, Adlerian play therapists use toys and expressive materials, sand tray figures that may be connected to traumatic experiences (such as death-related figures, authority figures like police officers, and parental figures); and the application of metacommunication, creative drama activities, metaphors and storytelling, and role-playing to appropriately respond to children who have been traumatized and help them gain insight into the impact of the trauma on how they see themselves, the world, and others.

The fourth core assumption in trauma-informed care is to *Resist Retraumatization*. Many children who have been traumatized are reluctant to talk directly about what happened to them. By forcing these children to tell the story of the trauma, the therapist may risk re-traumatizing them–this would be a violation of the tenets of AdPT, which state the child can use the play to communicate without ever having to tell the story of the traumatic thing that happened to them. In AdPT, the therapist allows the child to communicate through metaphor rather than direct communication. During Phase 4 of AdPT, the therapist may tell stories or use direct teaching to help the child learn skills to help avoid future retraumatization. Clinical Case Study

Cecilia is a 7-year-old only child who was sexually abused over a period of several months by a male college student, who sometimes babysat for her. Her behavior had recently changed, with her becoming clingy with her parents, asking them not to leave her with babysitters, and crying whenever her parents left her at daycare. Cecilia's parents had noticed that she had started hesitating to try new things, had gotten very shy and withdrawn around adults, and was struggling at school, which had not been the case earlier. After several months of this behavior, she told her mother that "Gerald touches my privates whenever he babysits me. Sometimes it hurts. He's not supposed to do that, is he?" Her parents believed her, reported the incidents to Child Protective Services, and immediately brought her to Jean, an Adlerian play therapist, to help her work through her feelings about the abuse and to help her regain confidence, self-esteem, and a sense of self-efficacy.

After consulting with Cecilia's parents and observing her behavior in the playroom during Phases 1 and 2 of the play therapy process, Jean recognized that the sexual abuse had detrimentally affected Cecilia's mastery of the Crucial Cs of Courage, Capable, and Connect. Cecilia had difficulty separating from her parents to go to the playroom, and once she got to the playroom, she would only play with toys and art materials she had at home, frequently saying, "I know how to play with this." When she encountered trouble making things in the playroom work the way she wanted them to work, Cecilia would give up, often with comments like, "I can't figure that out." or "That's too hard for me. I'm not good at things like that." Since Cecilia's parents reported that before the sexual abuse, Cecilia had confidently tried new things and believed she could figure out anything, regardless of the difficulty, these patterns suggested to Jean that Cecilia was struggling with Courage and Capable as a result of the abuse. Cecilia seldom made eye contact with Jean and chose not to interact with any of the other children in the waiting room of Jean's office. Her parents reported that she was withdrawn and shy when she was around older, bigger children at school and in their neighborhood, and she did not like to be touched by any adults, which had not been the case before the sexual abuse. This signaled to Jean that Cecilia's Connect was also impacted by the abuse. Cecilia always hugged her parents and looked to them for approval—she seemed confident that she was important to her parents and that they would listen to her and respect what she had to say, which indicated to Jean that her Count remained strong.

Jean planned a series of directed play activities to help Cecilia gain insight in Phase 3 and support her in making shifts in some of her thoughts, feelings, and behavior in Phase 4. Because Cecilia refused to discuss the abuse with Jean, instead acting out scenes in the dollhouse where children needed to hide from adults who would hurt them, Jean decided she would need to use a metaphor to help Cecilia. Jean's goal was to help Cecilia understand that many older children and adults could be trusted not to hurt her and to renew her belief that she was courageous enough to try new activities and that she could successfully master difficult tasks (Courage and Capable). She also wanted to help Cecilia recognize that she could make and keep friends, discerning who was safe and interested in friendship (Connect). Jean told a series of stories about a little mouse (CeCe) who always hid in a hollow tree because she was afraid that other creatures would hurt her. An owl had once nipped her tail trying to capture her for lunch, so she had overgeneralized that other animals would always be dangerous to her. With the help of a neighboring hedgehog, CeCe determined that not everyone was dangerous and that she had many resources for keeping herself safe and distinguishing when another creature was dangerous. CeCe, the mouse, went on other adventures, learning to try new things, make friends, trust herself, and believe in her abilities. Jean invited Cecilia to take over telling the stories and invent new adventures for CeCe. She also requested that Cecilia join her in playing in the dollhouse, with a variety of other characters coming to the door and asking to come into the house, with Cecilia deciding whether those creatures were safe enough to let them enter. As time passed, Cecilia duplicated CeCe's progress in the playroom and other situations. She started being willing to play with other children in the neighborhood and at school, was increasingly willing to try new activities, and expressed confidence in her abilities. Jean felt that her lagging Crucial Cs had been restored and worked with Cecilia's parents to continue to support her development of Courage, Capable, and Connect, along with continuing to foster Count.

Limitations

While AdPT has shown effectiveness in treating a wide range of childhood issues, including trauma, its application with sexual abuse victims presents unique challenges. While AdPT can be a valuable approach for working with sexually abused victims, like any therapeutic method, it has limitations. AdPT focuses on a child's overall well-being and emphasizes the exploration of basic life tasks, such as social interaction, belongingness, and personal achievement. As such, it may not always adequately address the specific traumatizing experiences of all childhood sexual abuse victims, who sometimes require specialized attention to their unique trauma-related issues (Fortuna et al., 2017). Because of this limitation, it may be necessary to combine AdPT with additional modalities like Trauma-Focused Cognitive Behavioral Therapy (TF-CBT) (Cohen et al., 2006, 2017) or Eye Movement Desensitization and Reprocessing (EMDR) (Adler-Tapia et al., 2011). Specific training related to the impact and treatment of sexual abuse is crucial for Adlerian play therapists to offer effective and ethical support. Unintentional retraumatization is a potential risk in AdPT, emphasizing the need for therapist expertise, trauma-informed practice, and ongoing education. While play provides a non-threatening medium for accessing traumatic memories, it can also trigger distressing emotions and flashbacks. Inadvertently exposing sexual abuse victims to distressing play themes or situations during therapy sessions may compound their trauma rather than facilitate healing (Johnson, 2019). The effectiveness of AdPT can be influenced by the child's age and developmental stage, requiring tailored interventions. Therapists using AdPT should have a solid understanding of trauma-informed care and interventions specific to sexual abuse (Evans, 2020). Inadequate training may lead to incomplete or ineffective support. In Adlerian therapy, involving the family is often important (Kottman & Meany-Walen, 2016). In cases of sexual abuse, however, involving the family may be challenging due to trust issues or the involvement of the perpetrator, limiting the therapist's ability to address systemic family issues. While AdPT acknowledges cultural influence, it may not explicitly address cultural nuances related to sexual abuse, necessitating cultural sensitivity from therapists.

Conclusion

AdPT, rooted in the foundational principles of Individual Psychology, offers a holistic and goal-oriented approach to addressing the needs of sexually abused children. Emphasizing the importance of social interest, goal-oriented behavior, and the pursuit of belonging and significance, AdPT aligns with the core tenets of Adler's theoretical framework. The therapeutic process, divided into four phases, focuses on building an egalitarian relationship, exploring the client's lifestyle, gaining insight, and reorienting through skill-building and practice.

Therapists employing AdPT with sexually abused children must be well-trained, continuously educate themselves, and collaborate with other professionals when needed. Integrating multiple therapeutic modalities based on individual needs and circumstances can enhance the overall effectiveness of the therapeutic process. Additionally, involving parents/caregivers in therapy may present challenges, requiring careful consideration of trust, family dynamics, and the presence of the perpetrator. AdPT offers a valuable framework for promoting a child's overall well-being and resilience. Its application with sexually abused children demands a nuanced and specialized approach. Therapists must be attuned to the unique needs of this population, continually refine their skills, and engage in ongoing collaboration and education to provide ethical, effective, and culturally sensitive support.

Considerations for Practice: Key Takeaways

- AdPT, rooted in Alfred Adler's Individual Psychology, offers a holistic perspective in understanding children. The basic tenets, such as the importance of belonging, purposive behavior, and the innate capacity to belong, guide therapists in addressing the psychological needs of sexually abused children.

- The emphasis on Courage, Connect, Capable, and Count (Crucial Cs) provides a valuable framework for assessing and enhancing a child's well-being. Adlerian play therapists tailor interventions based on the child's strengths and struggles with these Cs, promoting a sense of belonging, positive self-esteem, and interpersonal skills.
- AdPT, while effective for various childhood issues, may not comprehensively address the specific trauma-related issues of all sexually abused victims. Specialized attention to trauma-related issues, such as those requiring TF-CBT or EMDR, may be necessary.
- Therapists should be aware of potential unintentional retraumatization and continuously update their knowledge on trauma-informed practices.

References

Adler, A. (1954). *Understanding human nature* (W. B. Wolf, Trans.). Fawcett Premier. (Original work published 1927)

Adler, A. (1958). *What life should mean to you.* Capricorn. (Original work published 1931)

Adler, A. (2011). *The practice and theory of Individual Psychology.* Martino Fine Books. (Original work published 1925)

Adler-Tapia, R., Settle, C., & Shapiro, F. (2011). Eye movement desensitization and reprocessing (EMDR) psychotherapy with children who have experienced sexual abuse and trauma. In P. Goodyear-Brown (Ed.), *Handbook of child sexual abuse: Identification, assessment, and treatment* (pp. 229–250). Wiley.

Akay, S., & Bratton, S. (2017). The effects of Adlerian play therapy on maladaptive perfectionism and anxiety in children: A single case design. *International Journal of Play Therapy, 26*(2), 96–110. https://doi.org/10.1037/pla0000043

Akay-Sullivan, S., Sullivan, J., & Bratton, S. C. (2016). The courage to be imperfect: A boy's journey toward becoming a child. *Journal of Individual Psychology, 72*(4), 273–389.

Cohen, J. A., Mannarino, A. P., & Deblinger, E. (2006). *Treating trauma and traumatic grief in children and adolescents.* Guilford Press.

Cohen, J. A., Mannarino, A. P., & Deblinger, E. (2017). *Treating trauma and traumatic grief in children and adolescents* (2nd ed.). Guilford Press.

Evans, C. (2020). Adlerian play therapy and trauma. *The Journal of Individual Psychology, 76*(2), 217–228.

Fortuna, L. R., Alvarez, K., Ramos Ortiz, Z., Wang, Y., Mozo Alegría, X., & Cook, B. L. (2017). Mental health, migration stressors and suicidal ideation among Latino immigrants in Spain and the United States. *European Journal of Public Health*, *27*(3), 484–490.

Greenwood, M., & Eldredge, K. (2022, January). *Trauma-informed Adlerian play therapy*. Association for Humanistic Counseling. https://www.humanisticcounseling. org/news/4dd1bve7affr9vsk49bl4j6k2zn8df

Gupta, S., & Garg, S. (2020). Causes and effects of child sexual abuse. *International Journal of Innovative Science and Research Technology*, *5*(5), 1867–1870.

Izzaty, R. E., Cholimah, N., & Astuti, B. (2016). The implementation of an integrative model of adventure-based counseling and Adlerian play therapy value-based taught by parents to children to increase adjustment ability of preschool children. *Asia Pacific Journal of Multidisciplinary Research*, *4*(4), 36–45.

Johnson, V. (2019). Re-traumatization in child development and mental health services. *Journal of Trauma & Dissociation*, *20*(4), 475–491.

Kottman, T., & Meany-Walen, K. (2016). *Partners in play: An Adlerian approach to play therapy*. American Counseling Association.

Kottman, T., & Meany-Walen, K. (2018). *Doing play therapy: From building the relationship to facilitating change*. Guilford.

Lew, A., & Bettner, B. L. (1996). *A parent's guide to understanding and motivating children*. Connexions Press.

Lo Iacono, L., Trentini, C., & Carola, V. (2021). Psychobiological consequences of childhood sexual abuse: Current knowledge and clinical implications. *Frontiers in Neuroscience*, *15*, 771511. https://doi.org/10.3389/fnins.2021.771511

Meany-Walen, K. K., Bratton, S.C., & Kottman, T. (2012). Effects of Adlerian Play Therapy on reducing students' disruptive behaviors. *Journal of Counseling and Development*, *92*(1), 47–56.

Meany-Walen, K. K., Bullis, Q., Kottman, T., & Dillman Taylor, D. (2015a). Group Adlerian Play Therapy with children with off-task behaviors. *Journal for Specialists in Group Work*, *40*(3), 294–314. https://doi.org/10.1080/01933922.1056569

Meany-Walen, K. K., Kottman, T., Bullis, Q., & Dillman Taylor, D. (2015b). Effects of Adlerian Play Therapy on children's externalizing behavior. *Journal of Counseling and Development*, *93*(4), 418–428. https://doi.org/10.1002/jcad.12040

Meany-Walen, K. K., & Teeling, S. (2016). Adlerian Play Therapy with students with externalizing behaviors and poor social skills. *International Journal of Play Therapy*, *25*(2), 64–77. https://doi.org/10.1037/pla0000022

Snow, M. S., Buckley, M. R., & Williams, S.C. (1999). Case study using Adlerian Play Therapy. *Journal of Individual Psychology*, *55*(3), 328–341.

Substance Abuse and Mental Health Services Association (SAMHSA). (2014). *SAMHSA's concept of trauma and guidance for a trauma-informed approach*. https:// ncsacw.samhsa.gov/userfiles/files/SAMHSA_Trauma.pdf

CHAPTER 7

CHILD-CENTERED PLAY THERAPY AND CHILDHOOD SEXUAL ABUSE

THE POWER OF RELATIONSHIP

Dee C. Ray, Amber-Lea Martinez and Bonnie L. Stice

Child-Centered Play Therapy (CCPT) is a therapy of relationship. The relationship between therapist and child is considered the healing factor that promotes the child's holistic development and unleashes the child's natural tendency toward optimal health. In CCPT, the child experiences safety, acceptance, empowerment, and trust. For children who have been sexually abused, these are the dimensions of adult-child relationships that have been exploited and violated. The CCPT therapist seeks to provide healing of these relational disruptions by walking alongside the child in their journey toward reconciling their experiences with the perception of self. The organism of the child can be trusted to move toward health when provided with an environment in which the child experiences therapeutic authenticity, acceptance of all parts and experiences of the child, and empathic connection with the person of the child.

The environment and relationship fostered within CCPT subverts the power differential that exists outside of the playroom in which the child is typically powerless (Ray, 2011). This may be particularly befitting for treatment of CSA survivors who display tendencies to please adults (Reyes & Asbrand, 2005). In CCPT, children are given an opportunity to experience self-responsibility and a feeling of being in control, free from the conditions placed on them by the adults in their lives (Landreth, 2024; Ray, 2011). Over the last 40 years, there has been a steady amount of literature examining play therapy as potentially effective with children who have been sexually abused, but the topic remains underresearched and deserves greater attention.

DOI: 10.4324/9781003451549-9

Overview and Basic Tenets of CCPT

CCPT is the most widely used and researched play therapy approach, as well as the most enduring child counseling intervention, with its inception dating back over 80 years (Ray, 2011). Based on person-centered theory proposed by Carl Rogers (1951), Virginia Axline (1947) adapted person-centered principles to meet the developmental needs of children in the form of play therapy. Recognizing play as children's natural form of communication, Axline developed methods of therapy that used play as a tool of communication to build the necessary and healing conditions of the therapeutic relationship.

The primacy of the healing relationship in CCPT is grounded in the theoretical constructs of person-centered propositions presented by Rogers (1951). Rogers' developmental theory provides a roadmap for recognizing the person's innate qualities and the impact of events occurring between the person and the environment that may lead to maladaptive or unhealthy self-structures for the organism. According to person-centered theory, each person is the center of their own reality, perceiving events and experiences from their own unique lens. This perception is reality for the person. Each person is born with a self-actualizing tendency, the drive to maintain and enhance the organism (Rogers, 1951). Behavior, which is accompanied by emotion, is the goal-directed attempt of each person to meet the needs of the organism within the perceptual field. Evaluational interactions with others may result in perceived "conditions of worth" in which the child feels a sense of worth only under specific conditions that may or may not be consistent with the organismic valuing process. When a child denies awareness of significant sensory and visceral experiences, they are not symbolized in the self-structure, which can result in psychological maladjustment.

The practice of CCPT is predicated on the belief that a child enters the world with a propensity to move toward enhancing the self and relationship with others. As the child interacts with others over the course of development, the child develops a perception of self that is constructed from the introjections of conditions of worthiness or absence of such conditions. When a child receives messages of self-worth tied to meeting adult and peer expectations, the child develops a self-structure that is estranged from the innate organismic tendency, leading to problematic behaviors and emotions.

Emanating from the theoretical constructs of CCPT is the essential practice of offering intervention in which a child is provided an environment absent of conditions of worth. The CCPT environment is marked by three therapist attitudinal conditions including genuineness and authenticity of the therapist, therapist's unconditional positive regard for the child, and therapist's empathic understanding of the whole child (Ray, 2011; Rogers, 1957). Through attention to genuineness, the therapist seeks to operate from a high level of personal awareness in which the therapist is open to both internal and external experiences, allowing accessibility to emotional responses and motivations for behaviors. Through this genuineness, the child experiences the therapist as known, trustworthy, and safe. Through unconditional positive regard, the therapist sends messages of believing in the child's capability, self-direction, and worthiness. Valuing the language of play as the child's primary language is one way to send a message of unconditional positive regard for the child, while following the child's lead in therapy serves as another message of trust in the child's natural movement toward health. The therapist's ability to experience accurate empathic understanding and communicate this understanding to the child facilitates the child's sense of worthiness and meets the relational needs of the child.

CCPT Theory in Action

Due to extensive outcome research, CCPT is recognized as a promising evidence-based practice by multiple entities including California Evidence-Based Clearinghouse for Child Welfare (https://www.cebc4cw. org/) and Title IV – E Prevention Services Clearinghouse (*https://preventionservices.acf.hhs.gov/*). Based on the belief in the child's organismic valuing process, CCPT offers an intervention in which the child leads the play or verbal interaction in therapy. The therapist trusts the child to direct therapy toward what the child needs. The therapist's role is to facilitate an environment in which the child feels free to pursue play or conversation that meets the child's needs. The therapist sends nonverbal messages of care, understanding, and relational connection in order to experience and convey the attitudinal conditions of genuineness, unconditional positive regard, and empathic understanding. As an evidence-based intervention, CCPT offers a specific verbal protocol that includes categories of therapist responses including tracking behavior, reflecting content, reflecting feeling, returning responsibility, encouragement, facilitating creativity, reflecting relationship, reflecting larger meaning, and limit setting (see Ray, 2011). The environment of CCPT also involves the careful selection of diverse play materials that allow for a child's full expression of experiences, emotions, and thoughts (see Landreth, 2024).

CSA and CCPT

Children who have experienced CSA often exhibit a wide range of post-traumatic behaviors, from internalizing symptoms such as fear, depression, and nightmares to externalizing symptoms including aggression, sexualized behaviors, and hypervigilance (Kendall-Tackett et al., 1993; Narang et al., 2019). Additionally, child survivors of CSA often experience lower self-esteem than children who have not experienced CSA (Kendall-Tackett et al., 1993) as well as high levels of shame (Narang et al., 2019) impacting their overall self-concept. CSA's impacts are deep and broad, impacting multiple facets of a child's experience.

Theoretically, CCPT therapists conceptualize childhood sexual abuse as an egregious and damaging evaluational interaction with the environment; in this case, interaction with a specific person or persons. Developmentally, any child is vulnerable to the conditions of worth introjected from persons in the environment. In the case of CSA, children are particularly vulnerable to a perpetrator who asserts conditions that may demand compliance, subjugation, and pain in order to please the adult (Hawkins, 2017). From these experiences, there are deleterious consequences to the self-structure. The child may develop a self that perceives worthiness through meeting these conditions with all others, losing contact with the internal organism altogether. Or the child may dissociate and deny symbolization of the experience to the self, moving further away from the core of self (Hawkins, 2017). CSA represents a disruption in relationships that leads to a disruption in the self-structure. Hence, CCPT offers healing by providing an environment and relationship characterized by "depth of relating and trust in the client's own self-directed process to provide the reparative experience of real empowerment" (Hawkins, 2014, p. 24).

In CCPT, the child's innate actualizing tendency is trusted to lead play therapy in the direction of accurately symbolizing their experiences in order to integrate experiences into a healthy self-structure. CSA leaves the child feeling powerless, helpless, and defenseless (Hawkins, 2014). In contrast, CCPT avoids the replication of these experiences that are often echoed through other mental health interventions in which the therapist leads the child toward goals set by the therapist believed to be best for the child. For children who have been sexually abused, the CCPT therapist seeks to provide a wholly different experience for the child in which the child is free to explore their experiences and internalized perceptions at their own pace. The child learns to trust their own experience, motivations, and process in the context of a safe relationship and through the language of play, the antithesis of the child's abuse experiences.

CSA Research and CCPT

CCPT has been shown to be effective with children who have experienced trauma (Humble et al., 2019; Parker et al., 2021; Ray et al., 2022), yet there has been little research exploring CCPT specifically with CSA survivors. In Humble et al.'s (2019) review of a handful of studies (N=6) exploring the use of CCPT with children who have experienced trauma, they found that participation in CCPT resulted in improvements in self-concept and competence, internalizing problems, externalizing problems, and posttraumatic stress symptoms. However, studies encompassed various and diverse outcomes that produced non-significant effects among other variables. In a much larger review of CCPT trauma studies (N=32), Parker et al. (2021) found that CCPT studies reported significant improvements in internalizing, externalizing, and total behavior problems for children who had experienced adverse childhood experiences. Finally, Ray et al. (2022) conducted the largest study to date on outcomes for children who experienced multiple adverse childhood experiences and participated in CCPT. Through a randomized controlled design, Ray et al. reported that children who participated in CCPT improved in social-emotional competencies and reduced behavioral problems at a statistically significant level with moderate effect size over children in a waitlist control group. These results are promising for the impact of CCPT participation with children who have experienced multiple or single trauma events yet there has been little examination of CCPT with children who have experienced the specific adverse childhood experience of sexual abuse.

In a small study, Scott et al. (2003) investigated the impact of ten sessions of CCPT on mood, self-concept, and social competence in children who exhibited behaviors of sexual abuse ranging in age from 3 to 9 at post-treatment and two-month follow-up. Findings were mixed with children reporting higher levels of competence but parents not reporting significant change. Scott et al. found that the children who experienced the most lifetime trauma also exhibited the most reliable change in CCPT, hypothesizing that family functioning or personal resiliency may support play therapy's effectiveness with this group. Scott et al. (2003) concluded that CSA treatment should involve families and parents. Reyes and Asbrand (2005) measured the impact of 9 months of play therapy (N = 18) on children's trauma symptoms resulting from sexual abuse. Play therapists identified mostly as CCPT but were trained in other methods. The authors found that child self-reported symptoms of anxiety, depression, posttraumatic stress, and sexual distress saw statistically significant drops. In addition, there was a substantial decrease in trauma symptoms for children who reported clinical levels of symptoms at pretest. Overall, these studies support CCPT's potential effectiveness in treating children who have been sexually abused, while elevating a need for more in-depth research on the topic.

Clinical Case Study

Emeric, a 5-year-old boy, was brought to the counseling clinic by his parents, Mr. and Ms. Bailey, after discovering Emeric had been sexually abused by his uncle for the past year following Emeric's sexually inappropriate behaviors with other children at his preschool. During the intake appointment, the play therapist met with Mr. and Mrs. Bailey to gather information regarding Emeric, discuss their concerns, and orient them to the play therapy process. With the primary goal of developing a relationship with the parents in this first parent consultation (Ray, 2011), the play therapist used genuineness to create a reciprocal relationship with the parents, empathic understanding to better understand the parents' concerns, and unconditional positive regard to accept the parents' experiences without pushing them to change or parent differently. Using these core attitudinal conditions is invaluable within a child-centered perspective (Landreth, 2024) and extends into work with parents as well as with children. Mr. and Mrs. Bailey expressed both fear and concern for Emeric's well-being, powerlessness regarding how to best support him through healing, and guilt for feeling unable to protect him. The play therapist assured the Baileys that they would have regularly scheduled parent consultations to address their parenting concerns and provide them with the support they need. The Baileys were unsure of the therapeutic process, wondering how Emeric would "get better just by playing," but were receptive to the therapist's explanation of play therapy and how they would create a relationship and a space that allowed Emeric to lead his own healing.

The next week, as the play therapist introduced herself to Emeric in the lobby, he shrank toward his parents and was hesitant to follow the therapist to the play therapy room. As they slowly walked to the play therapy room, Emeric's eyes flitted around, taking in his new environment with caution. The play therapist introduced the space to Emeric in a manner consistent with CCPT (Landreth, 2024), communicating trust in his self-directed play (i.e., "in here, you can choose to play with these toys in lots of ways that you'd like"). After briefly exploring the play therapy room, Emeric eagerly gravitated toward toys that made him feel powerful (i.e., the king crown, the sword, the gun) and used these toys to exert control over the therapist (i.e., bossing them around, handcuffing and blindfolding them, attacking them).

Throughout the session, the play therapist used her nonverbal presence as well as reflections of feeling, reflections of content, and tracking statements to convey the four healing messages: I hear you. I'm here. I understand. I care (Landreth, 2024). Emeric's self-directed play facilitated communication (Schaefer & Drewes, 2014); he expressed through play his desire to be powerful and in control while providing his play therapist with an empathic glimpse into his world of powerlessness. Concurrently, Emeric presented as hypervigilant, overly aware of other people in the clinic or loud noises in other play therapy rooms. In these moments, Emeric would often try to leave the play therapy room, run toward the clinic lobby, or attack the play therapist with the sword. Responding to Emeric's hypervigilance, the therapist reflected his feelings of fear while also creating structure and safety by utilizing ACT limit setting (Landreth, 2024): A-acknowledge feelings (i.e., "I know you're angry"), C-communicate limit (i.e., "but I am not for hitting"), T-target alternative (i.e., "You can hit the bobo").

As the play therapist continued to convey acceptance and care within their relationship, Emeric began using his play to explore and express more aspects of himself, including pieces of himself that he had previously rejected for fear of being wholly rejected. Emeric began undressing the dolls and exploring their body parts. He reenacted sexual acts with the people figurines and would then bury them in the sand, hiding them from his play therapist. Throughout this play, the therapist did not express a desire for Emeric to play differently, instead conveying to

Emeric trust in his process, empathy with his experience, and acceptance in his reactions to that experience. Through play, Emeric began to involve a lizard toy in his play stories, often using the lizard as the direct target of his anger, calling him "bad" and "nasty" and burying him in the sand. As Emeric engaged in this abreactive play (Schaefer & Drewes, 2014), the play therapist reflected his anger and disgust toward the lizard. As these feelings, which previously brought up feelings of shame within Emeric, were accepted by the therapist within the therapeutic relationship, Emeric's cathartic play with the lizard intensified. Emeric began engaging in traumatic reenactment with the lizard, alternating between using the sword to "slice" the lizard's private parts and rubbing the lizard's private parts gently. At times, Emeric would play out sexual acts between the lizard and other animals. As this play became more intense and repetitive, the play therapist stayed in his play and continued to provide him with a relationship of safety and understanding.

Within the therapeutic relationship, Emeric was able to use play as a means of fostering emotional wellness (Schaefer & Drewes, 2014) by processing his feelings of fear, anger, and shame while also experiencing moments of joy, love, and connection. As Emeric continued to process his experiences within the context of a safe relationship, he began to increase his personal strengths (Schaefer & Drewes, 2014), developing a stronger self-concept through a deeper understanding of himself. Emeric's integration of his experiences into his self-structure resulted in a sense of strength and empowerment. Emeric's self-regulation and self-control increased as well, and limits were set less frequently by the therapist. Both the therapist and Mr. and Mrs. Bailey noted decreased levels of concerning behaviors and increased positive social interactions. Through regular parent consultations, the Baileys worked with the play therapist to discover new ways of relating to Emeric, using CCPT-based parenting skills such as reflective listening, encouragement, and ACT limit setting. True to his name, Emeric, a French name meaning strength and resilience, experienced relational healing following a relational trauma and experienced love and trust within relationship.

Limitations

CCPT is designed as an intervention that strengthens a child's self-concept and relational connections with others, indicating that CCPT is functionally beneficial for all children. However, for children who have experienced sexual abuse, research is limited in the correlation of outcomes between CCPT and CSA. CCPT is not an educational intervention; hence, CCPT practices typically will not include teaching children about sexual abuse, sexual boundaries, or ways in which they can keep themselves safe from future abuse. Although these are worthy goals and necessary for children's safety, the CCPT therapist works with other systemic partners to provide these educational opportunities to victims of CSA rather than provide them directly. The focus for the CCPT therapist is providing a relationship that builds the self-structure of the child; a relationship that emphasizes the worthiness of the child, allowing them to embrace the idea that they deserve to be safe and use the tools to keep themselves safe.

Considerations for Practice: Key Takeaways

- CCPT offers a relational, reparative intervention for victims of CSA to counteract the relational violations they have experienced.
- CCPT facilitates the empowerment of victims of CSA by allowing children to integrate their experiences and perceptions into their self-concept at their own pace, the antithesis of what they have experienced with their perpetrators.
- CCPT therapists need to be prepared to work with victims of CSA through considerable knowledge of CSA and through the ability to accept and journey with children through their darkest of thoughts and actions.
- Because CCPT focuses on empowering the child's self-concept through building a sense of worthiness, CCPT therapists will likely employ adjunct systemic partners to provide for the educational needs of CSA victims.

References

Axline, V. (1947). *Play therapy.* Ballantine.

Hawkins, J. (2014). Person-centered therapy with adult survivors of child sexual abuse. In P. Pearce & L. Sommerbeck (Eds.), *Person-centered practice at the difficult edge* (pp. 14–26). PCCS.

Hawkins, J. (2017). Living with pain: Mental health and the legacy of childhood abuse. In S. Joseph's (Ed.), *The handbook of person-centered therapy and mental health: Theory, research and practice* (pp. 275–295). PCCS.

Humble, J. J., Summers, N. L., Villarreal, V., Styck, K. M., Sullivan, J. R., Hechler, J. M., & Warren, B. S. (2019). Child-centered play therapy for youths who have experienced trauma: A systematic literature review. *Journal of Child & Adolescent Trauma*, *12*(3), 365–375. https://doi.org.libproxy.library.unt.edu/10.1007/s40653-018-0235-7

Kendall-Tackett, K. A., Williams, L. M., & Finkelhor, D. (1993). Impact of sexual abuse on children: A review and synthesis of recent empirical studies. *Psychological Bulletin*, *113*(1), 164–180. https://doi.org/10.1037/0033-2909.113.1.164

Landreth, G. L. (2024). *Play therapy: The art of the relationship*. Routledge.

Narang, J., Schwannauer, M., Quayle, E., & Chouliara, Z. (2019). Therapeutic interventions with child and adolescent survivors of sexual abuse: A critical narrative review. *Children and Youth Services Review*, *107*, 104559. https://doi.org/10.1016/j.childyouth.2019.104559

Parker, M. M., Hergenrather, K., Smelser, Q., Kelly, C. T. (2021). Exploring child-centered play therapy and trauma: A systematic review of literature. *International Journal of Play Therapy*, *30*(1), 2–13. http://dx.doi.org/10.1037/pla0000136

Ray, D. C. (2011). *Advanced play therapy: Essential conditions, knowledge, and skills for child practice*. Routledge.

Ray, D. C., Burgin, E., Gutierrez, D., Ceballos, P., & Lindo, N. (2022). Child-centered play therapy and adverse childhood experiences: A randomized controlled trial. *Journal of Counseling & Development*, *100*(2), 134–145. https://doi.org/10.1002/jcad.12412

Reyes, C. J., & Asbrand, J. P. (2005). A longitudinal study assessing trauma symptoms in sexually abused children engaged in play therapy. *International Journal of Play Therapy*, *14*(2), 25–47. https://doi.org/10.1037/h0088901

Rogers, C. R. (1951). *Client-centered therapy: Its current practice, implications and theory*. Houghton Mifflin.

Rogers, C. R. (1957). The necessary and sufficient conditions of therapeutic personality change. *Journal of Consulting Psychology*, *21*(2), 95–103. https://doi.org/10.1037/h0045357

Schaefer, C. E., & Drewes, A. A. (Eds.). (2014). *The therapeutic powers of play: 20 core agents of change* (2nd ed.). Wiley.

Scott, T. A., Burlingame, G., Starling, M., Porter, C., & Lilly, J. P. (2003). Effects of individual client-centered play therapy on sexually abused children's mood, self-concept, and social competence. *International Journal of Play Therapy*, *12*(1), 7–30. https://doi.org/10.1037/h0088869

CHAPTER 8

COGNITIVE BEHAVIORAL PLAY THERAPY WITH SEXUALLY ABUSED CHILDREN AND ADOLESCENTS

Angela M. Cavett

Childhood sexual abuse (CSA) refers to sexual activity with a child or adolescent including sexual activity that the child or adolescent may not understand and does not or cannot give consent to (Centers for Disease Control and Prevention, 2024). There is some variation across different studies in the estimates of the prevalence of CSA. Recent studies that include sexual abuse online show rates for females increased from to 31.6% (previously 19.8%) and for males from to 10.8% (6.2% previously) (Finkelhor et al., 2024).

The short- and long-term psychological impact of CSA include anxiety, posttraumatic stress disorder (PTSD), depression, and attention problems (Strathearn et al., 2020), problems with relationships and difficulty regulating emotions (Amedee et al., 2019). Some fit the criteria for PTSD, others for Complex PTSD (CPTSD), and a small portion do not fit the criteria for either and are referred to as resilient in the literature (Hébert et al., 2024). Those with PTSD show hyperarousal, avoidance, and reexperiencing. Those with Complex PTSD also have symptoms related to disturbance of self-organization. Children and adolescents who have been sexually abused show deficits in executive functioning (Amedee et al., 2024).

Treatment for Symptoms Following Childhood Sexual Abuse

Trauma-Focused Cognitive Behavioral Therapy (TF-CBT) has been found to be effective in decreasing psychological symptoms including depression and anxiety in children and adolescents who have been sexually abused (Cohen et al., 2017). Additionally, executive functioning has improved for children and adolescents who received treatment with TF-CBT.

DOI: 10.4324/9781003451549-10

Cognitive Behavioral Play Therapy (CBPT) was developed by Susan Knell (1993). CBPT, including play-based TF-CBT, allows for the efficacy of cognitive behavioral approaches with play-based interventions. Play may be included across each of the TF-CBT components to adapt treatment for younger populations (Cavett & Drewes, 2012). Before TF-CBT was introduced, there were play therapy interventions for all TF-CBT components. which were regularly used by play therapists (Crisci et al., 1998).

CBPT for CSA includes the following components: parenting (including relationships and regulation), relaxation, psychoeducation and safety planning, affect regulation, cognitive coping (including self-concept), trauma narrative processing, and exposure.

Integrative Attachment Informed Model (I AIM)

CBPT for CSA has empirical support, especially for those with PTSD. For those with CPTSD, assessments of symptoms that differ from those with PTSD may result in better treatment specificity. For instance, Hébert and colleagues (2024) suggest that assessing security of attachment may result in better outcomes as attachment-based interventions could supplement TF-CBT. This is the approach this writer uses, the Integrative Attachment Informed Model (I AIM) (Cavett, 2011a, 2011b, 2011c, 2012, 2013, 2015). It is a neurosequential model informed by the work of Dr. Bruce Perry. I AIM is a tiered approach with three tiers based on the caregiver–child relationship. Depending on the need for attachment-focused work, the therapist begins with attachment-based interventions including Theraplay and family therapy without the patient present for caregiver training and to provide psychoeducation to the caregiver. As the caregiver–child relationship is strengthened and caregivers become more attuned, CBPT is implemented. I AIM includes CBPT at Tier I. Tiers II and III are only utilized if CBPT, including playful TF-CBT are not appropriate due to attachment concerns in the caregiver–child relationship which inhibit the effectiveness of CBPT alone. Where many cognitive behavioral therapy models are not neurosequential, I AIM utilizes the power of CBT in play when it is necessary but honors that it is not necessarily sufficient, rather depending on Theraplay and nondirective play to fill the neurosequential needs of the child on an individualized basis.

Relationship/Regulation

The relationships children and adolescents have with their therapists, caregivers, teachers, peers, and others are important for healing post CSA. The relationship between the child and caregiver is assessed and deficits are a focus of family sessions. The relationship with caregivers impacts children and adolescents who have been traumatized. Social support, especially that provided by caregivers, has a significant impact on responses to sexual trauma. Including caregivers in therapy is essential. This includes both sessions with the caregiver alone and with the client and caregiver. Coregulating the caregiver so they can coregulate the client is necessary. Only then can the therapist assist the caregiver in supporting the child or adolescent, teaching them emotional regulation.

I AIM, which includes Theraplay at Tiers II and III, focuses on attachment, attunement, and developing relationships that can provide coregulation. I AIM is an integrative model of CBPT and Theraplay. Although some children and adolescents can self-regulate, many need coregulation from the caregiver. Sessions building security in the caregiver–child relationship prior to CBPT can be helpful. For insecure attachment, evidenced by the caregiver not being attuned to the child, the session can include Theraplay. Theraplay interventions allow the parent to develop neuroception and attunement with the child or adolescent prior to CBPT.

Relaxation

Once a child or an adolescent can be coregulated by a caregiver, they can build skills to self-regulate including the ability to use relaxation techniques in CBPT. Playful mindfulness meditation can allow for relaxation, increased emotional awareness, and regulation. A tactile, proprioceptive mindfulness exercise can be balancing on the balance board while thinking about the bodily sensations associated with this activity. Feeling, smelling, and seeing slime can provide connection to the body during sessions and serves as a form of grounding. Playful relaxation exercises allow for emotional and physiological calming. For instance, one may use the Bee Breathing exercise.

Taylor and her therapist sit back to back. The therapist holds a bee puppet which she raises as they breathe in, pauses while at the highest point as their breaths also pause, then they buzz together as the therapist lowers the bee puppet and again a pause at the bottom before inhaling again as the bee puppet "flies" up. The vibration of the therapist's and Taylor's backs help coregulate as the breaths in calm both. Playful relaxation exercises may allow for safe physical touch. When children and adolescents have been sexually abused, appropriate touch can be healing to healthy boundaries.

Psychoeducation and Safety Planning

Psychoeducation is done early in therapy and as needed throughout each of the components. Psychoeducation should include information about common responses to trauma, including symptoms of PTSD and depression, as well as information about how therapy works and how it will be helpful. Psychoeducation on CSA may include bibliotherapy, play-based interventions, and caregiver–child education.

CSA prevention education includes discussion of definitions, frequency, boundaries, and information about anatomy terminology. Children and adolescents often use imprecise language related to CSA (Sullivan et al., 2022). Abusers often gravitate toward victims with incorrect terminology. When words are used that may be confusing or misleading, such as calling a girl's vagina a "lasagna" instead of labia and vagina, many disclosures or questions about what is happening to them may not be understood by caregivers or professionals. Sexual abusers are more likely to abuse children and adolescents who use names for sexual parts that are not medical terms (Briggs, 1997). Psychoeducation includes boundaries and a client's right to set limits around their own bodies. The manipulation and "tricks" used by sexual abusers are also an area requiring psychoeducation.

Affective Regulation

Children and adolescents who have experienced CSA often present with symptoms of PTSD or CPTSD. For both, the symptoms include intrusive reminders of the trauma, avoidance of trauma reminders, negative mood and cognition, and arousal alternations (American Psychiatric Association [APA], 2013). Emotional regulation for children and adolescents who have experienced CSA can be problematic. Emotional regulation is defined as the experience, occurrence, and expression of emotions.

Emotional regulation includes being able to express emotions in a manner that their goals can be met.

Interventions for affect modulation consists of labeling, quantification, physiology, and modulation of feelings. One CBPT intervention is feelings charades. Many interventions are created in sessions by the child or adolescent. For example, Sara, an 8-year-old female who was sexually abused by her father, wanted to move about in session. She placed dolls with feeling faces and feeling words on the ground and closed her eyes. She ran over the tops of the dolls. She asked the therapist to toss them into a pile after she had stepped on them. She did this several times until they were all in a pile. She then told the therapist, "Those are my feelings. They are like a landmine." This allowed for further processing of how the child's feelings felt out of control and the child felt like feelings, especially anger and sadness, seemed to pop up out of nowhere to overwhelm her like a landmine. This child, like most others, was bored talking about feelings with a CBT worksheet. The words on the paper seemed academic, distant, and disconnected from their experiences. Incorporating play therapy with CBT components happens through an integrative directive/nondirective approach and allows the child or adolescent to feel more control and to allow for developmentally appropriate learning. This approach also helps develop mastery over CSA. Sara used CBPT to express herself. This was done through full-bodied expression and enactment of emotions.

Cognitive Coping

Knell originally developed CBPT (1993). CBPT utilizes concepts across CBT models. Within CBT, there are three main mechanisms; cognitive structures, cognitive operations/processes, and cognitive products. Cognitive structures are schemas. Schemas are the lens through which the client sees their life. Schemas develop early in life and are a mental representation of one's perceptions of self, others, and the world. Cognitive operations or processes include cognitive distortions. Appraisal of situations consistent with the schema confirms the unconscious belief system. If situations do not confirm one's unconscious schema, a cognitive distortion is formed to reject unconfirming information. This allows for the schema to be maintained through the distortion. Schemas drive cognitive operations such as cognitive distortions and cognitive products, including automatic thoughts.

Cognitive behavioral therapists often use techniques such as speech bubbles to help children and adolescents understand the concept of a thought and have a means of expressing it. Having gingerbread people drawn on a page with thought bubbles can be used to process thoughts that clients have had in scenarios in the past week or month and eventually during narrative processing of CSA. Children are introduced to the cognitive triangle including how thoughts impact mood and behavior. The Magnetic Cognitive Triangle (Cavett, 2010) allows for movement and processing of changes over time of triggers, feelings, thoughts, and behaviors and using Socratic techniques.

Appraisal of a person's experiences influences the emotional and behavioral responses to the experience. How one thinks of the experience, such as to whom blame is attributed, impacts emotion, such as shame and behaviors. Cognitive coping can be positive or negative. Negative cognitive coping post CSA may include anger and self-blame. Cognitive coping skills in CBPT include cognitive restructuring or altering negative coping skills such as self-blame and anger.

Automatic negative thoughts are thoughts which are unhelpful and inaccurate such as a child or adolescent believing they are responsible for their CSA. CBPT interventions can include identifying and confronting automatic negative thoughts. For example, Sasha was sexually abused by her stepfather. She wanted to be with her stepfather on nights when her mother was at work because he would give her attention and gifts as part of sexual grooming which eventually progressed to sexually abusive intercourse. In her nondirective play, themes related to self-blame were identified, and directive interventions were utilized to follow up on the themes shown in play. She indicated that she felt partially responsible for her CSA because she "allowed" it to occur to get the candy and internet access to games. In therapy, we made a list of ANTS, Automatic Negative Thoughts. Each was listed on a paper shaped like black ants. Her mother was asked to help us think of other automatic thoughts she had heard or wondered if Sasha had. The contributions from her mother were discussed and unraveled with Sasha. The therapist introduced an ant puppet and the concept of reducing automatic negative thoughts. Sasha and the therapist used the puppet while discussing and practicing strategies to decrease the ANTS.

Within CBPT for victims of CSA, there are many interventions which can be utilized during cognitive restructuring to reduce self-blame and negative, inaccurate perceptions of self. Clay may be used to form shapes reminiscent of negative thoughts and then "smashed." In Feelings Bowling, the pins can have negative thoughts written on papers taped to the pins and then knocked down. Symbolism, bilateral movement, and playfulness all contribute to the effectiveness of these CBPT interventions.

Trauma Narrative

CSA impacts victims' view of the self, world, and others. CBPT theorizes that after CSA, victims may have beliefs about the trauma and their environment that are negative. Children and adolescents who have experienced CSA may feel ongoing environmental threat. Trauma from CSA often decreases a sense of safety and increases a sense of threat (Ehlers & Clark, 2000). Trauma memories must be processed. This includes developing an understanding of attributions of blame.

Children and adolescents with PTSD following CSA often have memories of that are not integrated in a healthy manner. Victims may not integrate trauma memories secondary to CSA to avoid the memories or due to other negative coping methods. Psychoeducation related to remembering and using positive coping skills related to processing CSA lead to healthy responses to sexual trauma while avoidance, suppression of traumatic memories, and rumination without processing are unhelpful. This psychoeducation needs to be for the victim and caregivers. Negative appraisals of the trauma include feeling that the world is dangerous, and people are not to be trusted (Ehlers et al., 2003).

Matthew chose to do his trauma narrative in the dollhouse. The structured narrative included many elements that were consistent with the documentation from the Children's Advocacy Center (CAC) and Matthew's statements to others. It showed a verbal account of his experiences. The therapist transcribed his account and, over several sessions, filled in corresponding feelings and beliefs. After doing his narrative, Matthew had about 20 minutes to use nondirective play. His nondirective play appeared related to his narrative but with more depth and physiological sensations, such as tearing and pain. It seemed to show his feelings of powerlessness. It showed the conflict between sexual grooming and violations.

Integrating nondirective play with directive CBPT allows the advantages of both approaches. It seems nondirective play allows for depth that is not verbalized and directive CBPT approaches allow for processing and making sense of the complexity of CSA.

Matthew began playing with a cat puppet. He stroked its fur gently at first, but then began to smack it with his hand and then his fist. He took the toy mixer from the play kitchen, and he set the puppet with its body under the mixer's beater and made a sound. He stopped for a few moments and played with cracked toy eggs. This seemed to be a play break, meaning the intensity of the material was high, a break was needed, and Matthew played something less emotionally evocative. He returned to the mixer and pretended to use the beaters to hurt the cat. He picked up the cat puppet and stroked it, saying to the therapist that he was going to name it "Number Two." He told the cat puppet that it was named "Number Two" because it was not pee which is "Number One." Matthew stated, "Number Two" was "poop."

Exposure

In vivo exposure for an adolescent can include imaginal exposure to the innocuous stimuli such as this example. Jasmine was sexually abused and trafficked by her uncle. When he took her home to her mother's after the sexual abuse, he would stop at a local gas station. Following disclosure, Jasmine had panic attacks when proximal to the gas station. At first, she attempted to avoid the gas station. However, this was not possible. In caregiver sessions, exposure was described. Jasmin's mother was supportive in wanting to help her daughter function without avoidance. Although in vivo exposure is a form of exposure that is done "in life," play scenarios that allow for miniaturization of the anxiety provoking stimuli can facilitate mastery. After a brief check-in related to her past week during which her mother noted she had a panic attack while they were getting fuel, Jasmine and the therapist used a box to create a play gas station and toy cars and the doll house were used to play out being at home, at school, and at the gas station. Initially, the therapist observed Jasmine's play and noted verbalizations that were related to fear. Over the course of several sessions, the therapist helped Jasmine think of alternative cognitions. Three coping skills, butterfly tapping, grounding and tightening, and relaxing her fists to reduce physiological arousal were practiced within the play. Jasmine then created a hierarchy for in vivo exposure and completed this with encouragement and support from her caregiver.

Limitations of Cognitive Behavioral Play Therapy With Children Who Have Been Sexually Abused

Cognitive Behavioral Therapy, despite the empirical validation it has, is severely limited in its application with children including those who have been abused. With play, it is greatly improved. However, even CBPT is limited without being integrated into a model that allows for additional processing. For instance, the somatic aspects present after trauma are not addressed with standard CBPT. The relational aspects are touched on with CBPT, but not at a deep enough level. The "cortex" level processing can be done, but more is needed for lower brain change. This can be addressed with the addition of attunement-focused therapies that include the dyad of the caregiver and child. This can be done by including Theraplay or other attachment-based models.

Conclusion

CBPT can be an effective treatment for CSA. Key components include parenting (including relationships and regulation), relaxation, psychoeducation and safety planning, affect regulation, cognitive coping (including self-concept), trauma narrative processing, and exposure. Directive interventions can assist in developing skills related to relaxation and affect modulation. The trauma narrative and cognitive processing, both utilizing play, allow for processing and altering of cognitive distortions, often noted as significant symptoms following sexual abuse. Although CBPT is a directive intervention, nondirective play enhances it and seems to allow for deeper processing and experiences that are not easily verbalized or processed directly.

Considerations for Practice: Key Takeaways

- CBPT is the play-based implementation of CBT, including that based on TF-CBT. CBPT can pull on the concepts of the most studied treatments, Cognitive Behavioral Therapies, for children who have been sexually abused, while allowing play to enhance said treatments.
- CBPT directly addresses cognitive distortions, which are significant symptoms of those who have been sexually abused.

- CBPT within a model such as Integrative Attachment Informed Model (I AIM) allow for an integration of CBPT and attachment-informed therapy and interventions to improve the caregiver–child relationship.
- CBPT may include both directive and nondirective play to enhance the child's ability to express their feelings and experiences and to learn relational and coping skills.
- As CBPT is a cognitive therapy that focuses on the cortex, adjunctive therapies, such as Theraplay, can address relational, attunement-based goals for the child and important people in their support systems.

References

Amedee, L. M., Cyr, C., Jean-Thorn, A., & Hébert, M. (2024). Executive functioning in child victims of sexual abuse: A multi-informant comparative study. *Child Abuse & Neglect, 152*, Article 106737. https://doi.org/10.1016/j.chiabu.2024.106737

Amedee, L. M., Tremblay-Perreault, A., Hébert, M., & Cyr, C. (2019). Child victims of sexual abuse: Teachers' evaluation of emotion regulation and social adaptation in school. *Psychology in the Schools, 56*(7), 1077–1088. https://doi.org/10.1002/pits.22236

American Psychiatric Association. (2013). *Diagnostic and statistical manual of mental disorders* (5th ed.). American Psychiatric Association.

Briggs, F. (1997). *Child protection: A guide for teachers and child care professionals* (1st ed.). Routledge.

Cavett, A. (2011a, April 30). *Playful healing: Counseling traumatized children and adolescents* [Conference presentation]. South Dakota Counselors Association Conference, Sioux Falls, SD.

Cavett, A. (2011b, June 13). *Integrating play into trauma-focused TF-CBT* [Conference presentation]. Division of Child and Family Services, Las Vegas, NV.

Cavett, A. (2011c, February 11). *Reactive attachment disorder: Diagnosis, treatment, and collaborative efforts* [Conference presentation]. West Fargo Public Schools, West Fargo, ND.

Cavett, A. (2012, June). *Treating attachment disorders in children* [Conference presentation]. Nevada Department of Children and Family Services, Las Vegas, NV.

Cavett, A. (2013, August). *Integrating play-based interventions with cognitive behavioral therapy* [Conference presentation]. American Psychological Association Conference, Honolulu, HI.

Cavett, A. M. (2010). *Structured play-based interventions for engaging children and adolescents in therapy*. Infinity Publishing,

Cavett, A. M. (2015, October 6). *Cognitive behavioral play therapy* [Conference presentation]. Association for Play Therapy International Conference, Atlanta, GA.

Cavett, A. M., & Drewes, A. A. (2012). Play applications and trauma-specific components. In J. A. Cohen, A. P. Mannarino, & E. Deblinger (Eds.), *Trauma-focused cognitive behavioral therapy for children and adolescents: Treatment applications* (pp. 124–148). The Guilford Press.

Centers for Disease Control and Prevention. (2024, May 16). *About child sexual abuse*. U.S. Department of Health & Human Services. https://www.cdc.gov/child-abuse-neglect/about/about-child-sexual-abuse.html

Cohen, J. A., Mannarino, A. P., & Deblinger, E. (2017). *Treating trauma and traumatic grief in children and adolescents* (2nd ed.). Guilford Press.

Crisci, G., Lay, M., & Lowenstein, L. (1998). *Paper dolls and paper airplanes: Therapeutic exercises for sexually traumatized children*. Kidsrights.

Ehlers, A., & Clark, D. M. (2000). A cognitive model of posttraumatic stress disorder. *Behaviour Research and Therapy*, *38*(4), 319–345. https://doi.org/10.1016/S0005-7967(99)00123-0

Ehlers, A., Mayou, R. A., & Bryant, B. (2003). Cognitive predictors of posttraumatic stress disorder in children: Results of a prospective longitudinal study. *Behaviour Research and Therapy*, *41*(1), 1–10. https://doi.org/10.1016/S0005-7967(01)00126-7

Finkelhor, D., Turner, H., & Colburn, D. (2024). The prevalence of child sexual abuse with online sexual abuse added. *Child Abuse & Neglect*, *149*, Article 106634. https://doi.org/10.1016/j.chiabu.2024.106634

Hébert, M., Amedee, L. M., & Tremblay-Perreault, A. (2024). Identifying PTSD and complex PTSD profiles in child victims of sexual abuse. *Journal of Child Sexual Abuse*, *33*(5), 1–19. https://doi.org/10.1080/10538712.2024.2403996

Knell, S. M. (1993). *Cognitive-behavioral play therapy*. Jason Aronson.

Strathearn, L., Giannotti, M., Mills, R., Kisely, S., Najman, J., & Abajobir, A. (2020). Long-term cognitive, psychological, and health outcomes associated with child abuse and neglect. *Pediatrics*, *146*(4), e20200438. https://doi.org/10.1542/peds.2020-0438

Sullivan, C., St. George, S., Stolzenberg, S. N., Williams, S., & Lyon, T. D. (2022). Imprecision about body mechanics when child witnesses are questioned about sexual abuse. *Journal of Interpersonal Violence*, *37*(13–14), NP12375–NP12397. https://doi.org/10.1177/0886260521997941

CHAPTER 9
DEVELOPMENTAL PLAY THERAPY WITH SEXUALLY ABUSED CHILDREN

Kim Vander Dussen

The foundation of developmental play therapy is safe relationships that utilize the therapeutic use of touch to help children heal. This may seem counterintuitive in the treatment of childhood sexual abuse as touch has been exploitive to these children. Developmental play therapists seek to establish relationships that help the child experience nurturing touch and regain ownership over their bodies. The following chapter will explore the role of safe and caring touch in helping children heal. While much progress has been made in understanding the importance of touch in healing, it is an area that deserves further research attention.

Developmental Play Therapy

In the early 1970s, Viola Brody coined her approach to psychotherapy with children, developmental play therapy (Brody, 1997a). In this pioneering approach, Brody was deeply rooted in play therapy and is recognized as a significant contributor to the development of the field. Through play, children explore their emotions and experiences. Developmental play therapy is grounded in helping children to understand and cope with their feelings and challenges. Children express themselves, communicate, and work through emotional and psychological issues through play therapy. Understanding child development and the attachment process is at the root of this model. Most notably, Brody highlighted the use of safe and caring touch in facilitating healing processes and promoting healthy attachment bonds. Brody detailed the importance of this process in helping children grow and heal. It would take several decades for science to understand the importance of touch in health processes and further reinforce the developmental play therapy model.

DOI: 10.4324/9781003451549-11

Tiffany Field is the director of the Touch Research Institute in the Department of Pediatrics at the University of Miami School of Medicine. During her career, she has authored a plethora of research connecting the therapeutic use of touch to improved health and developmental outcomes for children (Field, 2014). There is a powerful impact of skin-to-skin touch on human biological processes. Within the context of attachment, skin-to-skin contact promotes the production of oxytocin in the body, the hormone associated with love. In conjunction with promoting attachment bonds, the impacts of skin-to-skin contact in parent-child relationships extend well beyond the first years of life (Vittner et al., 2018; Bigelow & Power, 2020).

Touch within the context of developmental play therapy can be defined as any physical contact between the clinician and the client, initiated by the client or the clinician. It is also considered that some contact, particularly initiated by a child in play therapy, is inevitable. Touch may occur in individual, dyadic, family, or group therapy.

It can be assumed that using touch in therapy is a complex issue that should be examined and contemplated. The Association for Play Therapy provides a document entitled The Paper on Touch (2022) that highlights clinical and ethical considerations when deciding whether therapeutic touch might be useful in treating any case. Considering clinical motivations, training, supervision, and thoughtfulness in applying touch are critical.

Additionally, clinicians must address cultural and diversity factors when implementing touch. It should be noted that in many healing traditions of different ethnic and cultural groups, touch is vital. Neurodivergent children might also have neurological profiles that impact how they experience touch, and this should be considered and assessed when implementing the therapeutic use of touch (Dunn, 1997, 2007). Children may actively seek touch due to sensory needs or experience touch with great discomfort. Notably, children may not be able to articulate what their felt experience of touch is, so clinicians should be mindful of the need to gather additional information or consult with other professionals.

Children who have been sexually traumatized deserve special consideration when evaluating the application of the therapeutic use of touch. Each case should be addressed and well-documented individually. It is often said that sexually abused children become untouchable. Clinicians and other adults err on avoiding all touch to circumvent any misattributions of intent and to honor a child's agency over their body. In developmental play therapy, victims of childhood sexual abuse can experience healthy boundaries and appropriate touch within a safe and caring relationship (Brody, 1997a). It can be used to treat the overwhelming dysregulation that often results from sexual abuse. This can be a critical piece in healing as therapeutic touch may be utilized to help a child experience coregulation in the wake of sexual trauma.

There are six guiding principles in developmental play therapy for healing and therapeutic interactions between children and the adults who work with and provide care that require explanation and articulation within the context of the treatment of sexually abused children. The first identifies that a child who experiences themselves "as touched develops a sense of self." (Brody, 1997a, p. 7). The experience of being touched helps a child develop a relationship with the adult who touches them. As expected, this experience has been broken by an adult for a sexually traumatized child. Therefore, it can be argued that creating a safe and caring touch, done with thought, consideration, and training, can bring about healing. The importance of touch within the context of developmental play therapy is to help the child reclaim their felt sense of self and felt sense of "other" through carefully considered consensual touch. Children in developmental play therapy can choose to accept or reject the touch, but in doing so, they are provided the felt experience of self (Brody, 1997b).

The second guiding principle is that "for a child to experience themselves touched, a capable adult must" provide the touch (Brody, 1997a, p. 7). In this way, a caring, safe adult who knows what it is to be touched gives this same experience to the child. This capable adult must know how to provide the kind of healthy relationship that allows a child to feel touched in a safe, caring way. This emphasis on safety and care may seem self-evident, but it is the foundation of the therapeutic relationship between a child and their therapist. All play therapy theories and frameworks share a belief in the healing power of the play therapy relationship (Drewes & Schaefer, 2015).

The third guiding principle in developmental play therapy is that in order "to be a toucher, the adult must first learn to be the one touched" (Brody, 1997a, p. 7). This issue is complex in that being touched evokes powerful feelings and memories, most notably your own experiences of being touched as a child.

The fourth guiding principle is of utmost importance, and its consideration should be thoroughly examined, as mentioned previously. Children must allow themselves to be touched to feel touched. Touch for sexually abused children has been associated with pain and suffering

(Brody, 1997b). It should never be coerced or forced upon a child. What, then, does a clinician do? Gestures may be offered. For example, cupping a child's hand while handing them a requested object, developing a special handshake that is a greeting ritual if the child is amenable to that idea, high fives, or responding positively when the child initiates some small contact. Therapists must stay engaged and attuned and not withdraw as children begin to grow increasingly comfortable and safe in the therapeutic relationship. With time, children will become increasingly grounded in their bodies and will allow safe and caring adults to be close to them.

The fifth guiding principle is that at birth, first experiences of being *seen* come through being touched (Brody, 1997a). Our most powerful first experiences of touch come from our parents. Skin-to-skin contact in those first moments of life brings with it our first experiences of coregulation. Research supports that providing mother and infant with skin-to-skin contact within the first hour of life has a multitude of health benefits for the child, including an increase in physiological stability-heart rate, decrease in cortisol, and respiration (Phillips, 2013). Brody asserted that for humans, touch precedes all other more complex ways of relating (Brody, 1997b).

The final guiding principle is that the therapist must provide "the relationship the child needs to feel touched, the adult controls activities that take place in a Developmental Play Therapy session" (Brody, 1997a, p. 8). From Brody's perspective, the clinician creates the experiences in sessions in which the child feels touched. The therapist is responsible for providing a therapeutic environment in which a child can experience being seen and healed. The activities identified by Brody (1997a, 1997b) are categorized as noticing the child, touching the child, responding to the child's cues, and bringing to the attention of the child an adult who meets their needs.

These activities are not mutually exclusive and are defined rather broadly. In application, a host of play therapy theories and clinical frameworks focus on noticing the child by being present, empathic, and attuned. Responding to the child's cues and bringing their attention to the therapist's genuine, empathic, and safe presence encompasses many approaches. What sets developmental play therapy apart in therapy activities is the use of safe, caring touch.

Literature Review

The last 40 years have seen a surge in literature on childhood sexual abuse (CSA). In addition to public awareness, research including incident rates, assessment, developmental impact, short- and long-term effects, and intervention has left clinicians with vast resources. The evidence for play therapy treatment interventions is growing but remains in development. Metanalyses on play therapy indicate strong effect sizes in multiple domains including decreasing anxiety, reducing posttraumatic symptoms, and improving relationships between children and caregivers (LeBlanc & Ritchie, 2001; Ray et al., 2015; Parker et al., 2021; Slade & Warne, 2016).

An early study by Mitchum (1987) examined the effects of Developmental Play Therapy on a group of sexually abused children in treatment with their nonoffending mothers. The children selected for treatment were screened for problems with tolerating touch post-victimization. All children in the study were highly symptomatic, suffering from the impact of the trauma of sexual abuse as detailed in this text. Throughout 10 sessions, the children and their mothers participated in activities that involved safe and playful touch. Some of these activities were one-on-one, between the parent and child. For example, an intervention described was called "Race Track." The parent pretended the back of their child was a racetrack and the parent's thumbs were competing in a race across the child's back. Other interventions were group-based. One such intervention was called "Pass It On." Here, the group of parents and children sat or stood in a circle and passed on a touch around the circle, ranging from things like a pat on the back or a handshake. Progress was noted as fearfulness and tears at the beginning, to joy and laughter at the end. All mothers reported increased cooperation (a decrease in problematic behaviors) and increased playfulness at home. While certainly promising, more qualitative measures of the outcome of Developmental Play Therapy with victims of CSA are needed.

Clinical Case Study

Vanessa is a 3½-year-old Hispanic female. At the time of referral, she was in the process of being adopted by her aunt and uncle after a year and a half in relative placement. Vanessa was removed from the home of her biological parents due to sexual abuse and neglect by her father. The abuse was discovered during an investigation by law enforcement into child sexual abuse material (CSAM), formerly referred to as child pornography. Vanessa refers to her soon-to-be adoptive parents as Mommy and Daddy. It should be noted throughout this case study that the Mommy and Daddy referenced are these adoptive parents.

Vanessa's parents brought her to treatment due to significant problems with dysregulation after she was "kicked out" of preschool due to her unregulated and somewhat aggressive behavior with peers and with school staff. "Meltdowns" at home would sometimes last an hour or more, ending when she fell into an exhausted sleep. She would often alternate between being clingy to refusing contact or comfort at home.

Vanessa was open with her parents about the abuse she experienced. During bathtime, she shared stories where she was either abused or witnessed the sexual acts of others. The sensory experience of bathing and being bathed were activating events for her. Vanessa's parents responded with empathy and concern but felt unsure of how to respond to her memories. Her parents had raised three older children who were adults, making Vanessa the only child in the home.

Vanessa's preschool teacher reported that other children seemed quite reactive to her. At least once a week, Vanessa could be found in the preschool director's office crying, lying on the floor, and kicking anyone who attempted to get close to her. Hence, there is a need for developmentally sensitive therapy.

The therapy structure involved an initial observation play session with Vanessa and her parents followed by a series of sessions with the child and the clinician only. During the observation session with her parents, Vanessa was able to initiate touch but turned away at contact initiated by her parents. In her first individual play therapy session, she was aware of the clinician and responded, but she kept several feet away.

The goals of treatment were as follows: aid in processing and recovery from childhood sexual abuse, improve coregulation, decrease anxiety, and improve overall mood.

Vanessa's parents were oriented to some principles of play therapy and the use of touch in developmental play therapy. Safe and caring touch was emphasized in order to provide co-regulatory opportunities for Vanessa. She was naturally drawn to sand and water and frequently centered her play in these areas. Her parents were guided through interactions that would allow them to safely and gently initiate touch with Vanessa, from touching her hands to affectionally cradling her.

Vanessa progressed to initiating some touch but struggled with being touched. If at any time she rejected their contact, she was allowed to remain in control. Through gently tracking her and acknowledging her feelings and the themes present in play her parents would stay in contact and attuned with her. Vanessa would seek contact with the clinician as she became increasingly comfortable in sessions. Some examples of safe and caring touch ranged from gently cradling her hand when she would ask to have a toy or other object in the playroom handed to her, to gently rubbing her back, head, or hands when she was engaged in play. All of these were modeled by the clinician with her parents and then, eventually, initiated by the parents with Vanessa in treatment to help the parents navigate any anxiety about initiating physical contact with her.

A key principle in treatment was that the adult that touches had to allow themselves to be touched. This was a critical step in treatment. One goal that was particularly meaningful for her mother was to be able to kiss affectionately as parents do with their children. It was something that Vanessa never initiated. Yet, her mother desperately wanted to experience it and would reference her culture as one where physical displays of affection were important.

In play therapy, Vanessa was drawn to the medical toys and play emphasized healing dolls and a brown teddy bear. She would place bandages on the bear which provided an opportunity to have her parents ask her for any boo-boo's that she had. Gradually, Vanessa identified boo-boo's on her arms or legs and allowed her parents to place band-aids on them. Although there were no real injuries, it was an opportunity to allow safe and caring touch and created an opportunity for nurturing from her parents.

Approximately three months into treatment, Vanessa allowed her parents to kiss the boo-boos. Sessions progressed in this way, with increasingly more physical contact between Vanessa and her parents. Vanessa also included me in her interactions and allowed safe contact between us.

Toward the end of treatment, Vanessa would greet me in the waiting room with a gentle hug around my legs or, if I crouched down in time, she would hug me as well. Some sessions were challenging as she acted out what she experienced through direct recollection or unconscious processes. Her parents were afforded time each week to process the sessions. Within a year, all reports indicated that Vanessa was doing well at home, in school, and with peers.

Limitations of Developmental Play Therapy in Treating Childhood Sexual Abuse

The greatest challenge with developmental play therapy is navigating the complex issues around touch. Again, the Paper on Touch developed by the Association for Play Therapy (2022) is an invaluable resource for play therapists and other clinicians who want to navigate these issues thoughtfully. Issues around consent and the absence of any coercion are of critical importance. The implementation of the principles of this approach requires training, supervision, and/or consultation. That requires time and resources on the part of the clinician.

The other significant limitation is the lack of recent research on the topic of touch in therapy. Janet Courtney has developed a model called First Play which is an infant mental health and developmental play therapy model (Courtney et al., 2017). This is where current research efforts connected to Developmental Play Therapy are occurring.

Conclusion

Sexually abused children have been deprived of personal agency, and many models developed over the years fail to accommodate and acknowledge the power of children to set their boundaries. The early years of developmental play therapy were more directive, but the focus has always been on the safety and well-being of children. A core value of genuine, empathic, attuned connection pervades all play therapy theories and models. Developmental play therapy is no exception.

Considerations for Practice: Key Takeaways

- The integration of safe-caring touch, in an intentional, therapeutic way, requires training, supervision, and consultation.
- Touch can be a potent tool in play therapy that can help sexually abused children gain agency and develop a healthy relationship with touch.
- Current iterations of models based on developmental play therapy focus on establishing healthy, secure attachment relationships.

References

Association for Play Therapy. (2022). *Paper on touch.* https://cdn.ymaws.com/www.a4pt.org/resource/resmgr/resource_center/Paper_on_Touch_2022__-_Final.pdf

Bigelow, A. E., & Power, M. (2020). Mother-infant skin-to-skin contact: Short- and long-term effects for mothers and their children born full-term. *Frontiers in Psychology, 11,* 1921. https://doi.org/10.3389/fpsyg.2020.01921

Brody, V. A. (1997a). *The dialogue of touch: Developmental play therapy* (2nd ed.). Jason Aronson.

Brody, V. A. (1997b). Developmental play therapy. In K. J. O'Connor & L. M. Braverman (Eds.), *Play therapy theory and practice: A comparative casebook* (pp. 160–183). John Wiley & Sons.

Courtney, J. A., & Nolan, R. D. (Eds.). (2017). *Touch in child counseling and play therapy: An ethical and clinical guide*. Routledge.

Drewes, A. A., & Schaefer, C. E. (2015). The therapeutic powers of play. In A. A. Drewes & C. E. Schaefer (Eds.), *Handbook of play therapy* (pp. 35–60). John Wiley & Sons.

Dunn, W. (1997). The impact of sensory processing abilities on the daily lives of young children and their families: A conceptual model. *Infants & Young Children, 9*(4), 23–35.

Dunn, W. (2007). Supporting children to participate successfully in everyday life by using sensory processing knowledge. *Infants & Young Children, 20*(2), 84–101. https://doi.org/10.1097/01.IYC.0000264477.05076.5d

Field, T. (2014). *Touch* (2nd ed.). MIT Press.

LeBlanc, M., & Ritchie, M. (2001). A metanalysis of play therapy outcomes. *Counselling Psychology Quarterly, 14*(2), 149–163.

Mitchum, N. T. (1987). Developmental play therapy: A treatment approach for child victims of sexual molestation. *Journal of Counseling & Development, 65*, 320–321. https://doi.org/10.1002/j.1556-6676.1987.tb01296.x

Parker, M. M., Hunnicutt Hollenbaugh, K. M., & Kelly, C. T. (2021). Exploring the impact of child-centered play therapy for children exhibiting behavioral problems: A meta-analysis. *International Journal of Play Therapy, 30*(4), 259–271. https://doi.org/10.1037/pla0000128

Phillips, R. (2013). The sacred hour: Uninterrupted skin-to-skin contact immediately after birth. *Newborn and Infant Nursing Reviews, 13*(2), 67–72. https://doi.org/10.1053/j.nainr.2013.04.001.

Ray, D. C., Armstrong, S. A., Balking, R. S., & Jayne, K. M. (2015). Child-centered play therapy in the schools: Review and meta-analysis. *Psychology in the Schools, 52*(2), 107–123.

Slade, M. K., & Warne, R. T. (2016). A meta-analysis of the effectiveness of Trauma-Focused Cognitive Behavioral Therapy and play therapy for child victims of abuse. *Journal of Young Investigators, 30*(6), 36–43.

Vittner, D., McGrath, J., Robinson, J., Lawhon, G., Cusson, R., Eisenfeld, L., Walsh, S., Young, E., & Cong, X. (2018). Increase in oxytocin from skin-to-skin contact enhances development of parent–infant relationship. *Biological Research for Nursing, 20*(1), 54–62.

CHAPTER 10
FILIAL THERAPY WITH NONOFFENDING CAREGIVERS AND FAMILIES OF CHILDREN WHO HAVE BEEN SEXUALLY ABUSED

Daire Gilmartin and Risë VanFleet

Childhood sexual abuse (CSA) hurts all members of the family. These stresses can potentially tear families apart while robbing children of their greatest source of trust and comfort – their caregivers and siblings. This chapter explores the pressures that follow CSA on all family members and describes Filial Therapy (FT) to help children and families cope and heal in ways that place family support at the center of the process.

Overview and Basics of Filial Therapy Theory

Filial Therapy was developed over 60 years ago by Drs. Bernard and Louise Guerney to strengthen family attachments and relationships while helping children overcome problems. It is a psychoeducational and theoretically integrative approach that effectively interweaves major theories, including humanistic, psychodynamic, behavioral, interpersonal, family, cognitive, systems, and more (Guerney & Ryan, 2013; VanFleet, 2014; VanFleet & Topham, 2016b).

FT includes caregivers as the primary change agents while the therapist teaches, processes, and supports them. In FT, the therapist teaches caregivers to conduct nondirective play sessions (VanFleet et al., 2010), supervises them as they conduct those sessions one to one with their children, processes the sessions with the caregivers, and eventually helps them shift the play sessions to the home environment for generalization of the skills learned. Caregivers learn skills of empathy, attunement, structuring, and boundary-setting, and gain deep understanding of their children through the natural developmental phenomenon of play. This understanding from children's primary attachment figures has a profound

DOI: 10.4324/9781003451549-12

and positive impact on the healing process offered through play-based interventions.

The Impact of CSA on Families

The Impact of CSA on Caregivers

Caregivers of children who have been sexually abused can suffer significant mental health difficulties and stress, including posttraumatic stress (Cavanaugh et al., 2015; Jobe-Shields et al., 2016). They frequently have a multitude of complex reactions to the disclosure of their child's abuse, including shame, guilt, sadness, and betrayal, commonly questioning how someone they trusted could abuse their child. Caregivers who have had their own abuse experiences often experience heightened reactions (Gabriel-Vacher et al., 2022). They can experience complex and mixed feelings about their failure to protect their child but also about the abuser, especially if the abuser is a known and trusted person.

These reactions strain couple and family relationships. They can feel helpless and disempowered, with low-stress tolerance (Hernandez et al., 2009). The caregiver–child relationship and co-parenting relationships can be destabilized at a time when the whole family requires support, guidance, understanding, connection, and skills to help stabilize the family.

The Impact of CSA on Siblings

The literature has explored the impact of CSA on non-abused siblings and emphasized the importance of including them in therapeutic interventions (Tener et al., 2021; McElvaney et al., 2022b). Siblings may have known about or witnessed the abuse. Others may not know what has occurred but sense the change in their family and wonder what has happened. They can feel left out, wonder if they did something wrong, and vicariously experience many complex feelings. Siblings might worry about all family members or those with whom they are no longer permitted contact.

Filial Therapy (FT) as an Intervention of Choice Where CSA Has Occurred

At a time of intense child and family stress, FT's strengths-based approach can assist at the multiple levels outlined while remaining flexible to the individual needs of the child and family (VanFleet & Topham, 2016a). It has been applied successfully as a preventive approach as well as a treatment of choice with many child and family challenges, including CSA (Costas & Landreth, 1999), and across numerous cultures and countries. Sixty years of research have demonstrated its effectiveness, and FT is considered an evidence-based intervention (Bratton et al., 2005; Cornett & Bratton, 2015; VanFleet & Guerney, 2003; VanFleet et al., 2005).

Given CSA's negative impact on children and families, Topham et al.'s (2011) research is noteworthy. It demonstrated that higher levels of parental distress and poorer child emotional regulation were predictive of the largest reduction in child behavior difficulties and larger increases in parental acceptance of their children from a FT program. It is a valuable intervention that can be used standalone or as an adjunct to other therapies.

VanFleet and Sniscak (2003) listed 15 reasons FT is suitable as a treatment of choice for children who have suffered maltreatment and their families. It is an empowering and flexible model supported by attachment and FT research which emphasizes consistent positive development in overall family communication and functioning (Topham & VanFleet, 2011). It can have greater influence on long-term psychological benefits for children and families impacted by CSA than the traditional model of individual counseling (McElvaney et al., 2022a).

The Power of Play and the Collaborative Relationship

Nondirective caregiver–child play sessions are at the core of FT, an approach that helps create an open, inviting, and safe atmosphere for children whose trust in adults may be damaged (Gilmartin & McElvaney, 2020; Jee et al., 2014). Children choose how and what they play as well as the nature and extent that they involve their caregivers. This creates safety for children who may not wish to discuss their abuse verbally. Nondirective play sessions encourage the expression of difficult feelings, thoughts, and needs, often symbolically or thematically (Ryan, 2007; VanFleet et al., 2010). Caregiver–child play, in this manner, offers an understanding of children's internal worlds (VanFleet, 2014). FT helps caregivers learn to interact with their children in ways that mirror early infant healthy parent-child relationships and promote secure attachment (VanFleet & Sniscak, 2003), which may have been weakened due to CSA. The therapist works collaboratively with caregivers to help them

respond with attunement, empathy, and healthy boundaries, which promote relational warmth, connection, and support (VanFleet & Topham,
2011). These special caregiver–child play sessions communicate to children that they are fully accepted, safe, wanted, and prized, which can
help mitigate many of the complex negative feelings and thoughts sexually abused children experience. By including caregivers in an integral
way, this approach mitigates the helplessness that many caregivers feel
post CSA.

Caregiver–Child Relationship

Limited progress can be made in helping sexually abused children without
the full involvement of their parents or caregivers (VanFleet & Topham,
2011; Gabriel-Vacher et al., 2022). With its focus on the child-caregiver
relationship, FT strengthens its connection at a time when children are
extremely vulnerable. The therapist works in close collaboration with
caregivers to help them offer special play times with their children that
are structured with healthy boundaries, that are emotionally warm, compassionate, understanding, and fun, while also fully respecting the child's
need for autonomy and self-expression (VanFleet & Topham, 2011), at
a time when control has been taken away.

In developing their use of FT skills, caregivers learn to accept, validate, and communicate understanding of the child's internal and emotional world, allowing children who are experiencing very complex and
conflicting thoughts about themselves and what happened to feel vali-
dated, understood, and accepted. The therapist prepares caregivers to
handle sexual abuse and trauma themes that might emerge during the
play and then supports them in responding in ways that further children's
healing while processing the caregivers' own feelings.

During the post-play session feedback, caregivers debrief with the
therapist, exploring challenges, refining their skills, learning about
emerging play themes and their connection with the child's internal
world, and discussing personal reactions. This can increase awareness and
acceptance of their own emotional reactions and responses, as well as
those of their partner/spouse and wider family. The play sessions can be
intense and emotionally evocative for caregivers as they gain insight into
what the child has experienced, their needs, thoughts, and feelings. The
therapist endeavors to meet the caregivers' full experience, responding
with empathy, which in turn allows them to feel safe to expose their own

vulnerabilities and struggles, opening them to a deeper understanding of their child's experiences.

Caregivers who feel sidelined, helpless, incompetent, and guilty because of CSA are viewed as the primary agent of therapeutic change. The caregiver–therapist relationship is a collaborative partnership, one that is recognized as being especially important in working with families where trust has been betrayed and power misused (Madsen, 2007). This helps build caregiver confidence and efficacy. Within the co-parenting and couple relationship, which can be stressed with the fallout from the abuse, this process can enhance understanding and acceptance while helping improve children's difficulties (VanFleet & Topham, 2011; Wickstrom, 2009).

Sibling Involvement

FT typically encourages each primary caregiver and all the children in the family to take part in the one-to-one play sessions, as healing and mastery of the trauma of CSA is needed by the entire family. This offers a way for non-abused siblings to be included in the therapeutic response (McElvaney et al., 2022b). When CSA occurs, caregiver attention is commonly drawn away from the other children in the family, who may appear unaffected. Filial therapists, therefore, advocate for each child to be involved in some way. When each child is offered a special playtime with a caregiver, they can feel heard, understood, and accepted, so their own resolution can occur. This family therapy approach assists caregivers in attuning to each child and connecting with them at a time when families can be fragmented and disconnected.

A Composite Clinical Case Study

Laura, aged eight, disclosed to her older sibling Joy (14) that she was sexually abused by her maternal cousin Martin, aged 20, over the course of 3 years. This happened on multiple occasions when Martin babysat the children. Laura shared a bedroom with her sister Alex (10). Laura had given a statement to police, as had other family members.

Family assessment at a local trauma clinic revealed reports that Laura was angry and aggressive toward her parents and sister Alex, sad and withdrawn, experiencing sleep disruption and nightmares, and was struggling in all relationships in her life. She was very angry with her parents for failing to protect her and with Alex for not helping her when Martin abused her in their bedroom. Joy had begun to stay out of the home and had started drinking alcohol. Following a period of shock and disbelief, Laura's parents, Doug and Mary, described feeling upset, angry, betrayed, conflicted, and guilty. They were no longer in contact with the maternal side of the family, who did not believe the allegations. There were occasional tensions in the marital relationship as Doug sometimes blamed Mary for the CSA. Both parents were eager to help Laura and mentioned they had previously been unaware of how hard this was on their other two children.

Following the assessment, Laura attended individual nondirective play therapy and educational sessions, while her parents attended individual and joint parent support meetings to help process what had happened to them individually and as a family. Filial Therapy was then recommended. Mary decided to continue individual therapy while starting FT with Doug. Joy attended individual therapy with parent involvement and agreed to have regular "special times" with her parents that included walks on the beach and swimming which seemed better suited to her age.

During the training phase, Doug struggled with empathic listening and the nondirective nature of the sessions; however, with further discussion of the rationale, consistent practice, and encouragement, Doug's competence and confidence strengthened. After completing the training phase, Laura and Alex engaged in weekly supervised play sessions, alternating their playtime with Doug or Mary.

Laura used animal puppets during her first few play sessions with each parent. These animals were very aggressive and angry, picking on younger animals and attempting to bite and hit their parents. The animals alternated between behaving nicely and changing rapidly to aggressive play. Both Doug and Mary set appropriate limits and reflected the intense feelings expressed. During the feedback discussion with the therapist, both expressed concern about this "violence." Through empathic listening and gentle inquiry, the therapist helped them understand that this is normal. They began to see how this play could be reflective of Laura's experiences with her cousin. This was both difficult and exciting for them, as they could see Laura's feelings of victimization, confusion, fear, loneliness, and sadness. With the therapist's help, they realized Laura was showing her internal world and that she felt safe with them during the play sessions. With this insight, her parents felt encouraged and gradually learned to deepen their empathic responses in the play sessions to more accurately reflect aspects of Laura's experiences of CSA. Over time, Laura's play became less aggressive and more nurturing, caring for the baby and holding tea parties for the family.

Alex was initially quieter in her play sessions, but with her parents' acceptance and patience, she played more freely. She played a scene where aliens entered the dollhouse and killed the family. Together with the therapist, Doug and Mary hypothesized that this play reflected the huge disruptions to their home life that the CSA had caused. In their play sessions, her parents reflected the metaphor, "The bomb went off and changed everything. That makes them sad and lonely." As the play sessions progressed, Alex's play showed more hope as the people came back to life. This also paralleled positive changes that were occurring in the family relationships.

After the therapist observed four play sessions of each parent and their skills were solid, the family began home sessions. Although the family was still feeling the impact of the CSA, the parents said they were feeling more connected with each other and the children, less stressed, and more competent. The children's behavior gradually returned to normal, and the family was able to discuss what had happened more openly. The parents brought any concerns about play sessions or these discussions to the therapist.

During the skill generalization stage of therapy, Mary and Doug continued play sessions while successfully using play session skills in daily life. Although challenges continued, they felt stronger as a couple and as co-parents. At the time of discharge, both parents were pleased with how their family was functioning and believed they could address concerns that arose from the CSA while moving forward with their lives.

Limitations and Adaptations of This Approach With Victims of CSA

1. Fortunately, FT is a flexible approach that can be implemented creatively at the appropriate time in a multi-modal therapeutic regimen. However, caregivers and children may need to complete individual work first when caregivers are very stressed, children are highly distressed, or court proceedings might require child or caregiver testimony.
2. Witnessing the impact of CSA as shown in their children's play can be very hard for caregivers. It is important that therapists work with

caregivers in person to be able to offer appropriate preparation and support.

3. Caregivers may initially find it difficult to understand that play can help them cope with the enormity of their situation.

4. There can be logistical challenges, such as enlisting others to watch the children at key times during sessions, especially when the family's resources are fragmented by the CSA.

5. FT might be contraindicated when caregivers have their own history of abuse that is triggering for them.

Conclusion

The needs victims of CSA are myriad, as are those of their caregivers and siblings. Research has shown that treatment of choice must include non-offending caregivers, and siblings should not be left out of the process. Filial Therapy, with its theoretical integration, empowerment emphasis, and whole-family involvement, offers empathy, acceptance, skills, and understanding to all members of the family through the medium of play. While it is not always the first intervention to be applied, it provides a central intervention that helps strengthen family attachments and relationships in ways that have been shown to be healing. While caregivers learn to support their children through special nondirective caregiver–child play sessions, therapists in FT offer support to the caregivers as they struggle to understand what has happened to their child and family and strive for mastery over the trauma.

Considerations for Practice: Key Takeaways

- FT should be considered a central intervention with CSA and can be used in conjunction with other interventions.
- FT requires considerable training. Training from Certified FT Instructors is available via the International Institute of Filial Therapy Professional Education, which maintains fidelity to the Guerney approach.
- FT might not be the first treatment used, but it should be considered at whatever point the child, caregivers, and siblings are ready for it.
- Practitioners of FT must also have appropriate training in CSA.
- Therapists working with this population must work with caregivers as collaborative partners and offer understanding and support to caregivers.

References

Bratton S. C., Ray, D., Rhine, T., & Jones, L. (2005). The efficacy of play therapy with children: A meta-analytic review of treatment outcomes. *Professional Psychology: Research and Practice, 36*(4), 376–390. https://doi.org/10.1037/0735-7028.36.4.376.

Cavanaugh, C. E., Petras, H., & Martins, S. S. (2015). Gender-specific profiles of adverse childhood experiences, past year mental and substance use disorders, and their associations among a national sample of adults in the United States. *Social Psychiatry and Psychiatric Epidemiology, 50*(8), 1257–1266.

Cornett, N., & Bratton, S. C. (2015). A golden intervention: 50 years of research on filial therapy. *International Journal of Play Therapy, 24*(3), 119–133. https://doi.org/10.1037/a0039088.

Costas, M., & Landreth, G. (1999). Filial therapy with nonoffending parents of children who have been sexually abused. *International Journal of Play Therapy, 8*(1), 43–66. https://doi.org/10.1037/h0089427

Gabriel-Vacher, N., Miranda, I., Olhaberry, M., Capella, C., Morán-Kneer, J., Núñez, L., Alamo, N., & Meza, C. (2022). The adverse childhood experiences of caregivers of children who have been victims of sexual assault: Their relationship with the parental alliance in child psychotherapy (Experiencias adversas tempranas de cuidadores de niños/as que han sido víctimas de agresiones sexuales: su relación con la alianza parental en la psicoterapia infantil). *Studies in Psychology, 43*(3), 688–707. https://doi.org/10.1080/02109395.2022.2139347

Gilmartin, D., & McElvaney, R. (2020). Filial therapy as a core intervention with children in foster care. *Child Abuse Review, 29*(2), 159–166. https://doi.org/10.1002/car.2602

Guerney, L. F., & Ryan, V. M. (2013). *Group filial therapy: A complete guide to teaching parents to play therapeutically with their children.* Jessica Kingsley.

Hernandez, A., Ruble, C., Rockmore, L., McKay, M., Messam, T., Harris, M., & Hope, S. (2009). An integrated approach to treating non-offending parents affected by sexual abuse. *Social Work in Mental Health, 7*(6), 533–555. https://doi.org/10.1080/15332980802301440

Jee, S. H., Conn, A. M., Toth, S., Szilagyi, M. A., & Chin, N. P. (2014). Mental health treatment experiences and expectations in foster care: A qualitative investigation. *Journal of Public Child Welfare, 8*(5), 539–559. https://doi.org/10.1080/15548732.2014.931831

Jobe-Shields, L., Swiecicki, C. C., Fritz, D. R., Stinnette, J. S., & Hanson, R. F. (2016). Posttraumatic stress and depression in the nonoffending caregivers of sexually abused children: Associations with parenting practices. *Journal of Child Sexual Abuse, 25*(1), 110–125.

Madsen, W. C. (2007). *Working collaboratively with multistressed families* (2nd ed.). Guilford Press.

McElvaney, R., Lateef, R., Collin-Vézina, D., Alaggia, R., & Simpson, M. (2022a). Bringing shame out of the shadows: Identifying shame in child sexual abuse disclosure processes and implications for psychotherapy. *Journal of Interpersonal Violence, 37*(19–20), NP18738–NP18760. https://doi.org/10.1177/08862605211037435

McElvaney, R., McDonnell Murray, R., & Dunne, S. (2022b). Siblings' perspectives of the impact of child sexual abuse disclosure on sibling and family relationships. *Family Process*, *61*(2), 858–872

Ryan, V. (2007). Filial therapy: Helping children and new carers to form secure attachment relationships. *The British Journal of Social Work*, *37*(4), 643–657. https://doi.org/10.1093/bjsw/bch331

Tener, D., Katz, C., & Kaufmann, Y. (2021). "And I Let It All Out": Survivors' sibling sexual abuse disclosures. *Journal of Interpersonal Violence*, *36*(23–24), 11140–11164. https://doi.org/10.1177/0886260519897326

Topham, G. L., & VanFleet, R. (2011). Filial therapy: A structured and straightforward approach to including young children in family therapy. *Australian and New Zealand Journal of Family Therapy*, *32*(2), 144–158. https://doi.org/10.1375/anft.32.2.144

Topham, G. L., Wampler, K. S., Titus, G., & Rolling, E. (2011). Predicting parent and child outcomes of a filial therapy program. *International Journal of Play Therapy*, *20*(2), 79–93. https://doi.org/10.1037/a0023261

VanFleet, R. (2014). *Filial therapy: Strengthening parent-child relationships through play* (3rd ed.). Professional Resource Press.

VanFleet, R., & Guerney, L. (2003). *Casebook of filial therapy*. Play Therapy Press.

VanFleet, R., Ryan, S. D., & Smith, S. K. (2005). Filial therapy: A critical review. In L. Reddy, T., Files-Hall, & C. Schaefer (Eds.), *Empirically based play interventions for children* (pp. 241–264). American Psychological Association.

VanFleet, R., & Sniscak, C. C. (2003). Filial therapy for attachment-disrupted and disordered children. In R. VanFleet & L. Guerney (Eds.), *Casebook of filial therapy* (pp. 279–308). Play Therapy Press.

VanFleet, R., Sywulak, A. E., & Sniscak, C. C. (2010). *Child-centered play therapy*. Guilford Press.

VanFleet, R., & Topham, G. (2011). Filial therapy for maltreated and neglected children: Integration of family therapy and play therapy. In A. Drewes, S. C. Bratton, & C. E. Schaefer (Eds.), *Integrative play therapy* (pp. 153–175). John Wiley & Sons.

VanFleet, R., & Topham, G. L. (2016a). Filial therapy. In K. O'Connor, C. Schaefer, & L. Braverman (Eds.), *Handbook of play therapy* (2nd ed., pp. 135–164). John Wiley & Sons.

VanFleet, R., & Topham, G. L. (2016b). Integration of family therapy and play therapy. In A. Drewes, S. Bratton, & C. Schaefer (Eds.), *Integrative play therapy* (pp. 153–175). Wiley & Sons.

Wickstrom, M. F. T. A. (2009). The process of systemic change in filial therapy: A phenomenological study of parent experience. *Contemporary Family Therapy: An International Journal*, *31*(3), 193–208. https://doi.org/10.1007/s10591-009-9089-3

CHAPTER 11
GESTALT PLAY THERAPY WITH SEXUALLY ABUSED CHILDREN AND ADOLESCENTS

Felicia Carroll

The scope of trauma that comes with the violation of a child's or adolescent's body shatters the child's organismic sense of self-experience. Not only do victims express this shattering in varied ways, but they also express powerlessness to regain organismic integration and a sense of well-being. As a Gestalt play therapist, this author has experienced waves of confusion, anger, sorrow, and helplessness while entering into the victim's world while supporting their therapeutic journey toward wholeness. The child's journey toward reintegration can bring understanding and strength to us both as he eventually engages with the challenges of growth and development into his future.

This chapter on Gestalt Play Therapy will include what has been learned from clients and their families as well as what has been learned from gifted mentors, such as Violet Oaklander (2015, 2006), Jan Hindman (1989, 1991), and Joyce Mills (Mills & Crowley, 1986). Over the years, research and clinical literature on recovery from the trauma of childhood sexual abuse (CSA) have become more comprehensive. In this chapter, the author integrates the principles of Gestalt play therapy and the treatment approaches of Hindman with victims of CSA, as well as others writing about the effects of sexual trauma. The influence of Mills (Mills & Crowley, 1986) was significant in re-configuring a trauma assessment developed by Hindman (1989, 1991) into a trauma narrative using storytelling elements. In recent years, the necessity of a victim having a coherent and cohesive narrative about their CSA that supports the reintegration of a sense of self and secure attachment to caregivers has been stressed by neuroscientists such as Siegel (2011) and Cozolino (2002, 2017). The *gestalt* of these elements, which informs the Gestalt play therapeutic process, will be represented in the following sections.

DOI: 10.4324/9781003451549-13

Overview and Basic Tenets of Gestalt Play Therapy

Gestalt play therapy is a process-oriented, experiential therapy that focuses on the integrated functioning of all aspects of the child: senses, body, emotions, and intellect (Carroll, 2025). The clinical interest is in how the child's maladaptive use of these organismic functions impairs his ability to be engaged in his life situation. Most children who have experienced CSA have redirected their natural aggression toward contacting their needs and the environmental resources to meet those needs. Consequently, they can become constricted, fragmented, lacking in grade and liveliness. These symptoms may be behavioral, affective, interpersonal, or more likely, a combination of many adaptations to an unsupportive environment. With therapeutic intervention these symptoms can become life patterns in coping with various stressors. Gestalt play therapy is a process whereby the child's energy can find its intended direction in the service of meeting the ongoing developmental and growth needs (Carroll, 2025). Such fulfillment brings the child into more nurturing interactions with all of life (Carroll, 2009; Taylor, 2014).

The process of Gestalt play therapy provides for the varied and unique facets of child, family, and community support: the neurodevelopmental level of the child in understanding the experience of violation, the relationship of the perpetrator to the child and others in family and community, and the child's history of support or maltreatment. The complexity of such treatment requires flexibility, sensitivity, and clinical skills that can encompass all that is demanded. The various interventions available through the Gestalt approach (Oaklander, 2006, 2015) supports the Gestalt play therapist to be creative and fully engaged with the child, family, and community.

The Therapy Process

The creativity of both child and therapist, using expressive play modalities, experiments, and dialogue, forms the direction and nature of the therapeutic process. Gestalt play therapy aims to restore a client's natural, unique aliveness with healthy growth and development. Oaklander (1982):

> Helping the child become aware of her organismic regulation is a prime goal of the Gestalt therapist. As a child becomes more aware of her functioning in the therapy experience – who she is, what she feels, what she likes and does not like, what she

needs, what she wants, what she does, and how she does it – she becomes aware and integrated. She has more choices for emotional expression, meeting her needs, and exploring new behaviors. This awareness happens through the various experiences and experiments that the play therapist provides in the process of therapy

(p. 65).

Fundamental Principles

Gestalt play therapy is a dynamic interaction of the following elements, creating a supportive experience for the child who has been sexually abused. The process of therapy is nonlinear and not a treatment protocol. The therapist's choices and creative interventions are based on the unique needs and interests of the child in support of his sense of self and integrated functioning, as well as the clinical skills of the therapist. (Carroll, 2025)

Authentic Relationship

A relationship between the therapist and the child needs to be one where the child feels safe and trusts the therapist to provide safety and understand of the child's situation and perspective. This relationship in Gestalt play therapy is based on mutuality, feeling with and for one another, and respect for boundaries. It is a collaborative, creative endeavor where agendas are minimized. The Gestalt play therapist is nonmanipulative with the child or members of the child's family. With discernment, the therapist's authenticity marks the nature of the interactions between all people involved, especially with the child.

Organismic Regulation

Being in contact involves the client being aware of their physical and sensory ability to be engaged in interactions with their body, emotions, and thoughts. Most children in psychotherapy have difficulty staying in contact, which indicates that the client is adapting their body or emotional response to cope with a problematic or painful issue. These protective patterns can become self-sustaining without therapeutic support. This is especially the case with the child who has been sexually abused.

Providing the child with experiences that support healthy body processes is essential to regain confidence in the natural self-regulating functions of his organism.

Phenomenology: Self-Support and Narrative

No two persons take in the outside world with "the same eyes." Every perception of inner and outer experience is unique to the individual and the understanding and meaning given to those experiences. In Gestalt play therapy, the therapist uses a non-analytical process that allows the child to share the depth of his experience and his meaning with the therapist. Providing the child with experiences of making choices, mastery, and using their energy for self-support is a part of sessions. As this occurs, the child can become more able to identify emotions and express them safely and effectively.

Most children who have been traumatized by violations of their bodies develop faulty beliefs about their body, behavior, emotions, and relationships with others. Through the Self-Nurturing process (Carroll, 2009; Oaklander, 2006) and the development of a cohesive narrative of the child's trauma experience (Carroll, 2012; Cozolino, 2002, 2017), these beliefs can be re-evaluated, and new understandings integrated.

Field Theory

A comprehensive view of the child within his life space (i.e., field), is essential in understanding the nature of his symptoms, needs, and supports. The full geography of a child's life is considered in the assessment process. A significant assessment must be made of the relationship that persists between the child and his perpetrator and other significant people in his life. The Gestalt play therapist is cognizant of the history of neglect, stress, protection, safety, and security within relationships on a developing child. Understanding the child's relationships is even more important for the child whose body integrity has been violated for another's purposes.

Literature Review

Theodore Stripling (2021), in his article, *Gestalt Interventions Benefiting Children and Adolescents: A Literature Review*, cited several studies that indicated Gestalt play therapy has benefited children and adolescents in the following areas: emotional self-expression, conflict resolution, contact with therapists, well-being, self-esteem, communication skills, decreased depression, child anxiety, parent anxiety, and trauma symptoms.

Results of an internet search on Gestalt therapy with sexually abused children provided many research papers, dissertations, as well as assessment and treatment model development. These articles were global in scope, with studies from Brazil, Iran, South Africa, South Korea, and the United States. Several other articles discussed the benefits of utilizing the Gestalt approach with other modalities such as equine therapy, family therapy, and community health care systems.

Clinical Case Presentation

Initial Sessions

I was astonished to learn that Nathan had to request his own therapist by writing a note to his cousin's therapist. Nathan's cousin had been removed from the home after his sexual abuse of Nathan was discovered. Nathan's family had immigrated to the United States about two years before Nathan was born. When Nathan was 9 years old, his aunt and 14-year-old cousin moved in with them, seeking safety from domestic violence. That therapist referred Nathan's family to me two months after his cousin had received support. Nathan and his family had met with his therapist during the assessment for his cousin's therapy. Unfortunately, Nathan was not referred to therapy until after meeting with his cousin's therapist. Then Nathan wrote a note asking for his own therapist. That therapist referred Nathan's family to me two months after his cousin had received support!

I met with Nathan's parents and learned that his therapy for sexual abuse had been overlooked. They had hoped it would not be needed. There was a police report made which described the acts of genital manipulation, anal penetration, and oral stimulation that had occurred over approximately four months. His parents were hesitant and found it difficult to discuss what had happened. They described how they discovered the behavior of the two boys, and his father had called the police. Their body language communicated their sense of shame, sadness, and guilt for what had happened to their son.

Nathan's father led our discussion. He explained that Nathan's cousin was his brother's son and that he had agreed to bring him and his mother to the United States for safety reasons. Nathan's family lived in a small home with only two bedrooms. Nathan and his cousin shared one of the rooms; the two women slept in the other. One night, his father, who slept on the couch, heard a disturbance in their room. He went to see what was going on and discovered them in one bed, naked. He separated the two, and Nathan began to cry and tell his father that sometimes his cousin would corner him in the house and threaten him to do "weird things." Almost every night, after they were in bed, his cousin would put his penis in his bottom.

Nathan's father called the police and told them what Nathan had said about his cousin. The police report was made, and the cousin was taken into custody through the juvenile system. Nathan's parents did not know what happened after that, except that his cousin had a therapist whom they had met twice. They learned at that time that members of his father's family had molested the cousin since he was a young boy. Nathan's father and mother were saddened by what they learned and blamed themselves for what had happened to Nathan.

I asked their permission to follow up on the police report and any other matters regarding Nathan's cousin's situation. I also informed them of Victim Witness funding, which could cover the cost of Nathan's therapy. I also received a Release of Information to confer with the other therapist and receive the status of his report to Child Protective Services.

When I met again with his parents, we included Nathan in the session. He was very eager and glad to come and meet with me. As we talked briefly about issues such as confidentiality and why he wanted a therapist for himself, I told Nathan that he was smart to write the note to his cousin's therapist and to find support for himself and his family. By the end of the session, Nathan and his parents seemed relaxed. Before they left this session, I discussed the parameters of confidentiality and that I am a mandated reporter. I assured them that I would discuss any reports with them before making additional disclosures. I expressed my appreciation for their support in signing the release of information.

This opening was essential to establish security for Nathan's therapy. When working with cases of CSA, it is important to take time to set the legal, ethical, and financial foundations for a child's therapy process. This structure and clarity are needed for the parents and child to begin trusting me and to feel secure enough to engage in his therapy. It was also clear that even with their initial hesitation, his parents were willing to do whatever was needed to help Nathan.

In the following initial sessions, Nathan and I established our friendship as he talked about his nightmares and worries about his cousin. He felt relief having everything stop and that his cousin was "in jail." His aunt moved out of the house and had a separate home since a court order prevented her son from contacting Nathan. I received a copy of the police report, and we reviewed it together. Nathan was glad that the report had all the information. He drew pictures of his house and put marks on the areas where his cousin would corner him – the bedroom, the laundry room, and the bathroom. He drew pictures of his fear when Nathan cornered him and pulled down his pants. He described being confused, frightened, anxious, angry, sad, and acutely lonely. His cousin was bigger and told Nathan not to tell anyone, or Nathan would get into trouble. Nathan told me about how scared he was and how worried that something was wrong with him for doing things that "were so disgusting and weird." He told me that once when his cousin put his penis inside of his anus, that blood came out. He worried if his body was okay.

Even though there had been a physical examination by the forensic doctor, I asked his parents to have Nathan see his pediatrician for a physical examination. Nathan told me he wanted to jump up and down when the doctor told him his body was okay. We jumped up and down in session. He drew a picture of himself as happy. In time, he became more relaxed and freer with his movements during our sensory and physical play.

Middle Sessions

Using water noodles, I introduced" Rough and Tumble" play (Panksepp, 1993). Subsequently, Nathan wanted to begin every session with an energetic, playful battle. In my office, all Rough and Tumble play is grounded in rules of safety, fairness, and respect for one another. This assured the boundaries of this energetic play and mitigated any anxiety that might have been aroused.

In his daily life, Nathan began playing soccer and spending time with classmates. He began to enjoy school, especially reading. The nightmares diminished, and he felt better about things in general. I attributed this to his finding support in our sessions, his cousin being contained, and the sensory, emotional, and energy interventions we participated in together.

As we worked together, I heard him express many self-statements, especially about not telling his parents what his cousin was doing. In one session, Nathan made a clay figure that represented his cousin. He also made a figure of himself. The figure of his cousin was much larger than Nathan's, which looked small and fragile. Nathan took the figures to the dollhouse, where he let the figures play out words and actions. The cousin's figure was threatening and forceful; Nathan's figure was quiet, without words. I asked Nathan to say to the figure of himself, "Even though you could not stop him, remember how small you were." He took a deep breath. "But I should have gotten away," he answered. "How could you have done that?" I asked softly. "I do not know," he said with a sad expression. Then he told me that his cousin choked him twice and made him do weird things. "You were small, Nathan, and could not stop him. You are very brave because you are stopping him now by telling me, your parents, and the police what happened." He sat quietly, and then, with tears in his eyes, he looked at me, "Yeah, I was really a little kid . . . then," was all he said.

Over several sessions, Nathan and I worked through many such feelings and judgments about himself as I used the elements of the Self-Nurturing process (Oaklander, 2006). He took home a boy figure that he used for himself in sand tray scenes. Each day he told the figure (himself) that he was brave to tell what had happened to him and stopping his cousin.

As I assessed his progress, I introduced the project of writing together his story and creating a book about what had happened (Mills & Crowley, 1986; Hindman, 1989). He was interested, so I mentioned this in one of the regular parent sessions, knowing their involvement would be necessary. His mother agreed to help Nathan find pictures that could go into the "book."

I wrote short pieces that talked about his cousin coming to live with his family and how the abuse first took place. Nathan illustrated sections of the story with the drawings he had done in earlier sessions, and we added the photographs that his mother sent. The narrative captured explicitly the molesting and penetration that happened, but more importantly, the sensations, emotions, and thoughts he had. When Nathan, as "editor-in-chief," would say, "That is right. That is the way it happened." I knew the words on the page had meaning and validation of his experiences. Sometimes, children will change my descriptive words and make the narrative truer to their experience.

The book closed with pictures and accounts of hiking and boat trips with friends and his other life activities. Letters of celebration and acknowledgment from family, community workers and me are there for him to read and re-read. A copy of the police report and the doctor's evaluation were also included. His "book" was important to him. It reminded him that other people can help him, that he has many friends, and that he enjoys sports and hiking with them. More importantly, he saw on those pages a special bravery, his bravery to tell the truth and to face the one who hurt him – even when he was bigger than him. We had a closing session for Nathan to read and show his book to his parents. After that, the book was his, and he took it home.

Closing Sessions

After we completed Nathan's narrative, I discussed with him and his parents the importance of a "Clarification Process" (Hindman, 1991). This is a sensitive process that must be supported by everyone involved. Nathan told me after meeting with his cousin in this session, that it meant a lot that his cousin had said that he was not to blame for what his cousin had done and that he was sorry for hurting and scaring him. His parents were loving and expressed their sorrow for what had happened and that they had not known to protect him. They shared their pride in him for what he had accomplished in therapy and in his life.

In our final sessions, they discussed what was developing in the family therapy and the supervised visits. Nathan said he initially felt nervous but more like doing things as a family again. The theme of bravery was present. His cousin never lived with them again as he and his mother returned to their previous home.

These developments indicated Nathan's restored integration of body, emotions, and strength in his sense of self. Even though the experience of the abuse can never be erased from the life memory of a client, the experience of Gestalt play therapy can provide the child with an experience of wholeness and wholesomeness about their body, self, and potential for healthy relationships and aliveness.

Limitations of Gestalt Play Therapy

Effective Gestalt play therapy is a function of support and involvement of significant people in the therapy process. Skills and discernment in including family and community systems are essential for long-lasting outcomes of organismic integration and the client's well-being. The effectiveness and limitations of any therapeutic approach are determined by the therapist's relational sensibilities, understanding of the unique trauma of each client, and the wise use of clinical interventions.

In this author's experience and the research review, there are no limitations if the therapist is trained in Gestalt play therapy and is informed by the theoretical principles of the organismic-relational paradigm of the Gestalt approach.

Considerations for Practice: Key Takeaways

- Secure support at all levels for a sense of safety and containment. This requires us to know that legal, ethical, financial, and medical issues have been identified and addressed in a way that allows the therapy to progress unhindered by unexpected obstacles in these domains.
- How the therapist talks with a child about their abusive experiences is what is either supportive or retraumatizing.
- Using the vocabulary of the child for the genitals and other parts of the body can ease any discomfort in the beginning.
- Writing a trauma narrative and creating a "book" with the story and accompanying pictures is very time-consuming for the therapist, yet very meaningful to the child.
- Providing experiences and clinical interventions that allow the child to work with the body and energy is essential.
- Be sure you have trained with an experienced therapist before doing a clarification session with the child and perpetrator.

References

Carroll, F. (2009). Gestalt play therapy. In K. J. O'Connor & L. D. Braverman (Eds.), *Play therapy theory and practice comparing theories and techniques* (2nd ed., pp. 283–314). John Wiley & Sons.

Carroll, F. (2009). Pitchfork princess: Transforming the torment of shame. *Interamerican Journal of Psychology, 43*(2), 260–267.

Carroll, F. (2012). Every child's life is worth a story. In J. Chang (Ed.), *Creative interventions with children: A transtheoretical approach* (pp. 187–191). Family Psychology Press.

Carroll, F. (2025). Gestalt therapy with children and adolescents. In D. A. Crenshaw, A. L. Stewart, & D. C. Ray (Eds.), *Comprehensive guide to play therapy* (2nd ed., pp. 73–91). Guilford Press.

Cozolino, L. (2002). The construction of the narrative self. In L. Cozolino (Ed.), *The neuroscience of psychotherapy: Building and rebuilding the human brain* (pp. 153–171). W.W. Norton.

Cozolino, L. (2017). From neural networks to narratives: The quest for integration. In L. Cozolino (Ed.), *The neuroscience of psychotherapy: Healing the social brain* (3rd ed., pp. 173–197). W. W. Norton.

Hindman, J. (1989). *Just before dawn: From the shadows of tradition to new reflections in trauma assessment and treatment of sexual victimization.* AlexAndria Associates.

Hindman, J. (1991). *The Mourning breaks: 101 "proactive" treatment strategies breaking the bonds of trauma for victims of sexual abuse.* AlexAndria Associates.

Mills, J. C., & Crowley, R. J. (1986). *Therapeutic metaphors for children and the child within.* Brunner/Mazel.

Oaklander, V. (1982). The relationship of gestalt therapy to children. *The Gestalt Journal Spring, V*(1), 64–74.

Oaklander, V. (2006). *Hidden treasure: A map to the child's inner self.* Karnac Books.

Oaklander, V. (2015). *Windows to our children: A gestalt therapy approach to children and adolescents.* The Gestalt Journal Press.

Panksepp, J. (1993). Rough and tumble play: A fundamental brain process. In K. Mac-Donald (Ed.), *Parent-child play: Descriptions and implications* (pp. 147–184). State University of New York Press.

Siegel, D. (2011). Attachment and mindfulness: Relational paths of the developing brain. In R. G. Lee & N. Harris (Eds.), *Relational child, relational brain: Development and therapy in childhood adolescence* (pp. 77–115). A Gestalt Press Book, Routledge, Taylor & Francis Group.

Stripling, T. (2021). Gestalt interventions benefiting children and adolescents: A literature review. *Gestalt Review, 25*(2), 197–221.

Taylor, M. (2014). *Trauma therapy and clinical practice: Neuroscience, Gestalt, and the body.* Open University Press.

CHAPTER 12

JUNGIAN ANALYTICAL PLAY THERAPY WITH SEXUALLY ABUSED CHILDREN

J.P. Lilly

Jungian Analytical Play Therapy (JAPT) (Jung, 1954, 1958, 1960, 1968, 1971) is not an easy method of treatment. Jung invented many of his own terms and expanded and deepened them over his years of writing. This approach is that change, and phenomenology of change is due to processes that we are unable to quantify. Although Jung did not write much about children, Wickes (1927) expounded Jung's theories for work with children. Allan (1998) was the pioneer who forwarded a Jungian Analytical Approach to play therapy with children. It has been found that Jung's theory and principles of change are applicable to children.

Basic Tenets of Jungian Analytical Play Therapy

JAPT is one that is not rooted in specific techniques or protocol. This approach receives each child into treatment as a unique individual who is processing their abuse in a meaningful way. The goal in JAPT is to champion the individual freedom of all children who cross the threshold of our playrooms by treating them as unique individuals working out their trauma in the best way they can. The JAPT therapist seeks to awaken the Self-Healer within each child that will ensure that the child is healing from within, and not from any outside agent. The goal is true transformational healing, not the elimination of a cluster of symptoms, although these symptoms are eliminated naturally when transformational healing is achieved.

JAPT considers the unconscious the seat of transformational healing. As a practitioner of this approach, one must become familiar with the language of the unconscious. Jung believed that the normal child lives psychologically in a state of unconsciousness from which various

DOI: 10.4324/9781003451549-14

isolated moments of consciousness appear. These "islands" of consciousness grow larger and larger until the ego develops. This allows for a more conscious awareness of self and others. The language of the unconscious is manifested in the child's life through symbols, images, metaphors, dreams, archetypes, and play themes.

An understanding of how sexual abuse affects children from a Jungian perspective begins with understanding the construct of the psyche, and the process of ego development (Moore, 2005). The psyche represents conscious and unconscious properties that are divided into a personal consciousness and the "collective conscious" (i.e., culture and social environments) (Elwood, 2020; Jung, 1960; Lilly, 2025; McRoberts, 2024). The collective unconscious where the entire history of humankind is contained. The JAPT approach accepts that this history is in each child manifests through the child's symbolic play. Play also becomes the mechanism by which the Self-Healer (Lilly, 2025) is manifested, an integral part of the child's unconscious that can be summoned when the child engages symbolically with their abuse.

The Ego (Jung, 1960) is a crucial part in the formulation of the psyche. As the Ego develops, it must now mitigate both unconscious and conscious activity. At birth, the Ego is emerging from a state of unconsciousness. For the first time the infant is confronted by situations that create "deintegration" (Fordham, 1973). Hunger, thirst, pain, and other experiences create this state of deintegration to the infant's Ego. The fragile and emerging Ego has limited resources to cope with this deintegration, and the child responds instinctively. The hungry infant experiences pain (Ego deintegration) and calls out for help (deintegration response). A nurturing caregiver comes to the aid of the child and feeds, changes, and comforts the child, creating "reintegration." Such is the process of Ego development, and the process by which the Ego creates "strength" (Fordham, 1973). Later, when more evolved cognitive developments are present, the child can accommodate or acclimate to new situations more fluidly and not be subjected to the same level of deintegration by applying previously learned scripts and schema to similar events. This process of adaptation was described by Piaget (1954) from a cognitive developmental perspective.

Sexually abused children and adolescents have been introduced to an external stimulus for which they do not have sufficient scripts, schema, coping skills, or experience to effectively engage and manage the effects of the abuse. Because this experience is so "traumatic," the experience is often repressed, and becomes a "protocomplex" (Peery, 2003). A protocomplex left without treatment becomes a complex which is "a collection of images and ideas, clustered round a core derived from one or more archetypes, and characterized by a common emotional tone." (Samuels et al., 1986). In simpler terms, it is a cluster of powerful emotions attached to an archetypal core. Jung indicated that a complex can and does act like "independent beings" (Jung, 1960). This means that this material is not conscious to the child, but the manifestations of the complex can be, and are manifested through the child's symptoms.

This author is frequently asked whether all children who have been sexually abused need therapy. While it is prudent to assess the damage, not all children who have experienced sexual abuse need therapy. Following the upper half of the model above, it is possible for a child to resolve their own trauma associated with sexual abuse. The event starts as a child is sexually abused as the "new or unfamiliar" event. The child experiences deintegration over the three levels of human experience: thinking, feeling, and behavior. However, the child has sufficient life experiences, sufficient support networks in her life, and sufficient ego strength to "engage" with the event. The event is not repressed into the unconscious because the child can engage it. The child engages what happened to them and can create healthy responses to what occurred. A few healthy adaptive cognitions to being sexually abused are: "It wasn't my fault"; "I am not for that"; "They are wrong, not me," and others. A few healthy adaptive emotions are anger, fear, frustration, feelings of betrayal, damaged trust, and others. Finally, healthy adaptive behaviors could be staying away from that individual, telling the truth, going to similar places only with people who are safe and protective. Having sufficient ego strength through supportive people, internal resiliency, previous life experiences, and other intangible means can assist children in engaging with their sexual abuse in an adaptive, healthy manner without the need for therapy.

Now let us consider a child that is sexually abused using the same model referenced above who doesn't have the same supportive networks available to them, both internally and externally. The model starts from the left and follows to the right. The child experiences the abuse, which is the new or unfamiliar event. The abuse negatively effects the child on all three levels of the human experience, cognitively, emotionally, and behaviorally, causing deintegration to the child's ego. The child has not developed the life experience or coping skills to effectively engage and manage this event. The experience overwhelms the child's ego and is repressed into the unconscious and becomes a complex – very powerful emotions attached to an archetypal core of abuse. This experience remains with the child in the unconscious, and because the complex has access to the ego by way of the unconscious, the child cannot have any peace or reprieve from the event and remains in an agitated state. If the material remains repressed in the unconscious, and the psychological movement of the child is to avoid engagement until sufficient ego strength is attained, and healthy, responsive coping skills can be adapted, time will pass without resolution. The complex continues to create deintegration within the child, but since the child lacks the ego strength to engage the material consciously, and the energy and emotions from the complex need to be addressed, the child engages in maladaptive homeostasis. This term means that the emotion and energy from the complex negatively affects the unprepared ego of the child, and is assuaged by avoiding engagement through maladaptive cognitions, emotions, and behaviors. Examples of these maladaptive, avoidant dynamics can look like cognitions such as, "it was my fault," "I'm to blame," "I wanted it to happen," "This is what I'm for, I'm a sex toy," and many others. Maladaptive emotions can be "It wasn't that bad," "I liked it," and "I like that person." Maladaptive behaviors can be seen as sexually abusing other children (a compensatory dynamic) or allowing oneself to be repeatedly abused (a confirmational dynamic). As much as the child tries to evade the experience, the complex is left unresolved and continues to "behave like independent beings" (Jung, 1960). This can lead the child to formulating maladaptive means to deal with the complex, with the intention to assuage the negative effects of the complex but avoiding meaningful engagement with it. Children's symptoms of abuse carry either a compensatory (making up for something) or a confirmational (playing it out as the child experienced it) (Lilly, 2025). Children rarely have the capacity of ego strength to engage effectively and in a healthy manner with traumatic events. The JAPT approach works diligently to make the connection between the child's symptoms and the relationship of those symptoms to the complex. We view these "symptoms" as a roadmap to the complex.

The JAPT approach believes that the complex remains active in the unconscious of children until it can be engaged and resolved, and that the symptoms persist, although they might manifest themselves differently over time. The goal of JAPT with the sexually abused child is to create a safe environment in which the complex can be engaged. The use of play is the only safe and consistent method by which this complex material can be accessed and engaged with children. The JAPT therapist uses play, the archetypes we use known as toys, art, metaphors, sand play, and other symbolic means to allow for this safe engagement of the complex material. Once that material is accessed, the child can call upon other unconscious material to combat, resolve, create, and allow the Self-Healer to come forward to heal the child. The JAPT doesn't enter the therapeutic relationship believing to know what that Self-Healer will look like but welcomes all symbolic material that the child generates as a means of engaging the complex and working toward that healing.

Play therapy is the perfect means by which unconscious engagement can occur. Play therapy provides sexually abused children the safety of the toys, which are symbolic representations of archetypal material, to engage with unconscious material in a safe manner. This safety, what Jung called "temenos" (Plaut et al., 1986), is augmented by the tender, caring, and safe relationship with the therapist. Creating the healthy, accepting relationship with the child is the JAPT therapist's primary role. As the sexually abused child feels safe within the therapeutic container, she will begin to use symbol, metaphors, and images to engage with the complex material. The JAPT therapist maintains several soft hypotheses regarding the symbolic material being used, the theme that is being created by the child with the material, and the theme's relationship to the complex. The maintaining of a several soft hypotheses by the JAPT therapists connects the therapist closely with the child on an unconscious level. There is a willingness on the part of the JAPT therapist to go to those unconscious places with the child, even if that place is uncomfortable for him.

Play that is engaging to the complex for children is powerful, and very disruptive to the psyche of children. Given that the complex contains powerful emotions, the JAPT therapist can witness or feel these powerful emotions attached to the archetypal core of the child's complex. Because it is so powerful emotionally when this contact is made, the child can only sustain that level of engagement for short periods of time. Ego deintegration will occur when conscious and unconscious contact is made with the complex. This process of deintegration serves as a witness to engagement with the complex. This process of deintegration when contacting complex material is followed quickly by reintegration. It is understandable for a child to be engaging in a powerfully emotional theme, to suddenly stop and begin to engage in something over which they have mastery. This author worked with a 5-year-old client who was painting a confirmational scene on the easel of how she had been sexually abused when she suddenly stopped painting and looked at me and began reciting the ABCs. The reciting of the ABCs was something over which she had mastery in her life and brought reintegration back to her psyche that had just experienced deintegration from complex engagement. The ebb and flow of deintegration and reintegration is a very normal process of complex engagement for sexually abused children in play therapy.

Naturally, the JAPT therapist is ever mindful of the symbolic material of the toys with which the child is intrigued, and how the child plays with that archetypal material. The toys hold their own specific symbolism for the child and have family, cultural and pancultural symbolism that extends beyond the child. The JAPT therapist works to understand the child's interpretation of the toy, the cultural meaning, and the pancultural meaning. It is not unusual for children to be attracted to toys with symbolic meaning to their culture about which they have no conscious knowledge. And to use those toys in meaningful themes for their healing. For example, during JAPT, a 6-year-old boy who was sexually abused created a Celtic knot out of the clay. He had no idea regarding his Celtic heritage, but he took the knot home, baked it, and, unknowingly to him, painted it in one of the colors of his family crest. He carried it in his pocket for two weeks, then brought it into the play therapy room and presented it to the therapist, indicating that he did not need it anymore. He had no knowledge about his heritage, but he used it to seal the healing that he had done. The JAPT therapist is sensitive and knowledgeable regarding the cultural and ethnic history of our clients.

While we maintain no active mental prescriptions in our minds about what sexually abused clients will do in the play therapy room, the JAPT therapist knows that the child has experienced a disruption to their ego functioning that has overwhelmed them. The dynamics of their symptoms reflect the relationship that sexually abused children have to their individual complexes. Some typical themes of children who have been sexually abused are powerlessness, worthlessness, manipulation, compliance, betrayal, and many others. It is not difficult to see these themes acted out in a confirmational manner in their play. It is also not uncommon to see the counterpart to these themes when healing begins to take place. Suddenly powerlessness becomes their individual power; worthlessness becomes inherent worth and value; manipulation becomes cleverness; compliance becomes integrity; and betrayal becomes trust to name only a few. Each dynamic of sexual abuse has its counterpart, and the healing journey for sexually abused children finds its' symbolic way to manifest itself to the play therapist open to see it.

Clinical Case Study

In this section I will refer to a 5-year-old boy with whom I worked years ago. He had been adopted from an orphanage in Russia. This young boy had three four-inch knives wounds on his body, cigarette burns on both of his arms, and anal fissures. He was the victim of a cadre of maltreatment including CSA.

Initially, JAPT work was about creating safety. At the end of one session, he began to work out his plan for engagement with his complex. At the end of the session, he took a predator animal from the shelf (a T-Rex dinosaur) and placed it in the garbage can. He projected the abuser archetype onto the T-Rex and had made a movement to remove it from his psyche. His ego was strengthening, and he was preparing for a confrontation with his "predator."

The confrontation happened in the next session; his attack was accompanied by intense complex energy as he was killing his predators. He gathered weapons, field tested his equipment, and enlisted me in the process of "killing" his predator. He turned out the lights of the playroom and we attacked the T-Rex, and I witnessed the complex energy that existed from his abuse as he powerfully, repeatedly, and savagely beat on the T-Rex. He continued to beat on the T-Rex until he was physically tired. He then placed the T-Rex back on the shelf.

I suggested a soft hypothesis to him that he might not be done. He acknowledged and communicated to me that there was more than one predator. At his direction, we began killing (shooting) the other predators on that shelf. He could sustain these attacks for about three- to four-minute intervals until he had to break to reintegrate. He reintegrated with drawing, playing in the water, talking to me, and playing with money in a very significant manner. Each time after reintegrating, he returned to his compensatory task and worked methodically and purposefully, killing more and more of the predators and dumping them in the trash. I was able to feel his anxiety in performing this heroic task, and I verbalized to him my feelings of anxiety associated with his journey. He acknowledged my comment with only a look, but he knew that

I understood his emotions. When his task was completed and he had killed all of the predators, I recognized the trash can not only as the repository of the dead predators from his life, but also as the container for them. I verbalized to him, "They can't hurt us anymore" (I used the word "us" because he had deputized me in the killing of the predators). He quipped "Yup, they can't," at which point he turned the lights back on and let out a resounding exhale.

Now with the predators all killed and buried in the trash can, he was faced with a dilemma. The shelf where the predators were was now empty. It was a metaphorical hole in his life. He then spent the next 15 minutes of his session rearranging the shelves. He put the weapons and toys of power in the empty shelf where the predators were. He moved around many shelves, and whatever did not work in his world, he threw out into the garbage. He ended up with the empty shelf being on the very bottom, symbolic of that part being gone from his early life. He finished his session by painting. He painted the entire paper blue, and in the midst of his painting he created a demonic figure in it. Eerily, it represented what he had overcome, and it was his unconscious communicating to him regarding his ultimate victory.

This young boy's journey had metaphorically placed him in front of his abusers. He undertook the hero's journey, like Hercules or Jason, and confronted them with courage and all the magical power his inflated ego could muster. "We" took that journey together and conquered the evil in his life. My part in bringing the unconscious into consciousness was to interpret the "container" and the properties of the container as the holder of garbage and as something from which things could not return. "We" were safe from the return of those evil predators; it was something that I saw, interpreted, and then expressed to my young, courageous friend. This is the task of the JAPT therapist when unconscious material manifests itself: to assist the child to consciously understand it, and in this case, understand it more fully. Interpretation is a high-level skill to be able to do it and allow the meaning of it to resonate with the child.

Limitations of Jungian Analytical Play Therapy With Childhood Sexual Abuse

JAPT requires highly skilled play therapists. It is not a beginner-level approach. The JAPT therapist must be able to conduct play therapy with basic skills of reflecting content, tracking behaviors, attending to the emotions of the child, and attend to the child's cognitions while at the same time understanding the symbolic meaning of the toys engaged, carry soft hypotheses regarding the themes being presented, and pace with the emotional and unconscious energy of the child. One should feel confident in one's ability to demonstrate basic play therapy skills before considering moving to a more in-depth process.

Another limitation of JAPT is that since the play therapist is considered part of the play therapy room, the therapist must have a deep understanding of their own psychological issues. Working in the unconscious can create a rich environment for countertransference of the therapist's issues to be transferred onto the child. It is important the clinician knows where they stop and the client begins so as not to contaminate the child's play. This is why it is important for JAPT therapists to "do their own work" with analysts who are trained to understand the manifestations of unconscious material.

JAPT is not suited to research. The dearth of quantifiable components leaves the JAPT approach grossly understudied and under-researched. JAPT will more than likely always be understudied as the unconscious is, and remains, unquantifiable to be measured. Unconscious dynamics like complexes, neuroses, and due to the theoretical position that the collective unconscious operates independently of the Ego on account of its origin in the inherited part of the brain, we cannot measure it.

Due to the inherited part of the psyche, each child comes to therapy with their own history of the world in their psyche. We have a collective beginning in the collective unconscious and as we grow in our cultures, we inherit that branch of symbolic meaning. It is incumbent on the JAPT therapist to be culturally sensitive, learn about the client's cultural heritage, and observe for any manifestations of those cultural symbols in therapy. This creates more work for the JAPT therapist not familiar with a particular culture.

Considerations for Practice: Key Takeaways

- There exists a systemic dynamic in families where children may be acting out unresolved unconscious material of a parent.
- CSA affects the child cognitively, emotionally, and behaviorally leading to a state of ego deintegration.
- Symptoms that result from CSA carry with them either compensatory or confirmational dynamics associated with the child's attempts to adapt to sexual abuse.

- Healing for the child comes by safely engaging the complex formulated by the abuse and is done so in play therapy by archetypal materials (toys, therapist, art materials, etc.).
- The unconscious is the source of true transformational healing for sexually abused children.

References

Allan, J. (1998). *Inscapes of the child's world: Jungian counseling in schools and clinics.* Springer.

Elwood, P. (2020). *A Jungian approach to spontaneous drawing: A window to the soul.* Routledge.

Fordham, M. (1973). Maturation of ego and self in infancy. In M. Fordham, R. Gordon, J. Hubback, K. Lambert, & M. Williams (Eds.), *The library of analytical psychology: Analytical psychology and modern science* (Vol. 1, pp. 82–94). Heinemann.

Jung, C. G. (1954). The development of personality. In *Collected works* (Vol. 17, p. 7). Princeton University Press.

Jung, C. G. (1958). *Collected works of C. G. Jung* (Vol. 11). Princeton University Press.

Jung, C. G. (1960). The structure and dynamics of the psyche. In *Collected works* (Vol. 8). Princeton University Press.

Jung, C. G. (1968). Psychology and alchemy. In *Collected works* (Vol. 12). Princeton University Press.

Jung, C. G. (1971). *The collected works of C. G. Jung.* Princeton University Press.

Lilly, J. P. (2025). Jungian analytical play therapy. In D. A. Crenshaw, A. L. Stewart, & D. C. Ray (Eds.), *Play therapy: Theory, research, and practice* (2nd ed., pp. 92–110). Guilford Press.

McRoberts, R. (2024). *Jungian counseling and play therapy: Classical theory for the digital age.* Routledge.

Moore, R. (2005). *The rape of the soul: Jungian perspectives on the sexual abuse of children.* CG Jung Institute of Chicago.

Peery, C. (2003). Jungian analytical play therapy. In C. Schaefer (Ed.), *Foundations of play therapy* (3rd ed., pp. 14–54). Wiley.

Piaget, J. (1954). *Construction of reality in the child.* Routledge.

Plaut, F., Samuels, A., & Shorter, B. (1986). *A critical dictionary of Jungian analysis.* Routledge.

Samuels, A., Shorter, B., & Plaut, F. (1986). *A critical dictionary of Jungian analysis* (1st ed.). Routledge. https://doi.org/10.4324/9780203713822

Wickes, F. (1927). *The inner world of childhood.* D. Appleton & Co.

CHAPTER 13
USING THERAPLAY TO TREAT CHILDHOOD SEXUAL ABUSE

Elizabeth Konrath

Childhood sexual abuse (CSA) is a complex, challenging issue. Therapists who work with victims are vigilant about the type of treatment we provide. We believe there is "a lot on the line" and hold a deep desire to "get it right." Our cautiousness is warranted. Research confirms that CSA has profound short- and long-term effects on the victim's mental and physical health and their relationships (National Child Traumatic Stress Network [NCTSN], 2023).

Different from other types of relational trauma, the context of CSA involves an adult directly dismissing a child's needs and violating their boundaries in service of the adult's desires. Therapists have the opportunity to model a relationship where the child's needs are not just honored but held at the center of our work. Those needs, which involve physical and emotional safety, healthy and appropriate touch, and joyful, delightful interactions with others, are met without conditions. This is one of the many reasons Theraplay is useful in treating CSA. Through this model, the child experiences a relationship where they are celebrated and nurtured without contingencies on what the child does for the adult.

In this chapter, we will explore the ways that Theraplay is an appropriate, beneficial model to use when working with families who have experienced CSA. The primary benefits include:

1. Use of touch: Theraplay emphasizes attunement and relational boundaries, including the safe and healthy use of touch, with emphasis on the child's needs for touch, not the adult's.
2. Family focused: Theraplay involves a caregiver for dyadic work and can be modified to include the whole family system to address safety in

DOI: 10.4324/9781003451549-15

relationships, correct role reversals, increase connection, and combat shame and isolation.

3. Developmentally appropriate: Theraplay is a play-based modality that prioritizes the child's developmental needs so that they feel seen, heard, and understood through play and relational attunement.

4. Improves self-worth: Theraplay focuses on helping children change their self-perceptions, improve self-esteem, and provides opportunities for children to experience playful, empowering interactions.

Research Support for Utilizing Theraplay With CSA

Research on treating complex trauma in childhood supports the use of Theraplay to help children heal from CSA. Polyvagal theory (Porges, 2011) offers insight into why certain therapeutic modalities are more effective than others in healing childhood trauma. Polyvagal theory, which explains how crucial it is for mammals to experience coregulation, safety, and connection provides evidence that supports Theraplay as an appropriate, beneficial modality to use for treating CSA. In this theory, Porges (2015) describes how the "social engagement system, (SES)" activates higher brain functions, such as playfulness, intimacy, and creativity. The SES can only be accessed when one's nervous system experiences safety. One's SES is activated when a person receives safety signals from others, including facial expressions, gestures, and tone of voice. Theraplay facilitates the opportunity for children to experience this safety, thus activating their SES to be social, connected, and coregulated by others (Lindaman & Hong, 2021). There is a strong overlap between the safe states that Polyvagal Theory determines are crucial to treating trauma and the way Theraplay promotes safety through direct, interpersonal engagement and attunement.

van der Kolk (2015) emphasizes the need for trauma-focused treatment to include visceral, sensory, and physical dimensions. He questions the reliance on talk therapy, highlighting the value of integrating modalities that incorporate movement and pleasure to build regulation (van der Kolk, 2015). Theraplay incorporate movement, increases pleasure, and builds regulation. Positive treatment experiences must be relational, relevant, repetitive, rewarding, rhythmic, and respectful (Perry, 2006). The Theraplay model utilizes all six of these R's naturally and effectively.

CSA is a systemic issue that warrants a systemic response (Gil, 2006). Sheinberg and Fraenkel (2001) state that CSA violates the entire family system's sense of security and disrupts attachments between family members. Additionally, Sheinberg and Fraenkel (2001) emphasize the benefits of working within the family system to strengthen safe attachment relationships and help families create a secure base for the children and nonoffending adults. Theraplay emphasizes prioritizing safety through dyadic relational work.

Effective treatment must address the physical needs of the child's nervous system (Gaskill & Perry, 2013). Theraplay offers "bottom-up" techniques that focus on the brain stem's regulatory and physiological systems, such as pulse and heart rate. Theraplay activities are whole-brain approaches that promote vertical (body and mind) and horizontal (left and right hemispheres) communication in the brain, building emotional and physical regulation (Konrath & Gil, 2021). Coregulation within a secure relationship is a critical sign of relational health. The Theraplay model teaches the caregiver how to be an external co-regulator for the child. Thus, safety, trust, and attachment are simultaneously supported.

Use of Touch

This is a touchy subject, so let's explore it in depth before we go further. The use of touch tends to be the biggest concern about Theraplay when treating CSA. Theraplay, based in attachment theory and research, is modeled after a healthy, secure relationship between an infant and caregiver. That relationship *must* involve touch to nurture, protect, and regulate the child. Touch is necessary to build healthy nervous systems, decrease stress hormones, and regulate other physiological needs (Ardiel & Rankin, 2010).

Despite decades of data emphasizing the cruciality of healthy touch, clinicians tend to be ambivalent about incorporating touch in therapy. Therapists express concerns that doing so could inadvertently facilitate children bringing up sexual themes in their play, crossing physical boundaries with therapists, or reenacting victim/victimizer dynamics (Gil, 2017). Clinicians express fears that if they touch clients who have been sexually abused, the clients will immediately and certainly be traumatized. The fear therapists could cause trauma to a child who already has suffered leads clinicians to avoid using touch at all with families of CSA. Even for therapists who attempt to model and facilitate healthy touch between a caregiver and child, if the therapist is afraid of triggering or confusing the child, they might behave awkwardly or rigidly. The child may interpret the therapist's behavior to mean that there is something wrong with the child.

CSA victims may develop a fear of touching or being touched, or they may have learned inappropriate physical boundaries. The experience of physical touch becomes perplexing and complicated: children may feel unprotected, vulnerable, and embarrassed, and yet may also have some pleasurable sensations in their bodies. In Theraplay, the clinician facilitates experiences of touch primarily between the caregiver and child. Caregivers might need clinicians to model how to provide touch in a gentle, attuned, appropriate manner, but the goal is to have the caregiver, not the therapist, provide the nurture and care to the child.

Children who experience CSA learn that their bodies are special for what they provide to the abuser. The Theraplay model counters this by teaching children that there are many unique and special things about themselves and their bodies that have nothing to do with sex or being hurt. Ways to incorporate healthy and safe touch in a Theraplay session are accessible in all four dimensions – structure, engagement, nurture, and challenge. The use of touch is purposeful in the activity, natural for the interaction, and regulating for the child. For instance, using crepe paper to measure a child's arms, feet, fingers, or hands provides structuring touch throughout the activity, in a manner where touch is functional. The practitioner facilitates the interaction between the caregiver and the child so that they are both experiencing the different body parts with delight (i.e., "Look how big your feet are growing!" or "Wow, your thumb is the same size as your mom's pinky finger.").

The Theraplay practitioner also models for the caregiver how to attune to the child's nonverbal communication regarding touch. If the therapist notices the child moved away from the therapist during an activity, the therapist might state, "Oh, I see Juan moved back from me when I scooted closer. He's letting me know he needs some space." I would provide that physical proximity in a playful way, where the child blinks at me, I scoot back and when they give me a thumbs up, I move a little bit closer.

Family-Focused Approach

It is important to note that all of the evidence-based treatments identified by the National Child Traumatic Stress Network [NCTSN] (2023) for CSA involve the family. CSA affects the relationship with the nonoffending caregiver. Abusers teach children many confusing messages about relationships; consequently, the child's relationships with other adults are impacted in ways that damage their sense of safety. In Theraplay, a child does not have to do anything to receive attention, delight, and connection from the adults. They receive it simply because of who they are. This provides a template for how we hope children can learn to navigate relationships, that their needs and wants matter and deserve to be respected.

The following is an example of how the Theraplay practitioner creates moments of coregulation during a Theraplay session. The practitioner begins a game with a balloon where they try to keep it up in the air. During this activity, the practitioner is providing structure ("Lets tap the balloon with just our thumbs . . . now with just our left hands . . . now let's try to pass it with our feet."), while maintaining attunement to the child. The practitioner pays attention to the child's nonverbal cues – their level of excitement, facial expressions, frequency of eye contact, and body posture. Based on these cues, the practitioner can moderate the amount of energy, movement, and physical proximity to the child. The practitioner may notice the child is becoming hyperaroused and continue the activity while sitting on the ground, or having the dyad hold hands to tap the balloon in order to better regulate the child. There are many ways to adapt these activities depending on the child's need and tolerance of regulation, connection, and engagement.

As with the typical Theraplay protocol, clinicians must be careful not to rush into caregiver–child dyadic work. It is crucial the practitioner to take time with caregivers to review the Theraplay principles, prepare for dyadic sessions, gather information about the nature of and impact of sexual abuse on the family, and build a trusting, attuned relationship with them. It is also beneficial if the practitioner can conduct an Adult Attachment Interview or the Parental Self Reflection Survey to gain deeper insight into the caregivers' own attachment strategies and history. As with any other modality, a caregiver who is actively abusing the child, abusing substances, or is not capable of a healthy attachment should not be included in Theraplay sessions. Other modalities should be considered.

In the standard Theraplay protocol, a caregiver is typically in the room from the very beginning of the dyadic sessions, but their level of involvement may vary depending on their capacity for attunement and empathy. For CSA, the presence of the caregiver in the room can be crucial in helping to build the child's sense of safety with the therapist. This is particularly true for a child who was isolated or alone with an adult when the sexual abuse occurred. Involving the caregiver in a more active, participatory role allows the child to feel protected. It also helps ease the child's expectations of what will occur in the session. For example, in a Theraplay session, the therapist introduces an activity to make a handprint of the child's hand. As we notice their nonverbal communication, that they are physically withdrawn or perhaps refuse to engage, we would not force the child to comply or coax them into participating. Instead, the practitioner would demonstrate the activity with the caregiver so that the child can observe and know what to expect.

Developmentally Appropriate

Play is the universal language of children. It is how they communicate, regulate, connect, and learn. Adults tend to prioritize words as the best way to understand and connect with children. But verbal communication is not typically a child's natural or most accessible way to connect or to communicate their feelings, thoughts, and experiences. This is why therapies that emphasize verbal expression are limited, and why Theraplay, an experiential, play-based modality, can yield growth for children and families.

Abusers place demands on children that far exceed their developmental capacities. Thus, at a time when children should be carefree, curious, playful, and cared for, they are instead required to keep secrets, negotiate adult needs, and most importantly, negotiate them alone (Konrath & Gil, 2021). Furthermore, disclosures for children who have experienced CSA can create tension, confusion, and conflict. Often, children have had to disclose their abuse to multiple people, multiple times. By the time they enter our office, the last thing they want to do is tell some stranger what happened to them. Fortunately, Theraplay does not emphasize verbal processing of abuse during sessions, so the child can feel less self-protective and more open to engaging.

Theraplay practitioners would not expect the child to verbally clarify if they felt uncomfortable or unsure about activities. Rather, we attune to the child's nonverbal communication to determine if they appear afraid or nervous, and then adjust based on what we perceive. Each activity is selected and designed to give the caregiver the experience of attuning to, accepting, and supporting their child. Consequently, the child feels seen, heard, and understood in their earlier language of play and nonverbal communication.

Self-Worth

CSA creates distortions of negative self-worth and shame. Building self-esteem and positive self-worth can be protective factors in decreasing a child's risk of being sexually abused in the future. Activities within the challenge dimension are helpful to improve self-esteem, feelings of empowerment, and pride. For example, in a cooperative cotton ball race, the child and caregiver work together to see how many times it takes them to blow a cotton ball on the floor across the room. As they play, the practitioner exclaims, "Wow, you have really strong lungs! You are so determined! You and your dad make such a great team." Both the child and the caregiver are experiencing the child's body as strong and capable, while also participating in a joyful, pleasurable interaction.

Theraplay works directly to counter the negative beliefs that the child has internalized about themselves from their abuser ("My needs don't matter. I am only here for other people to use. Adults don't protect me. It's my job to take care of this adult,") and replaces them with appropriate, secure beliefs about oneself in the world ("I deserve to be cared for. What I want and need matters. Grown-ups keep me safe.").

Sexual abuse is not exclusively about sex. Sex offenders appear to be seeking power and control over their victims. Children who have been sexually abused need and benefit from opportunities to experience empowerment. The structured choices that practitioners provide throughout Theraplay, such as asking, "Do you want the red balloon or the yellow balloon?" help children experience autonomy without putting pressure on them. Theraplay practitioners find a balance between providing enough structure to help the child feel safe, while also creating opportunities for the child to experience empowerment and control. The Theraplay model creates opportunities for mastery to directly challenge helplessness.

Limitations of the Model

While Theraplay can be appropriate in cases of CSA, it does have limitations. There are times where there is not a capable, willing caregiver available to participate. If this is the case, it is still possible to provide Theraplay as a modality, but with modifications. A clinician would need to make modifications regarding physical touch, the pace of the sessions, how nurture is provided, and flexibility toward the child's readiness to engage if there is no caregiver present.

Another potential limitation is that Theraplay does not provide the opportunity to verbally reprocess trauma. Depending on clinical needs, this process might be an important part of healing. With complex trauma, a combination of therapy approaches is necessary since no one single model helps all families. Therefore, integrating Theraplay with another modality, such as Narrative Therapy, TF-CBT, EMDR, or Filial Therapy, can be more appropriate than utilizing Theraplay independently. Another option would be to have pure Theraplay initially in treatment to secure the attachment and regulate the child, and then transition to a different modality for trauma-focused processing.

A challenge that can occur when working with CSA is managing sexualized behaviors. Theraplay practitioners should anticipate and be prepared for how to respond. Sexually abused children can become confused about boundaries, adult intentions, and disconnect from their bodies. I have had Theraplay clients who, particularly during nurturing activities, attempted to touch my private parts or show me their private parts. Situations like this require a clear, verbal response from the practitioner. In such instances, I have moved my body away from the child, and stated, "I am so sorry. I think that maybe when we were playing, I confused you. I want you to know that I will never touch your bottom or your private parts and you may not touch mine either." Often these behaviors can illicit feelings of shame in the child, so it is crucial to maintain connection to the child. Because caregivers might not feel equipped in the moment to respond to their child's behaviors, the therapist should be prepared to take the lead in addressing them calmly, without judgment.

In summary, Theraplay treatment can work directly to target treatment issues typically found in sexually abused children and their families. Theraplay is uniquely suited for this work because it prioritizes secure attachment, regulation, boundary-setting, the developmental needs of the child, strengthening caregiver capacities for providing components of healthy attachment, and giving the caregiver and child opportunities to restore a sense of mastery and control. Theraplay is delivered in a lively, physical, engaging way that promotes relational pleasure and joy and helps children reconnect with their bodies and with others safely.

Considerations for Practice: Key Takeaways

- Theraplay is structured to provide reparative experiences for the child. The practitioner facilitates attunement and opportunities for reparative, healing touch from the caregiver to the child.

- If a caregiver is not available, the therapist can still provide opportunities for the child to receive physical touch in a manner that is therapeutic, functional, and appropriate.
- Theraplay incorporates key principles of trauma treatment for victims of CSA.
- Theraplay focuses on preverbal, playful experiences and attunement but does not provide direct verbal trauma processing. Clinicians need training in other trauma-focused modalities to integrate into Theraplay.

References

Ardiel, E. L., & Rankin, C. H. (2010). The importance of touch in development. *Paediatrics & Child Health*, 15(3), 153–156.

Gaskill, R., & Perry, B. (2013). The neurobiological power of play: Using the neurosequential model of therapeutics to guide play in the healing process. In C. Malchiodi & D. A. Crenshaw (Eds.), *Play and creative arts therapy for attachment problems* (pp. 178–194). Guilford Press.

Gil, E. (2006). *Helping abused and traumatized children: Integrating directive and nondirective approaches.* Guilford Press.

Gil, E. (2017). *Post-traumatic play in children: What clinicians should know.* Guilford Press.

Konrath, E., & Gil, E. (2021). Using Theraplay to treat clients of child sexual abuse. In S. Lindaman & R. Hong (Eds.), *Theraplay: Theory, applications and implementation* (pp. 175–198). Jessica Kingsley Publishers.

Lindaman, S., & Hong, R. (2021). An overview of the Theraplay model. In S. Lindaman & R. Hong (Eds.), *Theraplay: Theory, applications and implementation* (pp. 27–64). Jessica Kingsley Publishers.

National Child Traumatic Stress Network (NCTSN). (2023). *Sexual abuse.* https://www.nctsn.org/what-is-child-trauma/trauma-types/sexual-abuse

Perry, B. D. (2006). Applying principles of neurodevelopment to clinical work with maltreated and traumatized children. In N. B. Webb (Ed.), *Working with traumatized youth in child welfare* (pp. 27–52). Guilford Press.

Porges, S. (2011). *The polyvagal theory: Neurophysiological foundations of emotions, attachment, communication and self-regulation.* W. W. Norton.

Porges, S. (2015). Play as neural exercise: Insights from the polyvagal theory. In D. Pearce-McCall (Ed.), *The power of play for mind-brain health* (pp. 3–7). http://www.mindgains.org.

Sheinberg, M., & Fraenkel, P. (2001). *The relational trauma of incest: A family based approach to treatment.* Guilford Press.

van der Kolk, B. A. (2015). *The body keeps the score: Brain, mind, and body in the healing of trauma.* Penguin Books.

PART III

APPLICATIONS OF BURGEONING MODELS IN TREATING CHILDHOOD SEXUAL ABUSE

❧❦❧

CHAPTER 14
DIGITAL PLAY THERAPY™ WITH SEXUALLY ABUSED
CHILDREN AND ADOLESCENTS

Jessica Stone

In the complex landscape of treating childhood sexual abuse (CSA), the pursuit of effective therapeutic methods to aid children and adolescents is an enduring endeavor. Traditional play therapy has long been a cornerstone in treating this vulnerable population, emphasizing essential elements like connection, safety, and validation. Contemporary play therapy extends the therapeutic space into the digital realm with Digital Play Therapy™ (DPT). DPT is a powerful modality that upholds these foundational cornerstones, incorporates key theoretical components, and provides a vehicle to advance treatment.

By creating an environment where both therapist and child can engage through digital activities, DPT offers a prescriptive and interactive approach to CSA treatment. This modality adapts to the language and experiences of the digital-native generation while maintaining the objectives of traditional therapeutic interventions. This chapter presents a brief overview of Digital Play Therapy, components of current CSA treatment conceptualizations and approaches, and a case example illustrating how DPT can be utilized with clients. Digital Play Therapy can revolutionize our approach to CSA treatment by offering an integrative, contemporary avenue for healing that aligns with the needs of our clients.

Digital Play Therapy™

Developed by Stone (2019, 2022), Digital Play Therapy is a modality for in-person and telemental health sessions. Defined as "a modality that utilizes highly motivating, immersive activities to incorporate areas of client culture and interest into the play therapy process to deepen relationships,

DOI: 10.4324/9781003451549-17

gather information, implement interventions, and advance the treatment plan forward" (Stone, 2022, p. 16), DPT provides a framework for conceptualizing and utilizing digital tools appropriately within a therapeutic setting.

The foundational cornerstones of DPT include speaking the client's language (Axline, 1947), prescriptive play therapy (Beutler, 1979; Beutler & Harwood, 2000; Schaefer & Drewes, 2016), the therapeutic powers of play (Schaefer & Drewes, 2014), and the 5Cs of DPT (Stone, 2019, 2022). DPT is inherently rooted in well-established psychological principles, drawing from the rich heritage of traditional play therapy while seamlessly incorporating the language and media that resonate with today's digital natives. It is a mode of therapy that honors the child's natural communicative and learning processes, acknowledging that for the contemporary child, digital is a commonly utilized language. DPT leverages this digital fluency to enter into and understand a child's worldview, providing a bridge to their inner experiences and thought processes (Stone, 2022). This integration into the child's world is not merely about translation from one medium to another; it is about full immersion into the child's cognitive and emotional landscapes (Johnston, 2021).

By utilizing DPT, therapists can offer a wide assortment of experiences that are deeply familiar to the child, yet expansive in their therapeutic potential. The digital landscape is rich with opportunities for metaphor, storytelling, interaction, and role-playing, all of which are integral to a child's exploration of self and environment. Digital Play Therapy provides a customizable and personalized therapeutic space, where interventions can be tailored to the child's individual needs, interests, developmental level, and therapeutic goals.

When a therapist analyzes the narrative, content, and interactions within the digital play space, they gain invaluable insights into the child's worldview and self-perception. The type of game chosen, the approach to problem-solving, the level of engagement, and the nature of interactions within the digital environment all contribute to a comprehensive conceptualization of the client. This analysis extends far beyond mere observation, delving into the child's personal agency, psychological presence, coping strategies, and social interactions. Through this lens, the therapist can discern patterns, strengths, and areas for growth.

In the specific context of treating childhood sexual abuse, DPT becomes a particularly potent tool. DPT's controlled and safe environment allows children and adolescents to navigate scenarios that parallel their real-world experiences in a way that feels comfortable to them. Therapists can introduce scenarios, characters, and narratives that enable clients to process their experiences. This approach not only facilitates a deeper understanding of the client's internal world but also offers avenues for healing and empowerment. The child or adolescent can have digital experiences that promote mastery, resilience, and the reclamation of personal power in engaging and transformative ways.

Childhood Sexual Abuse Play Therapy Treatment

Childhood sexual abuse resonates profoundly and touches the core of our humanity. It is a title for a concept and experience that includes incomprehensible boundary violations for a most vulnerable population. The long-lasting ramifications of sexual abuse often extend far beyond the immediate physical and emotional harm, seeping into the mental, emotional, and even spiritual well-being of the survivor. The violation not only shatters the child's sense of safety and trust and profoundly disrupts their developmental trajectory. Navigating the world with the heavy burden of this experience alters their self-perception, interpersonal relationships, and basic assumptions about safety and love. Providing thorough treatment and support for victims of CSA is crucial, as it helps restore a sense of wholeness and safety, assisting children and adolescents on the path toward healing and regaining control over their lives.

As mentioned, the play therapy protocol for treating CSA is grounded in essential concepts such as connection, safety, and validation. Connection refers to the establishment of a strong therapeutic alliance, allowing the child to trust the therapist and engage openly in the healing process. Safety encompasses both physical and emotional aspects; it assures the client that the therapeutic environment is a secure place to explore feelings and experiences without the risk of harm or judgment. Validation signifies the therapist's role in acknowledging and affirming the client's thoughts, feelings, and experiences, making them feel seen, heard, and understood. Together, these three elements create a holistic framework that facilitates emotional expression and aids in skill-building and resilience. The incorporation of these concepts within the play therapy protocol serves as the foundation upon which healing can occur, providing the child or adolescent with the necessary tools to navigate the complexities of their experiences and regain a sense of control and well-being.

As stated by Gil (2010), "The unfortunate reality is that children who are abused and maltreated can develop expectations of the world as unsafe and grow to believe that interpersonal relationships carry inherent dangers that will surface predictably" (p. 3). Play therapy seeks to provide safety within the relationship and interactions to counteract, balance, and process the CSA experiences of the child. Offering therapeutically sound options to a child is not just a matter of best practice, but a necessity for creating a treatment environment that is accessible and adaptable to their unique needs. By extending the reach of therapy into the digital space, clinicians gain the flexibility to "speak the client's language," meeting them in a medium that may be more comfortable and engaging for them. The goal is not merely to focus on the video game or app as a novel therapeutic tool, but to emphasize that the essential components of effective treatment can be embedded within these digital interfaces. Thus, the power of Digital Play Therapy lies not in the technology itself but in its capacity to foster deep connections, provide meaningful interactions, and validate the child's experiences. This approach enhances our ability to make therapy accessible and versatile, fulfilling our ethical obligation to ensure that every child and adolescent feels heard, seen, understood, and accepted, irrespective of the modality employed.

Traditional CSA Treatment Modalities

Traditional treatment modalities for child sexual abuse focus on creating a therapeutic relationship and environment that prioritizes the child's emotional and psychological healing (Gil, 2010). CSA treatment often centers on establishing a sense of safety, developing trust, and providing the child with coping mechanisms to manage the complex ramifications of the abuse. Therapists are wise to also consider salient words from Dr. Lenore Terr regarding CSA treatment:

> No one program for posttraumatic problems in children is perfect. What works for a child immediately may not work years later. What successfully erases a certain youngster's fears may not suffice for another young child's fears, even if the other child shares a similar genetic background and family environment and the same trauma.
>
> (2010, p. xiii),

Acknowledging the variety of treatment approaches available for CSA clients, which can be utilized at different times and with a variety of needs, this short chapter will focus on one approach to allow for a more in-depth exploration. Created by Goodyear-Brown, TraumaPlay™ is a "flexibly sequential play therapy model grounded in attachment theory and based on current understandings of the neurobiology of play, trauma, and the power of one to heal the other" (Goodyear-Brown et al., 2022, p. 78). Cornerstones of this play therapy model include "1) enhancing felt safety and security; 2) augmenting coping skills; 3) soothing the physiology . . .; 4) increasing emotional literacy; 5) leveraging play-based gradual exposure; 6) addressing the thought life . . .; and 7) making positive meaning of the post-trauma self" (Goodyear-Brown et al., 2022, p. 78; Goodyear-Brown, 2010, 2021). This model provides key cornerstones for the treatment of CSA and provides structure for the digital play therapist to strive toward within digital play therapy.

Felt Safety and Security and Augmenting Coping Skills

Building upon the established framework of TraumaPlay, the digital play therapist has a unique opportunity to translate these core principles into the digital realm. Digital environments offer a versatile platform for children to experience a sense of safety and security, which is paramount in the healing process. The interactive nature of digital play allows for the enhancement of coping skills in a controlled, predictable, and often customizable environment, providing children with a sense of mastery and control that may be lacking in their real-world experiences.

Soothe Physiology

Digital Play Therapy utilizes innovative tools to soothe physiology and regulate the nervous system of children undergoing therapeutic treatment (Stone, 2023). By incorporating biofeedback and neurofeedback within digital platforms, children can gain real-time insights into their physiological responses, empowering them with strategies to calm their bodies and minds. Mindfulness apps, with their guided relaxation exercises alongside rhythm and music games, provide a rhythmic and immersive experience that can induce a state of tranquility, which also helps to stabilize the nervous system. There are many different types of programs from which to choose that maintain similar goals.

Additionally, DPT offers interactive storytelling and art creation apps for emotional processing and expression, which can be especially calming. Virtual Reality (VR) offers serene, 3D, controlled environments for children to experience, which can be incredibly soothing (Stone, 2021; MacMahon, 2022). Gaming mechanics that promote flow states and physical activity games that encourage movement can contribute to decreasing stress responses (Russoniello et al., 2009; Reinecke, 2009; Roy & Ferguson, 2016). These various components of DPT work to create a therapeutic experience that not only engages children in the digital language they are fluent in but also aids in their physiological and emotional regulation.

Emotional Literacy

Through storytelling, character development, and interactive narratives, children can learn to identify, express, and manage a range of emotions in a safe and engaging context. Digital play experiences can improve a child's emotional literacy (Modafferi et al., 2016), which can be particularly empowering for children who have experienced trauma. These interventions offer them a language to communicate complex feelings they may struggle to express otherwise (Stone, 2024).

Play-Based Gradual Exposure

Play-based gradual exposure within digital play can be a delicate but effective process. By controlling the elements within the digital environment, therapists can help children confront and process traumatic memories at a pace that is comfortable for them, effectively titrating the child toward their therapeutic goals (P. Goodyear-Brown, personal communication, February 5, 2022). This methodical approach allows children to engage with challenging emotions and memories without becoming overwhelmed, promoting healing through incremental steps.

The "Thought Life"

Addressing the "thought life" of a child in the aftermath of trauma is essential. This refers to the process of "helping clients to identify cognitive distortions or false attributions related to the trauma and to replace negative self-talk with positive statements" (Goodyear-Brown et al., 2022, p. 78). Digital play can provide a reflective space where children can explore different scenarios and outcomes, fostering cognitive processing and reframing of traumatic experiences. By engaging with various roles and perspectives within digital games, children can gain insight into their own thought patterns and develop healthier, more adaptive ways of thinking.

Positive Meaning of the Posttrauma Self

Digital play environments can be particularly potent in facilitating the process of making positive meaning of the posttrauma self, as they allow children to build narratives of resilience and strength (Stone, 2022). Through mastering in-game challenges and developing their digital avatars, children can construct and experience a sense of positive identity formation, which is crucial in rebuilding a sense of self after trauma (Nielsen, 2015; Stone, 2024).

By incorporating the core elements of TraumaPlay into Digital Play Therapy, therapists can offer a modern, relevant, and engaging form of CSA treatment that resonates with the lived experiences of clients. Digital play not only provides an accessible and relatable platform for therapy but also enriches the therapeutic process by capitalizing on the natural affinity children have with the digital world. Digital play therapy enhances traditional childhood sexual abuse treatment, offering a familiar digital environment that supports healing and resilience in the modern child.

Clinical Case Study

Carla, a 14-year-old 9th-grade student, presented to process the sexual abuse she experienced as an 8-year-old child. She had attended individual and family therapy as an 8-year-old and returned to work through some complex experiences she was having as an adolescent. She reported confusion regarding her sexuality, identity, and worth.

To incorporate Carla's interest in digital tools, the therapist introduced an Artificial Intelligence (AI) image generation activity into the therapeutic offerings. For Carla, the therapeutic goals included key Therapeutic Powers of Play, including facilitating communication, increasing personal strengths, and fostering emotional wellness (Schaefer & Drewes, 2014). This integration of AI image generation allows Carla to express complex feelings and thoughts in a visual format, bridging the gap between digital fluency and emotional articulation.

AI image generation includes using artificial intelligence algorithms to create visual imagery based on components the user defines, that is, emotions, colors, environments, and included items. AI image generation uses the provided details to produce images that reflect the requested concepts or themes. For instance, if a client requests the AI image generation app to create something full of fear, the generator will provide options for the client to choose the most fitting. Within the realm of sexual abuse, it is important to note that apps will have limitations regarding the content it is asked to generate, that is, explicit sexual acts, etc.

Carla used the prompts "pain and helplessness" using the Wombo app, *Dream* (n.d.). She then chose the style of artwork she desired. As the app created the images, she could keep or regenerate them based on the congruence (with her experience) she felt the image depicted. As she searched through the generated images, she also refined her criteria. The development and ongoing refinement of prompts can significantly enhance client communication, thereby deepening our understanding of their experiences. Attending to the details of this process is very important.

Ultimately, Carla found an image that spoke to her experience and she was somewhat awestruck. The image depicted the ghostly resemblance of what looks like a female child, faceless and alone, in something that resembled an ocean. The emotion and power of this intervention were significant. Carla asked to have a digital version of the image. Future sessions included many elements of this image.

Limitations

While Digital Play Therapy™ (DPT) offers innovative avenues for engaging and treating children and adolescents who have experienced sexual abuse, there are potential limitations to consider:

1. **Accessibility and Digital Divide:** Not all clients can access the necessary technology equally. This digital divide can limit the availability of digital tools, potentially exacerbating disparities in mental health services.
2. **Technological Proficiency:** Both therapists and clients need to be comfortable with and skilled with digital tools.
3. **Privacy and Confidentiality:** Ensuring privacy and confidentiality is more complex in the digital age. Special care must be taken.

4. **Validation of Efficacy:** While DPT is grounded in established therapeutic principles, it is relatively new and requires continued research to validate its efficacy across diverse populations and establish evidence-based practices.
5. **Cultural and Individual Suitability:** Some digital tools and games may not be culturally relevant or appropriate for all clients.

Conclusion

Digital Play Therapy™ represents a significant advancement in the therapeutic engagement of children and adolescents recovering from sexual abuse. By integrating the time-honored principles of traditional play therapy with the interactive and immersive capabilities of digital tools, DPT offers a language and landscape that is inherently familiar to the digital-native generation. This approach aligns with today's youth's developmental and cultural environment and empowers them within their healing process. As we navigate the complexities of treating childhood sexual abuse, DPT stands as a testament to the evolving landscape of therapeutic interventions – where innovation meets the enduring need for connection, understanding, and healing. It is a modality that acknowledges the present challenges while holding a steadfast commitment to the well-being and resilience of the children we serve.

Considerations for Practice: Key Takeaways

DPT as a Modern Extension: DPT is a contemporary extension of traditional play therapy. DPT utilizes digital platforms to create therapeutic environments that are both familiar and engaging for the digital-native child.

- Therapeutic Foundations and Digital Applications: DPT is grounded in fundamental therapeutic principles presented within digital programs and therapeutic interactions.
- Customization and Personalization: DPT offers a customizable approach, allowing for personalized therapeutic interventions tailored to the child's individual needs, interests, and therapeutic goals.
- Insight Through Digital Interaction: A child's engagement with digital play provides deep insights into their worldview and self-perception, aiding therapists in developing a comprehensive understanding of the child.

- Engagement and Mastery in Healing: By guiding children through digital experiences that promote mastery and resilience, DPT becomes a powerful tool in play therapy treatment aligned with modern childhood's digital realities.

References

Axline, V. (1947). *Play therapy*. Houghton Mifflin.

Beutler, L. E. (1979). Toward specific psychological therapies for specific conditions. *Journal of Consulting and Clinical Psychology, 47*(5), 882–897.

Beutler, L. E., & Harwood, T. M. (2000). *Prescriptive psychotherapy: A practical guide to systematic treatment selection*. Oxford University Press.

Gil, E. (2010). Introduction. In E. Gil (Ed.), *Working with children to heal interpersonal trauma: The power of play*. Guildford Press.

Goodyear-Brown, P. (2010). *Play therapy with traumatized children: A prescriptive approach*. Wiley.

Goodyear-Brown, P. (2021). *Parents as partners in child therapy: A clinician's guide*. Guilford Press.

Goodyear-Brown, P., Worley, K., & Rubens, J. (2022). Camp nurture: An immersion in key components of TraumaPlay™. In C. Mellenthin, J. Stone, & R. J. Grant (Eds.), *Implementing play therapy with groups: Contemporary issues in practice*. Routledge.

Johnston, K. (2021). Engagement and immersion in digital play: Supporting young children's digital wellbeing. *International Journal of Environmental Research and Public Health, 18*(19), 10179. https://doi.org/10.3390/ijerph181910179

MacMahon, L. (2022, November 23). *Video games support young patients' social, emotional health*. https://news.ohsu.edu/2022/11/23/video-games-support-young-patients-social-emotional-health?fbclid=IwAR3cDj_vtWUxstbv4Ib5a2c49LH-HyYpQ3MLoK07vD943lJeA6LqScbxdZt8

Modafferi, S., Boniface, M., Crowle, S., & Middleton, L. (2016, October). *Creating opportunities to learn social skills at school using digital games* [paper presentation]. European Conference on Games Based Learning (ECGBL), Paisley.

Nielsen, D. (2015). Identity performance in roleplaying games. *Computers and Composition, 38*, 45–56.

Reinecke, L. (2009). Games and recovery: The use of video and computer games to recuperate from stress and strain. *Journal of Media Psychology, 21*, 126–142.

Roy, A., & Ferguson, C. J. (2016). Competitively versus cooperatively? An analysis of the effect of game play on levels of stress. *Computers in Human Behavior, 56*, 14–20.

Russoniello, C. V., O'Brien, K., & Parks, J. M. (2009). The effectiveness of casual video games in improving mood and decreasing stress. *Journal of Cyber Therapy and Rehabilitation, 2*, 53–66.

Schaefer, C. E., & Drewes, A. A. (2014). *The therapeutic powers of play: 20 core agents of change*. Wiley.

Schaefer, C. E., & Drewes, A. A. (2016). Prescriptive play therapy. In K. J. O'Connor, C. E. Schaefer, & L. D. Braverman (Eds.), *Handbook of play therapy* (2nd ed., pp. 227–242). Wiley.

Stone, J. (2019). *Digital play therapy: A clinician's guide to comfort and competence* (1st ed.). Routledge.

Stone, J. (2021, Fall/Winter). Trauma-informed virtual reality play. *Playground Magazine*, 13–16.

Stone, J. (2022). *Digital play therapy: A clinician's guide to comfort and competence* (2nd ed.). Routledge.

Stone, J. (2023). *Technology in mental health: Foundations of clinical use.* Routledge.

Stone, J. (2024). Inoculation, protection, and processing: The powers of video game use with trauma. In J. Stone, R. J. Grant, & C. Mellenthin (Eds.), *The repercussions of individual and collective trauma* (pp. 195–209). Wiley.

Terr, L. C. (2010). Foreword. In E. Gil (Ed.), *Working with children to heal interpersonal trauma: The power of play* (pp. ix–xiii). Guilford Press.

Wombo. (n.d.). *Dream.* https://dream.ai/

꧁꧂

CHAPTER 15

EMDR AND PLAY THERAPY

A PLAYFUL INTEGRATION FOR TREATMENT OF CHILDHOOD SEXUAL ABUSE

Ann Beckley-Forest and Annie J. Monaco

Integrating play therapy with Eye Movement Desensitization and Reprocessing (EMDR) harnesses both the therapeutic powers of play (Schaefer & Drewes, 2014) and an evidence-based approach to relieving posttraumatic stress and recovering from traumatic events – including experiences of childhood sexual abuse (CSA). The Adaptive Information Processing (AIP) model developed by Shapiro as the basis for EMDR therapy describes the healthy process by which we can learn and heal from adversity, as well address the maladaptive disruptions caused by efforts to cope with threatening experiences (2017). Betrayal trauma, such as CSA, is particularly disruptive to the flow of adaptive information associated with a sense of safety, wellbeing, and worthiness and is challenging to treat (Freyd, 1996). A play therapy-supported approach to the EMDR phases is designed to prepare the child to gradually retrieve and face the memories of such harmful experiences and re-establish the healthy flow of emotions, cognitions, and body sensations along channels which allow the victim to heal and move forward (Adler-Tapia et al., 2011).

A prescriptive or integrative approach to play therapy can create both safety and collaboration in the therapeutic relationship, increase emotional regulation and grounding through the incorporation of prescriptive play activities including mindfulness (Kestly, 2016), and support the victim's ability to gradually approach disturbing material through posttraumatic play and metaphor (Parker et al., 2021; Ryan & Edge, 2012). These elements are essential considerations to integrate EMDR into a play therapy setting to relieve distress through desensitization and dual awareness in a tolerable manner (Beckley-Forest, 2020; Marks, 2017;

DOI: 10.4324/9781003451549-18

Banbury, 2016). We draw on a variety of approaches and models within play therapy to support this integrative model, including child-centered play and the trauma-sensitive play therapy approaches of authors such as Gil (2011, 2016) and Goodyear-Brown (2012), which offer options to invite and hold the play of child and adolescent clients.

Victims of CSA may use dissociation as a survival strategy, and these dissociative symptoms must also be a focus of treatment to move forward with healing and internal coherence by integrating EMDR, play therapy, and other expressive modalities (Monaco, 2020; Waters, 2016; Wieland, 2015).

Overview and Basic Tenets of EMDR Within Play Therapy

A play therapy-supported EMDR approach flexibly incorporates the eight phases of EMDR into four main treatment goals originally described in Beckley-Forest and Johnson (2024).

1. **Stabilize and increase connection to present physical and emotional safety.** Play therapy strategies such as CCPT and child-responsive play increase here-and-now safety.
2. **Prepare for trauma exposure work.** Playful grounding and regulation, play therapy as a space for storytelling and accessing positive emotions, and containing negative ones.
3. **Gradual exposure to past traumatic experiences.** Posttrauma themes in the play bridge to desensitize distressing feelings and body sensations and move towards more adaptive beliefs about the self, adding bilateral or dual attention stimulation (BLS/DAS), such as tapping or rocking back and forth, drumming, or bilateral eye movements, keeping them present and expanding their integrative capacity. Metaphors and themes in the play which touch on traumatic material and may serve as a bridge to narrative work.
4. **Re-evaluate** on a consistent basis regarding how the processing of memories is affecting the present functioning and future goals for the child.

When CSA is a part of the trauma history, we also add a specific focus on dissociation, responding to the likelihood of more dissociative "parts" having formed to protect the child at the time of the abuse. We can use play therapy and creative interventions to understand and befriend these parts – an alliance which will be needed. Dissociation can complicate a trauma-focused treatment approach by fragmenting the experience, disrupting the timeline, and permitting the victim to detach from the unbearable experiences of the trauma. This may result in difficulty for adaptive information to flow (Silberg & Dallam, 2022).

Gestalt play therapy, relies on process-oriented invitations or prompts using projection and creative materials such as sand tray and art to make playful contact with the wounded or alienated parts of the self and increase self-compassion (Oaklander, 1992, 2001). An example of how an integrated intervention might look: The therapist invites a child to choose miniatures for the sand tray – "include the most grown-up part of you . . . the part that protects you by getting very loud and angry . . . . the part that remembers the bad things, etc." (Monaco, 2020). The child and therapist creatively explore what these different parts need and use the bilateral stimulation of EMDR to install/notice these moments of parts getting their needs met. Later, the child and therapist can connect with these parts of the self while exploring and unpacking the trauma memories for reprocessing.

Literature Review

The overall efficacy of EMDR with children is well-established in the literature (de Roos et al., 2011; Fleming, 2012; Barron, 2018; Moreno-Alcazar et al., 2017; Beer, 2018; Manzoni et al., 2021), along with the necessity for adaptation based on the child's stage of development, the availability of supportive caregivers, and the nature of the trauma (Rathore, 2018; Gomez, 2012). More specifically, EMDR has evidence effectiveness in treating victims of CS (Jiménez et al., 2020; Jarero et al., 2013; Bermudez, 2001). However, the scarcity of randomized, controlled studies, as in child mental health research more broadly, is also a concern in the case of EMDR with children.

The challenges of working supportively and playfully with resistance and avoidance of processing the trauma can be met by offering the EMDR protocol supported by the play, movement, and creativity of the play therapy room. The widespread use of EMDR by credentialed play therapists is relatively new, but we can lean on the evidence supporting EMDR with children as well as the literature on play therapy as a research-supported treatment option for survivors of CSA. This includes Gestalt play therapy (Dunn & Selemogwe, 2009) and flexibly prescriptive approaches such as that described by Gil and Smelser (2019). Some cases in the literature are descriptive of the use of both play techniques and EMDR in tandem to help survivors of CSA including an excellent example from Swinden (2018).

Considerable research on EMDR adult clients who experienced CSA indicates that one of the aspects of EMDR therapy that is beneficial in therapy is that EMDR does not rely on the client having to describe the experiences verbally for exposure work to move the nervous system positively. When the memory is retrieved and the client maintains dual attention to past and present through the bilateral stimulation, the brain does its work, and reprocessing is possible (Karaya & Soylu, 2019). Current research supports clinical wisdom that processing even highly distressing experiences is possible if the dual attention is strong and playful (de Jongh et al., 2019)

Clinical Case Example

Susan presented as a 5-year-old foster child. She was removed from her biological mother at age 3 for indicators of sexual abuse, which included bumps and scabs around her mouth, vaginal tearing, and a urinary tract infection. After two brief placements, Susan and her sister were placed with foster parents, Jane and Mark.

Assessment

Collaborative initial sessions with Susan's caregivers were an opportunity to provide stabilization, psychoeducation about trauma and dissociative symptoms, and understanding the parenting style and the child's fragmented parts. This family was at a crisis point and leaning toward disrupting the foster/preadoption plan due to Susan's aggression and sexually reactive behavior.

Details of the CSA were vague. Since EMDR relies on the retrieval of traumatic memory targets for processing to heal and shift current reactions and responses, every effort was made to collect information from the caseworker as well as make clinical conceptualizations based on the caregivers' observations and themes of the child's chosen play. The therapist explained the EMDR processing phases and how play and movement would be used to make the intensity of the processing manageable for the child as well as to give Susan a setting for projection of more of the details of traumatic memories while staying grounded.

In this prescriptive approach, we acknowledge the hard stuff that will become the focus of treatment but are cautious not to overwhelm the child and to attune closely while remaining playful. In this case, the urgency of moving quickly toward processing necessitated substantial support from the caregivers in moving toward the challenging work of processing the CSA.

In her first session in the playroom, Susan had the opportunity to explore, and while they colored mandalas, the foster mother briefly narrated the story of how Susan came to them, being careful to state only the known facts. The therapist then opened the conversation to include "there might have been other scary things that happened" such as maybe there were times you were hungry, or someone did something to you that you didn't like, or maybe you had nightmares. The child stopped drawing, looked at the therapist, and stated, "I will never talk about what happened to me" and returned to drawing. Therapist responded "Thank you for being honest. That tells me it is very hard to talk about and I think how we will make it easier is to use lots of fun and playful toys. Do you want to see all my play stuff now?" Susan jumped up and said "yes!" She and the foster mom sat on yoga balls and talked about one difficult thing at home (hitting her sister) and then the therapist prompted "okay, that was hard, now bounce!" Both bounced, fell on the floor, and laughed. The therapist stated, "That is how you will talk about the hard stuff in here and then, we will get all the yucky stuff out of your body and mind!"

In the next session, the therapist set a 3-minute timer and said "we can *only* talk about yucky stuff for three minutes, okay?" Susan nodded. The therapist asked her to put one bead at a time into a balloon and say something yucky that happened to her when she was living with her bio mom. Susan stated, "got hit, he (mom's boyfriend) touched me (pointed to private parts), and my sister got hurt." The therapist then quickly blew up the balloon so Susan could happily bounce the balloon and beads around the room.

Playful EMDR Preparation Phase

In the next few sessions, the therapist playfully introduced play and creative ways of describing emotions, thoughts, and body sensations through items such as emojis and thought balls, the 0–10 "yucky scale" and bilateral stimulation toys including magic wands, favorite puppets, musical instruments, and EMDR gadgets.

Processing Trauma Targets

Given the urgency, the therapist's plan included moving as quickly as possible to processing but keeping the duration of processing short and manageable. When Susan began placing the dolls in the doll house in sexual positions, the therapist reflected, "I wonder if this is what happened to you? Jane (foster mom), can you take the magic wand and tap her hands left, right, left, right while Susan thinks about the dolls and how they are lying in bed. I wonder if that is mom's boyfriend." (Susan nodded and put out her hands to be tapped). After less than a minute of tapping, the therapist asked the foster mom to playfully pick up Susan, hug her and tell her what a good job she did, and shift to bounding on yoga balls.

The foster parents shared the details of further disclosures with the therapist so they could become further bridges into playful EMDR processing. With every new memory fragment, a novel way of doing the BLS was introduced. Susan and her foster parents had a parade with musical instruments, funny hats, funny glasses, etc., marching during the narration of what happened (see Figure 15.1).

Figure 15.1 *Therapist Leading a Family in a Playful EMDR Processing Parade.*
Source: Digital image.

Post Processing

After the initial session of playful EMDR processing, the physical attacks and sexual touching of her sister stopped. Creatively exploring Susan's "parts" in the sand tray and helping these parts connect with each other on the inside was one aspect of the ongoing work (see Figure 15.2 for an example). Due to the improvements, the family decided to proceed with the adoption plan (see Figure 15.2 for an example).

Limitations of Playful EMDR With Victims of Childhood Sexual Abuse

The play therapy setting, along with physically active short bursts of focusing on the details of the abuse helps the process. Structural dissociation must be managed and considered throughout processing, using play therapy and expressive modalities to maintain a present sense of safety.

The exact nature of sexual abuse events is often unknown, and the therapist is often unable to confirm details. If the current caregivers are not capable of participating actively, it is difficult to do the processing of

Figure 15.2 *Sandtray World Example.*

serious events. There are greater challenges in incorporating parents/ caregivers who may be in various stages of acceptance of the nature of the CSA.

Conclusion

Using play therapy to support EMDR processing of CSA holds great promise in helping children and adolescents who may be dissociative or sexually reactive to stay more present and grounded and begin to integrate more positive cognitions, especially when current caregivers are able to support this process.

Considerations for Practice: Key Takeaways

- The practice of EMDR therapy requires specific training in the use of the EMDR protocol and the adaptations to the protocol for children.
- The use of EMDR in a play therapy setting to digest CSA can help the victim stay more present and grounded because the bilateral stimulation and movement keeps them from dissociating.
- Episodes of EMDR are short, playful, and involve a current safe caregiver whenever possible.
- Explicit processing of CSA can be challenging when disclosure is ongoing, and forensic work should be completed before treatment.

References

Adler-Tapia, R., Settle, C., & Shapiro, F. (2011). Eye movement desensitization and reprocessing (EMDR) psychotherapy with children who have experienced sexual abuse and trauma. In P. Goodyer-Brown (Ed.), *Handbook of child sexual abuse: Identification, assessment, and treatment* (pp. 229–250). Wiley.

Banbury, N. M. (2016). Case study: Play therapy and eye movement desensitization and reprocessing for pediatric single incident posttraumatic stress disorder and developmental regression. *International Journal of Play Therapy, 25*(3), 166.

Barron, I. G. (2018). EMDR therapy with children and adolescents. *Journal of EMDR Practice and Research, 12*(4), 174–176.

Beckley-Forest, A. (2020). Using both EMDR and prescriptive play therapy in adaptive information processing: Rationale and essential considerations for integration. In A. Beckley-Forest & A. Monaco (Eds.), *EMDR with children in the play therapy room: An integrated approach* (pp. 1–18). Springer.

Beckley-Forest, A., & Johnson, R. (2024). A play therapy-supported EMDR approach to treatment planning. In L. L. Wonders & M. McAfee (Eds.), *Play therapy treatment planning with children and families: A guide for mental health profession-als.* Routledge.

Beer, R. (2018). Efficacy of EMDR therapy for children with PTSD: A review of the literature. *Journal of EMDR Practice and Research, 12*(4), 177–195.

Bermudez, J. S. (2001). *The use of eye movement desensitization and reprocessing (EMDR) within a multi-modal treatment program for child victims of extrafamilial sexual abuse.* Carlos Albizu University.

de Jongh, A., Bicanic, I., Matthijssen, S., Amann, B. L., Hofmann, A., Farrell, D., Lee, C. W., & Maxfield, L. (2019). The current status of EMDR therapy involving the treatment of complex posttraumatic stress disorder. *Journal of EMDR Practice and Research, 13*(4), 284–290.

de Roos, C., Greenwald, R., den Hollander-Gijsman, M., Noorthoorn, E., van Buuren, S., & De Jongh, A. (2011). A randomized comparison of cognitive behavioral therapy (CBT) and eye movement desensitization and reprocessing (EMDR) in disaster-exposed children. *European Journal of Psychotraumatology, 2*(1), 5694.

Dunn, M., & Selemogwe, M. (2009). Play therapy as an intervention against sexual violence in Botswana. *Journal of Psychology in Africa, 19*(1), 127–129.

Fleming, J. (2012). The effectiveness of eye movement desensitization and reprocessing in the treatment of traumatized children and youth. *Journal of EMDR Practice and Research, 6*(1), 16–26.

Freyd, J. J. (1996). *Betrayal trauma: The logic of forgetting childhood abuse.* Harvard University Press.

Gil, E. (2011). Trauma-focused integrated play therapy (TF-IPT). In P. Goodyear-Brown (Ed.), *Handbook of child sexual abuse: Identification, assessment, and treatment* (pp. 251–278). John Wiley & Sons.

Gil, E. (2016). *Posttraumatic play in children: What clinicians need to know.* Guilford Press.

Gil, E., & Smelser, Q. K. (2019). Play therapy for children who have been sexually abused. In H. Kaduson, C. Schaefer, & D. Cangelosi (Eds.), *Prescriptive play therapy: Tailoring interventions for specific childhood problems* (pp. 145–159). Guilford Press.

Gomez, A. M. (2012). *EMDR therapy and adjunct approaches with children: Complex trauma, attachment, and dissociation.* Springer Publishing Company.

Goodyear-Brown, P. (2012). Flexibly sequential play therapy (FSPT) with sexually victimized children. In P. Goodyear-Brown (Ed.), *Handbook of child sexual abuse: Identification, assessment, and treatment* (pp. 297–319). Wiley.

Jarero, I., Roque-López, S., & Gomez, J. (2013). The provision of an EMDR-based multicomponent trauma treatment with child victims of severe interpersonal trauma. *Journal of EMDR Practice and Research, 7*(1), 17–28.

Jiménez, G., Becker, Y., Varela, C., García, P., Nuño, M. A., Pérez, M. C., Osario, A., Jarero, I., & Givaudan, M. (2020). Multicenter randomized controlled trial on the provision of the EMDR-PRECI to female minors victims of sexual and/or physical violence and related PTSD diagnosis. *American Journal of Applied Psychology, 9*(2), 42–51.

Karaya, A., & Soylu, N. (2019). Eye movement desensitization and reprocessing (EMDR) treatment for a patient diagnosed with posttraumatic stress disorder after sexual abuse. *Klinik Psikofarmakoloji Bulteni, 29*, 147–148.

Kestly, T. A. (2016). Presence and play: Why mindfulness matters. *International Journal of Play Therapy, 25*(1), 14–23.

Manzoni, M., Fernandez, I., Bertella, S., Tizzoni, F., Gazzola, E., Molteni, M., & Nobile, M. (2021). Eye movement desensitization and reprocessing: The state of the art of efficacy in children and adolescents with post-traumatic stress disorder. *Journal of Affective Disorders, 282,* 340–347.

Marks, R. P. (2017). When play therapy is not enough: Using eye movement desensitization and reprocessing/bilateral stimulation in combination with play therapy for the child with complex trauma. In A. Hendry & J. Hasler (Eds.), *Creative therapies for complex trauma: Helping children and families in foster care, kinship care or adoption* (pp. 164–180). Jessica Kingsley Publishers.

Monaco, A. (2020). Understanding and responding to dissociation in children with play-based approaches. In A. Beckley-Forest & A. Monaco (Eds.), *EMDR with children in the play therapy room: An integrated approach* (pp. 251–290). Springer.

Moreno-Alcazar, A., Treen, D., Valiente-Gomez, A., Sio-Eroles, A., Perez, V., Amann, B. L., & Radua, J. (2017). Efficacy of eye movement desensitization and reprocessing in children and adolescents with posttraumatic stress disorder: A meta-analysis of randomized controlled trials. *Frontiers in Psychology, 8,* 1750.

Oaklander, V. (1992). Gestalt work with children: Working with anger and introjects. In E. Nevis (Ed.), *Gestalt therapy: Perspectives and applications* (pp. 263–282). Gardner Press.

Oaklander, V. (2001). Gestalt play therapy. *International Journal of Play Therapy, 10*(2), 45.

Parker, M. M., Hergenrather, K., Smelser, Q., & Kelly, C. T. (2021). Exploring child-centered play therapy and trauma: A systematic review of literature. *International Journal of Play Therapy, 30*(1), 2.

Rathore, H. E. (2018). Trust and attunement-focused EMDR with a child. *Journal of EMDR Practice & Research, 12*(4), 255–268. https://doi.org.ezproxy.fau.edu/10.1891/1933-3196.12.4.255

Ryan, V., & Edge, A. (2012). The role of play themes in non-directive play therapy. *Clinical Child Psychology and Psychiatry, 17*(3), 354–369.

Schaefer, C. E., & Drewes, A. A. (2014). *The therapeutic powers of play: 20 core agents of change.* John Wiley & Sons.

Shapiro, F. (2017). *Eye movement desensitization and reprocessing (EMDR) therapy: Basic principles, protocols, and procedures.* Guilford Press.

Silberg, J., & Dallam, S. (2022). Dissociative disorders in children and adolescents. In P. F. Dell & J. A. Oneill (Eds.), *Dissociation and the dissociative disorders* (pp. 433–447). Routledge.

Swinden, C. (2018). The child-centered EMDR approach: A case study investigating a young girl's treatment for sexual abuse. *Journal of EMDR Practice and Research, 12*(4), 282–296.

Waters, F. (2016). *Healing the fractured child: Diagnosis and treatment of youth with dissociation.* Springer.

Wieland, S. (2015). Dissociation in children and adolescents: What it is, how it presents, and how we can understand it. In S. Weiland (Ed.), *Dissociation in traumatized children and adolescents* (pp. 23–62). Routledge.

⁘

CHAPTER 16
NATURE-BASED PLAY THERAPY
INTERVENTIONS FOR WORKING WITH SEXUALLY ABUSED CHILDREN AND ADOLESCENTS

Julie Blundon Nash

Nature-based play therapy is the integration of play therapy with ecotherapy and other nature-based therapies. In this modality, practitioners utilize the therapeutic powers of both nature and play to help clients overcome difficulties, and further their psychological growth and development. Nature-based play therapy sessions may take place completely outside in an enclosed therapy area or on public land, inside an office utilizing natural materials, or some combination of the two. Why the practitioner chooses to utilize nature-based play within a treatment course matters more than how, and there are multiple reasons to include nature-based play therapy treatments with sexually abused children and adolescents. While there is limited research examining the direct use of nature-based therapies with sexually abused children and adolescents, there is research supporting the use of nature-based therapies with adult survivors of childhood sexual abuse. The findings from these studies support current discussions of the therapeutic factors present in nature-based therapy and the therapeutic powers of play. The importance of these research findings and discussions will be further explored, as will the potential positive impacts of nature-based play therapy when treating symptoms of childhood and adolescent sexual abuse. In addition, this chapter includes the basic tenets of nature-based play therapy, limitations, and a clinical case study based on a composite sketch of clinical cases.

Overview and Basic Tenets of Nature-Based Play Therapy

Nature-based play therapy has roots in both ecotherapy and play therapy. Nature-based play therapy is not a theoretical orientation but is based on

DOI: 10.4324/9781003451549-19

the concept that experiences utilizing nature are psychologically healing and supportive, especially when the therapeutic factors of nature and play are activated. Nature-based play therapy is, therefore, a model or modality of implementing play therapy through which any theoretical orientation can be utilized while integrating the therapeutic powers of nature and play. The role and value of integrating nature into play therapy might differ depending upon the practitioner's theoretical orientation, but it is important to always conceptualize nature-based play therapy on theory as this allows the play therapist to function from a solid foundation of therapeutic work instead of hoping nature-based techniques will work.

Therapeutic powers of both play and nature are relevant and important to understand when utilizing nature-based play therapy. The 20 therapeutic powers of play have been fully explored in other resources and each of these is appropriate to integrate into the model of nature-based play therapy, with the understanding that the individual therapeutic power of play is the change agent or way in which play provides a therapeutic experience or benefit for the client. Naor and Mayseless (2021) have begun to outline the therapeutic factors of nature and include the natural environment, challenge, the role of nature, and expansiveness and interconnectedness. When these therapeutic factors are facilitated in nature-based therapy, providers are utilizing the aspects of nature that provide specific therapeutic benefits for clients. Activating and utilizing these powers combined with the therapeutic powers of play and play therapy theory leads to effective nature-based play therapy grounded in a solid theoretical foundation.

One way to create a solid theoretical foundation in nature-based play therapy is to utilize a prescriptive approach to case conceptualization. Within a prescriptive approach to nature-based play therapy, the play therapist works to connect the presenting problem, therapeutic powers of play and nature, and desired outcomes to create a course of treatment that meets the needs of the individual client. Specific to this model, the play therapist aims to fill in the blanks in the questions:

> Given that this presenting concern is likely occurring because of (hypothesis based on theoretical tenets), the fact that play is (characteristics) and nature is (nature characteristics), the therapeutic power/s of (therapeutic powers of play and nature), is/are facilitated or supported in play, which will likely lead to (desired outcome). Given that we want to achieve (desired outcome),

how would we do that by utilizing (specific therapeutic powers of play and nature) and (this/these play and nature characteristics)?

(Nash, 2024, p. 100)

Literature Review of the Application of Nature-Based Play Therapy With Victims of Childhood Sexual Abuse (CSA)

In looking explicitly at the use of nature-based play therapy with young victims of childhood sexual abuse, there is no research noted. There is, however, research supporting the use of nature-based therapies with adult survivors of childhood and adult sexual abuse, specifically regarding common symptoms or reactions resulting from such abuse, that supports the idea of utilizing nature-based play therapy with this population. Children and adolescents who have experienced sexual abuse are at risk for a variety of short- and long-term symptoms of psychopathology, including anxiety (Maniglio, 2013), rumination (Sarin & Nolen-Hoeksema, 2010), hypervigilance (McClintock, 2009), shame (MacGinley et al., 2019), and attention challenges and other symptoms of posttraumtic stress disorder (PTSD) (Strathearn et al., 2020). Researchers have begun to identify the role that nature plays in clients' attributions of symptom improvement. Moore and Van Vliet (2022) reported that clients who engaged in nature-based therapies identified themes of support derived from nature, including reduction of rumination and negative thinking, increased focus of current attention (similar to increased mindfulness), increased acceptance and emotional regulation, and reduction of dissociation. Rediron (2021) reported similar findings, with clients identifying three themes of "(1) exploring strength, (2) finding comfort in mindfulness, and, (3) reconnecting to spirituality" during and after their therapeutic time spent in nature-based settings. These themes suggest that nature itself is seen as not just a supportive adjunct to therapy but an integral part of the therapeutic change process.

Per self-reports, research on the impact of nature for young people and their subsequent mental health reveals promising trends when considering the impact of childhood sexual abuse. Time in nature has been shown to result in multiple physical benefits, thus increasing physical health and abilities (Roberts et al., 2019), both of which have an impact on mental health and stress levels. In addition, spending short amounts of time in nature over the course of a week has been shown to reduce physical biomarkers of stress, as measured through decreases in salivary cortisol and alpha-amylase levels (Hunter et al., 2019), both of which are produced by the body in higher amounts when stress activates the nervous system. The negative impacts of stressful life events are moderated by time spent in nature (van den Berg et al., 2010; Wells & Evans, 2003). Thus, integrating nature-based therapy into treatment for those impacted by childhood sexual abuse is likely beneficial.

Specific to helping children overcome mental health symptoms resulting from childhood sexual abuse, walking in nature has been shown to reduce rumination (Bratman et al., 2015), and themes within client reports support this finding (Moore & Van Vliet, 2022). In terms of anxiety symptoms, people who report a stronger connection to nature report lower levels of anxiety. Martyn and Brymer (2016) suggest that spending time in nature, thus building connections with the natural world, can help reduce and manage anxiety symptoms. Research has also shown that using nature-based guided imagery techniques can reduce symptoms of anxiety when compared to traditional guided imagery (Nguyen & Brymer, 2018). These findings are important to recognize within treatment for childhood sexual abuse as time in nature has also been found to support self-acceptance and reductions of episodes of dissociation and negative thinking (Moore & Van Vliet, 2022).

There is a plethora of research supporting the use of play therapy with children and adolescents who have experienced sexual abuse. For example, Reyes and Asbrand (2005) found that the severity of trauma symptoms, anxiety, depression, and other trauma-related stress variables decreased after children who experienced sexual abuse engaged in six months of play therapy. The efficacy of play therapy with children who have experienced sexual abuse has been noted through a variety of play therapy approaches (e.g., Knell & Ruma, 2003; Wilson & Ryan, 1994; Gil, 2012). Thus, play therapy is an effective and accepted approach for the treatment of mental health symptoms following childhood sexual abuse.

Taken together, these research findings support utilizing nature as part of treatment following childhood sexual abuse to strengthen positive mental states and encourage healing related to a number of common psychological symptoms. Research also supports the use of play therapy in treatment following childhood sexual abuse. Thus, the integration of nature-based play therapy for this population is more than fitting, given the research findings for the utilization of both play and nature-based therapies in the treatment of childhood sexual abuse.

Clinical Case Study

Jessa is a 9-year-old girl who entered treatment following her experience of childhood sexual abuse perpetrated by her uncle. She reported molestation that first occurred under the guise of "playing games," which continued to grow in intensity and invasiveness. Jessa eventually told her mother that she did not like playing these games, and her uncle's behaviors were reported and investigated by authorities. Her parents were understandably upset by these realizations and supported Jessa through sharing her story, yet sometimes struggled to keep their emotional reactions under control as they dealt with their anger toward the uncle. At the time she entered treatment, Jessa was exhibiting trouble concentrating at school, rumination (specifically related to feelings of shame and thinking she encouraged her uncle's behaviors), and depressive symptoms. She reported not feeling worthy of any friendships because she was "dirty" and "broken." It was "easier" for Jessa to stay by herself and not attempt to interact with her peers because of anxiety related to what they might be thinking about her.

After a brief explanation of the potential benefits of integrating nature-based play therapy, Jessa was offered the choice between indoor and outdoor play therapy sessions. She chose to use the outdoor play area whenever the weather was pleasant. Jessa enjoyed running up and down the length of the outdoor space, smacking her hand against the fence on one end and the wall of the office at the other as she tallied how many laps she ran. When she completed her self-imposed laps, Jessa would explore the outdoor space by walking around and making comments about her observations. She was particularly intrigued by a small flower garden plot but preferred observing that space from a distance.

Approximately three months into therapy, Jessa's session was held after a few days of heavy rain. The day of the session was bright yet damp, and Jessa was eager to get outside. She started running her laps but was distracted by the garden plot, which was rather muddy. There were some new flower shoots beginning to poke up, which had not been visible during previous sessions. Jessa was captivated by these, and without saying a word, she walked over and slowly began poking her fingers into the mud around the plants. She continued pushing her fingers into the mud until both hands were covered in sticky mud. After about five minutes of this play, Jessa smoothed the mud around the plant shoots and asked what was growing in the space. She asked if she could plant some flowers, too, and carefully selected a packet of seeds and placed them around one of the shoots, encircling it. Jessa smiled, then washed her hands off in a basin and said, "Look how strong those plants are. It's been raining for days, and that's what they needed to grow. They needed the rain and the mud before they could reach for the sun." Jessa then skipped away and spent the last few minutes of her session happily skipping around a picnic table.

Over the next few weeks, Jessa's mom reported that Jessa was making attempts to speak with some of the children in her class and came home a couple of times quite excited to tell her about a positive peer interaction on the playground. Jessa had not been taking any initiative to interact with peers prior to planting the seeds in session and usually reported that recess was boring because she played by herself. The metaphorical representation of dirtying herself during play therapy and then realizing the positive growth that can come from adversity appeared to benefit Jessa's peer interactions because of the changes she was able to make within herself and her self-concept. She had engaged in physically active play outdoors and benefited from the simple exposure to nature, but the ability to play and dirty herself in the mud was a turning point for her in nature-based play therapy.

Jessa continued to choose outdoor play for subsequent sessions, and her play themes began to shift. She reduced the amount of time spent in repetitive play (running fewer laps until she stopped that play completely) and shifted into more strength-building play. Jessa began looking for opportunities to challenge herself and often varied the activities in which she engaged as she gained confidence in her abilities. Sometimes, she would stack bricks and blocks of wood as high as she could, and other times, she would test her balance on a basic seesaw. Jessa's ability to focus and attend to her tasks grew, as did her positive thoughts toward herself. Her parents reported ongoing small improvements in her attention at school and overall mood at home.

Limitations of Nature-Based Play Therapy With Victims of Childhood Sexual Abuse

As with any form of therapy, there are potential limitations to consider when implementing nature-based play therapy. As much as possible, be aware of the client's sexual abuse and historical experiences. The outdoors might not feel like a safe therapeutic space if sexual abuse occurred outside or had some connection to the outdoor world. The outdoor world might even feel too open and expansive for clients who are dealing with traumatic experiences (especially anxiety-related symptoms) and thus prefer being in spaces where they have more control and physical boundaries. However, these reasons do not mean that nature should be fully excluded from play therapy. Nature can be brought into the playroom, or the client can work toward overcoming the negative associations through the safety of play.

Another potential limitation of using nature-based play therapy is not specific to those who have experienced childhood sexual abuse. Allergies and sensitivities must be discussed prior to taking clients outdoors and when bringing plant material inside the playroom. The safety of an outdoor play space and the access to help should the need arise should always be considered, as clients are often able to engage in different types of physical play outdoors and thus are at risk of different injuries than during indoor sessions.

Outside of these limitations, practitioners should remember that nature-based play therapy is not a theoretical model in and of itself. The practitioner must bring his or her own theoretical understanding to the treatment plan and process and view nature-based play therapy as a means of achieving treatment goals. If the practitioner is not clear on their own understanding of the client, situation, and desired outcome from a theoretical perspective, nature-based play therapy will not lead to the most useful treatment outcomes. In other words, this is not a model in which techniques can be administered to achieve a desired outcome without a solid understanding of the client, the client's needs, and the development of the presenting problem.

Conclusion

Nature-based play therapy allows practitioners to go beyond the physical constraints of a typical play therapy treatment space and integrate the healing benefits of the entire natural world when working with children and adolescents who have experienced sexual abuse. This modality encourages practitioners to integrate the most salient and curative aspects of both play and nature to create a healing environment in which children and adolescents who have experienced sexual abuse can safely explore their challenges while being supported by the practitioner and the world. Current research supports the idea of integrating these two forms of therapy, and new literature is continuing to explore the therapeutic benefits of both. The ongoing integration of nature-based play therapy will only continue to provide new therapeutic resources for children and adolescents who have experienced sexual abuse.

Considerations for Practice: Key Takeaways

- Experiencing a healing, larger world in a nature-based play therapy environment is salient when working with victims of childhood sexual abuse, as it creates opportunities to practice mindfulness, experience reductions in anxiety and depression, and experience acceptance within the world as a whole.
- A limitation of using nature-based play therapy with children who have experienced sexual abuse is related to understanding where the client's abuse occurred as well as how they react to open spaces. This does not mean that nature-based play therapy cannot be used with the client.
- Experiencing nature indoors can be a way to help clients overcome the sexual trauma experienced and may serve as a gateway to becoming more comfortable with the natural environment and creating a safe space in which to move outside.
- The benefits of exploring nature-based play therapy with children and adolescents who have experienced sexual abuse are worth the effort. Offering children and adolescents a fully immersive and integrated healing environment while providing nature-based play therapy and utilizing the therapeutic powers of both nature and play shows the value of honoring all aspects of our clients and their experiences.

References

Bratman, G. N., Hamilton, J. P., Hahn, K. S., Daily, G. C., & Gross, J. J. (2015). Nature experience reduces rumination and subgenual prefrontal cortex activation. *Proceedings of the National Academy of Sciences, 112*(28), 8567–8572. https://doi.org/10.1073/pnas.1510459112

Gil, E. (2012). Trauma-focused integrated play therapy (TF-IPT). In P. Goodyear-Brown (Ed.), *Handbook of child sexual abuse: Identification, assessment, and treatment* (pp. 251–278). John Wiley & Sons. https://doi.org/10.1002/9781118094822

Hunter, M. R., Gillespie, B. W., & Chen, S. Y. (2019). Urban nature experiences reduce stress in the context of daily life based on salivary biomarkers. *Frontiers in Psychology, 20,* 722. https://doi.org/10.3389/fpsyg.2019.00722

Knell, S. M., & Ruma, C. D. (2003). Play therapy with a sexually abused child. In M. A. Reinecke, F. M. Dattilio, & A. Freeman (Eds.), *Cognitive therapy with children and adolescents: A casebook for clinical practice* (pp. 338–368). Guilford Press.

MacGinley, M., Breckenridge, J., & Mowll, J. (2019). A scoping review of adult survivors' experiences of shame following sexual abuse in childhood. *Health & Social Care in the Community, 27*(5), 1135–1146. https://doi.org/10.1111/hsc.12771

Maniglio, R. (2013). Child sexual abuse in the etiology of anxiety disorders: A systematic review of anxiety disorders. *Trauma, Violence, & Abuse, 14*(2), 96–112. https://doi.org/10.1177/1524838012470032

Martyn, P., & Brymer, E. (2016). The relationship between nature relatedness and anxiety. *Journal of Health Psychology, 21*(7), 1436–1445. https://doi.org/10.1177/1359105314555169

McClintock, C. (2009). *Play therapy behaviors and themes in physically abused, sexually abused, and nonabused children* (Publication No. 3389042) [Doctoral dissertation, Baylor University]. Proquest Dissertations Publishing.

Moore, C. L., & Van Vliet, K. J. (2022). Women's experiences of nature as a pathway to recovery from sexual assault. *Journal of Humanistic Psychology, 62*(1), 123–150. https://doi.org/10.1177/0022167819847094

Naor, L., & Mayseless, O. (2021). Therapeutic factors in nature-based therapies: Unraveling the therapeutic benefits of integrating nature in psychotherapy. *Psychotherapy, 58*(4), 576–590. https://doi.org/10.1037/pst0000396

Nash, J. B. (2024). *Nature-based play therapy: A prescriptive approach to integrating the therapeutic powers of nature and play.* Routledge. https://doi.org/10.4324/9781003332343-7

Nguyen, J., & Brymer, E. (2018). Nature-based guided imagery as an intervention for state anxiety. *Frontiers in Psychology, 9*(1858), 1–10. https://doi.org/10.3389/fpsyg.2018.01858

Rediron, T. J. (2021). *Indigenous women survivors of child sexual abuse reflect on the power of nature engagement.* [Master's thesis, University of Saskatchewan]. Harvest. https://hdl.handle.net/10388/13529

Reyes, C. J., & Asbrand, J. P. (2005). A longitudinal study assessing trauma symptoms in sexually abused children engaged in play therapy. *International Journal of Play Therapy, 14*(2), 25–47. https://doi.org/10.1037/h0088901

Roberts, A., Hinds, J., & Camic, P. M. (2019). Nature activities and wellbeing in children and young people: A systematic review. *Journal of Adventure Education and Outdoor Learning, 20*(4), 298–318. https://doi.org/10.1080/14729679.2019.1660195

Sarin, S., & Nolen-Hoeksema, S. (2010). The dangers of dwelling: An examination of the relationship between rumination and consumptive coping in survivors of childhood sexual assault. *Cognition and Emotion, 24*(1), 71–85. https://doi.org/10.1080/02699930802563668

Strathearn, L., Giannotti, M., Mills, R., Kisely, S., Najman, J., & Abajobir, A. (2020). Long-term cognitive, psychological, and health outcomes associated with child abuse and neglect. *Pediatrics, 146*(4), 389–403. https://doi.org/10.1542/peds.2020-0438

van den Berg, A. E., Maas, J., Verheij, R. A., & Groenewegen, P. P. (2010). Green spaces as a buffer between stressful life events and health. *Social Science & Medicine, 70,* 1203–1210. https://doi.org/10.1016/j.soscimed.2010.01.002

Wells, N. M., & Evans, G. W. (2003). Nearby nature: A buffer of life stress among rural children. *Environment and Behavior, 35*(3), 311–330. https://doi.org/10.1177/0013916503035003001

Wilson, K., & Ryan, V. (1994). Working with the sexually abused child: The use of non-directive play therapy and family therapy. *Journal of Social Work Practice, 8*(1), 67–74. https://doi.org/10.1080/02650539408413968

CHAPTER 17
POSTTRAUMATIC PLAY WITH SEXUALLY ABUSED CHILDREN
CLINICAL INVITATIONS AND PROCESSING

Eliana Gil

Posttraumatic play refers to children's ability to "play out" traumatic memories (Terr, 1981, 1991, 1992). Unlike generic play, the play of traumatized children may be robotic, repetitive, and offer little emotional relief. Some children may be stuck in their traumatic memories and unable to resolve these events on their own. Clinicians should give children time to bring forth whatever they need to play out, pay close attention to the benefits gained, and understand that the intent of posttraumatic play is to resolve trauma. Clinicians are cautioned that posttraumatic play could be unsafe unless it brings relief. It could keep traumatized children in a state of disorganized retraumatization. Posttraumatic play is a beneficial resource many traumatized children possess, and clinicians are encouraged to stay attentive to inviting or welcoming posttraumatic play in the clinical environment (Gil, 2017).

Introduction to Posttraumatic Play

As this author worked with children, three dimensions of posttraumatic play have emerged: (1) the externalization of the traumatic material (through some form of narrative story, or the creation of art or sand therapy images). Children are capable of projecting fears and concerns directly into the stories they tell, thus allowing clinicians to interact with the stories or metaphors, rather than pushing too hard or getting too close to events that could cause children to withdraw; (2) The identification and accessing of resources (the appearance of possibilities, resources, hope); and (3) The restoration of personal control and orientation to the future. In other words, through posttraumatic play, children are able to

DOI: 10.4324/9781003451549-20

remember, manage, and process feared memories, identify ways to cope, and begin to visualize the possibility of more rewarding, protective, or nurturing interactions and empathic relationships (Gil, 2017).

Posttraumatic play is NOT guided by the clinician. It is the child's natural reparative system, and the job of the play therapist is to welcome the posttrauma play, provide literal symbols of trauma children can use, and observe and document the trajectory of the play. Posttraumatic play emerges when children feel safe, compelled to bring forward traumatic memories, or feel ready to explore challenging memories. Posttraumatic play may be facilitated by the child's comfort with the therapy environment and clinician; and is buffered by a trusting and safe relationship and when the child's reparative system is engaged.

Posttraumatic play is the child's natural way of initiating and utilizing gradual exposure (Gil, 2011, 2012, 2017). Children can be invited to play out their traumas utilizing a variety of expressive therapies, such as play, art, or sand therapies. These three modalities have a great deal in common because they invite the child to engage in activities that allow for a *safe enough distance* from the trauma, externalizing aspects of the experience while feeling safe (counterconditioning). In addition, the toys allow children to miniaturize and express fears and worries in the safest possible way. Through this play, the child can restore a sense of personal control (mastery), becomes an active rather than a passive teller of their traumatic story, tests out alternate endings, identifies and deploys resources, and begins to discharge feelings, sensations, and thoughts (Gil, 2011, 2012, 2017). Through this process, children experience a sense of personal power with the accompanying ability to distinguish between things that happened in the past and what's occurring in the present. The child's cognitive reassessment of interpersonal trauma also provides a framework for their understanding that they were not to blame for their abuse, as well as reformat their self-image and feelings of self-worth.

The clinician's role varies depending on theoretical orientation; however, clinicians are advised to set the stage for the child's use of posttraumatic play by providing unconditional witnessing and allowing the child to feel free of demands, agendas, or expectations. The witnessing clinician values the uniqueness of what unfolds in the child's process, in the here and now, without charting the course, but trusting the child's capacity to direct the therapy process. The clinician facilitates the child's introspection and offers a permissive environment in which children can say or not say what they want, and they are allowed to play out whatever might be on their minds (Gil, 2017; Ray, 2021; Stewart & Echterling, 2014). Clinicians differ in the ways they respond to children's stories although relationship-building and witnessing tends to occur early on in most situations.

During this uninterrupted process, free of expectations, traumatized children may engage in an internal process that they convey, transform, and take back into conscious awareness. This process is powerful with vulnerable children and does not necessarily replace or thwart other possible accompanying resources. For example, if a child is able to tell stories with small toys, include projective material, and begin to re-establish their footing, they can eventually release feelings of isolation and secrecy in favor of self-directed processing of difficult emotional material. One of the hallmarks of trauma work is giving children the opportunity to remember and externalize traumatic events so that they can recognize that the abuse is not happening to them in the present, but they are recalling it while they feel safe, that they can identify and show thoughts, feelings, and embodied memories, and that their story belongs to them, with or without modifications.

Victims of Childhood Sexual Abuse

Gil's career focused on working with child abuse and neglect cases, and childhood sexual abuse (CSA) cases in particular (Gil, 2011, 2012, 2017). CSA happens frequently, goes under-reported, happens to children of all ages, and happens to both genders. Vulnerable populations are targeted, and most perpetrators are within the family or trusted individuals.

CSA impacts child development and short- and long-term psychological, physical, emotional, and social well-being (Benuto & O'Donohue, 2015; Cashmore & Shackel, 2013; Chen et al., 2010; Conte & Vaughan-Eden, 2018; Kenney-Noziska, 2022; Lalor & McElvaney, 2010; Trask, Walsh, & DiLillo, 2011). Children can have externalizing and internalizing dysregulation and cannot always find ways to communicate their distress verbally.

CSA treatment is complex and demanding. A great deal of research supports the use of Trauma-Focused Cognitive Behavioral Therapy (TF-CBT) (Thielemann et al., 2022) and yet because this approach is primarily verbal and psychoeducational, many clinicians experience it as limiting with disengaged, uncomfortable, or withdrawn youth. Clinicians are currently integrating other approaches that might be viewed as more child-friendly (play, art, sand therapies, as well as attachment-based models such as Child Parent Psychotherapy). There has been great innovation in creating programs for traumatized children as well as research that supports evidence-based models for trauma treatment for children (Ford & Courtois, 2013).

This author encourages readers to familiarize themselves with posttraumatic play and at the very least have a willingness to consider that this child-initiated type of play has many reparative aspects and can be a portion of the bigger work necessary in treatment of traumatized children.

Clinical Case Study

Ten-year-old Amelia was adopted from an orphanage in Guatemala by a Caucasian couple in their 40s when she was 2 years of age. After she moved to the United States, she lived with her adoptive mother and father, two adopted brothers, and her maternal grandparents, Pancho and Gisella. When Amelia was 10 years old, she reported that her grandfather, whom she called "Abu," sexually abused her.

After her disclosure, Amelia received a forensic interview and medical exam at the local Children's Advocacy Center (CAC). During Amelia's interview, she made a clear outcry of sexual abuse by her grandfather. The grandfather moved out of the home and was later arrested. He served a short-term prison sentence before he was deported to Nicaragua. It is believed Pancho sexually abused Amelia for quite some time. The abuse included anal penetration and the medical exam was positive for anal tears. Although distressed, the parents responded protectively, and Amelia was referred for therapy.

I met with the parents weekly to help them deal with the shock and guilt and worry about Amelia's sexual abuse. I also met weekly individually with Amelia, who was painfully shy. Her mother had told her that I was a counselor who talked with children who had "bad things happen to them." When I met Amelia, I reiterated, "your mom is right, I do see children who have had their private parts touched, sometimes hurt," adding, "and yes, I do listen to children when they want to talk to me, but mostly, this is a place where you decide what toys to play with and what to do. You can draw, make a sand tray, play in the doll house, build something in the sand box, whatever you choose . . . those can be other ways of showing what happened and how you feel . . . . It's a different way of talking . . . . But for now, we're going to get to know each other a little by playing in the play therapy office together . . . ." Amelia looked visibly relieved that she didn't have to talk to me, especially after her CAC interviews.

I utilized child-centered play therapy (CCPT) and invited Amelia to explore the room freely. She was very drawn to the doll house, and I made sure that there were toys nearby that could represent her family. Knowing that she had a small dog and a rabbit, I made sure those objects were visible as well. Slowly but surely, she rearranged the furniture in the dollhouse specifying her room, her two brothers' room, her grandparents' room, and her parent's room. She put the dog with the boys and the rabbit in her room. She had mother cooking with her helping, and the mother doll called for the boys to wash up and come to dinner. I used reflective observations with her, but infrequently since my talking seemed to interrupt her flow. Another time she would show the morning time, and mom getting everyone off to school. Finally, she began talking about watching TV with her grandfather and used a Kleenex to cover the two dolls up. She had the grandmother sitting nearby, but sleeping. I noticed that the little girl and grandfather were covered up. She looked up and said, "Abu is sneaking bad touches." I repeated what she said "Abu is sneaking bad touches . . ." and "I wonder where his bad touches are going." Amelia said, "Inside my panties and in my butt hole." "Oh," I said, "Abu is sneaky touching and touching inside your panties, in your butt hole." Amelia nodded.

Over a period of about five months, Amelia's play was self-directed in the dollhouse where she had chosen to reveal herself to me. She spent lots of time showing me that her parent's relationship was happy and that they kissed a lot, that her brother Ricky followed her around like a puppy dog, that her brother Alex liked to talk on the phone a lot, that she tried to hide and lock herself in the bathroom, and that she tried to stay away from her grandfather.

She also showed me the first time that her grandfather Pancho touched her by asking, "Do you know what Abu did to me?" I said that I knew he had sneaky touched her private parts. Amelia corrected me in a clear voice. "Not just touch me, he hurted me!!" Eventually she told me that Abu had stuck his private in her butt and that blood came out, and that he hurt her. I matched her energy as I rephrased what she had told me, adding "Thank you so much for telling me that Abu not only touched you, he hurt you, and stuck his private inside your butt, and it bled, and hurt." I went on, "I'm so sorry that happened to you. Abu did something wrong and needs to learn that it is not okay for him to do that." "Yes," Amelia said, "he can't come back home until he learns to stop doing bad things." I agreed.

In her posttraumatic play, Amelia stated that "mommy and daddy didn't know that Abu was doing bad things." "No," I exclaimed, "Mom and dad didn't know that Abu was hurting you, he was doing sneaky touching and hurting." Amelia looked at me and asked "They got mad at him, didn't they?" I told her I thought they had but then suggested, "maybe you can show me with the mom and dad doll, what you think they said to Abu?" She acted out a whole lecture from parents to Abu about how he had done bad things. She added at the end, "just because someone did that to you, and hurt you, doesn't mean you can do to someone else." Then she said emphatically, "I won't hurt someone else just because he hurt me." I said, "that's right, because you already know that it was a bad thing to do . . . Abu still needs to learn that." This play prompted me to have a family session in which parents could talk about their feelings about Abu and what he had done. Everyone in the family could say they loved Abu and missed him (which mostly, they did), that they were still mad at him, and they were glad he was getting help so he never hurt anyone again.

Amelia did very well in treatment utilizing posttraumatic play intertwined with family therapy sessions. She returned to pre-abuse functioning within the first two years. Over the next five years, I met with the parents from time to time, they consulted with me about Amelia and her two brothers, and from time to time, I met with them as family to check in.

Limitations of This Approach With Victims of Childhood Sexual Abuse

The last three to four decades have generated a great deal of knowledge about the impact of CSA on development, brain structure, the nervous system, social and emotional problems, and long-term effects (Ford & Courtois, 2013). Social recognition of the high cost of childhood trauma has increased tremendously. Several books on trauma have been widely read and more and more discussion has ensued (van der Kolk, 2015). There is consensus about what needs to be addressed post CSA and some of the key principles which should be incorporated with any treatment model. A host of clinical approaches and evidence-based models continue to be designed in a trauma-informed way. Clinicians are advised to remain conversant with various models that promote positive treatment outcomes.

In terms of working with sexually abused children, Trauma-Focused Cognitive Behavioral Therapy has the greatest empirical support and has been touted as "the gold standard." This model has been funded for national distribution and most child-serving professionals have been trained and/or certified in this model which the research specifies has positive outcomes, most especially in decreasing symptoms of posttraumatic stress disorders.

Most clinicians now implement a hybrid model of Trauma-Focused Cognitive Behavioral Therapy. In addition, play therapists and neuroscientists have encouraged bottom-up activities with children that don't begin with conversations about abuse that require cognitive attention. Most child-serving professionals have found that many children are initially hyper- or hypo-aroused, may feel overwhelmed or shut down, and may be unable to engage in conversation or receive psychoeducation early on. Contemporary child therapists focus on uniquely-tailored interventions that first identify how the child is coping with stress, what their attachment world-views might affect, and/or how their brain and body functions are activated when they have unwelcome and intrusive sensory, affective, or cognitive memories. Many child therapists have a repertoire of activities and responses designed to quiet the nervous system and engage the child in relational health and safety.

Play therapy allows the child to experience personal power or control, access internal resources, and explore relational interactions with a safe and receptive other. Posttraumatic play is the child's natural gradual exposure which allows them to be the active change agent on their own behalf. Clinicians are encouraged to recognize and value this type of play, prepare for it, engage with it, and trust that injured children have the capacity to access either internal or external resources as they begin to feel safe. Posttraumatic play is their intuitive process and play therapists can ensure that they have the security and unconditional acceptance to self-repair. Obviously, not every child will have the capacity to engage in this form of play, and when they do not, we can "tickle the defenses," or make small invitations to see if children can find their way toward processing through their play. When children are not capable of posttraumatic play, clinicians will turn to other approaches to see if they can successfully invite children into the work that is needed.

Conclusion

Familial sexual abuse is more common than most clinicians anticipate and can evoke many responses. CSA tends to be secretive and chronic, going on for multiple years and across several developmental stages. If the abuse occurred out of the home, parents tend to feel tremendous guilt for not knowing about the abuse and may feel they somehow failed their children. When the abuse has been perpetrated by a trusted family member or friend, parents can feel a range of feelings toward family members in the role of victim and victimizer. Usually, when the victimizers are older adolescents or adults, they can be remanded to the juvenile or adult justice system and can be incarcerated. Sometimes, in cases of familial sexual abuse (an uncle, parent, and sibling) reunification work is necessary to address and correct prior relationship dynamics, and set new and healthy boundaries for everyone. Reunification can be successful yet the treatment process for the victimizer, victim, and family must be carefully undertaken, and treatment providers should be on the same page about how to proceed.

CCPT may serve an important benefit early on in treatment since it gives children a sense of mastery to use their own initiative in the play therapy office. Eventually, traumatized children will be able to bring their trauma to the therapy process by utilizing posttraumatic play, a remarkable and unique type of play that allows children to initiate gradual exposure and reap the benefits of that dynamic. Eventually children feel that they can have controlled recall, they can remember what happened, they can resolve lingering questions, and express their feelings in front of an unconditional witness. At a later time, they can also share that narrative with parents as appropriate. In cases of familial sexual abuse, individual child work is always achieved with intermittent family therapy meetings with an understanding that the abuse has affected everyone in the family in different ways.

Considerations for Practice: Key Takeaways

- Posttraumatic play is initiated by children and allows them to work at their own pace, while remaining in control of what they say/do with their traumatic memories.
- During posttraumatic play children gradually expose themselves to distressing traumatic memories. By miniaturizing the event with toys,

the child can take charge of the sequence of play, characters in the story, thematic material, resolution, challenges and resources.

- Trust the process. Given a safe, reparative, trusting relationship with a clinician, children may know what they need to address to feel better and move forward.
- It is useful to co-create a treatment process with children based on who they are, their developmental stage, their security, their coping strategies, etc. I won't know what type of play therapy will work best until I meet the child and attend to their needs. Do not come with agendas or protocols but consider your primary task to build a relationship.

References

Benuto, L. E., & O'Donohue, W. (2015). Treatment of sexually abused children: A review and synthesis of recent meta-analyses. *Children and Youth Services Review, 56*, 52–56.

Cashmore, J., & Shackel, R. (2013). The long-term effects of child sexual abuse. *Child Family Community Australia, 11*.

Chen, L. P., Murad, M. H., Paras, M. L., Colbenson, K. M., Sattler, A. L., Goranson, E. N., Elamin, M. B., Seime, R. J., Shinozaki, G., Prokop, L., & Zirakzadeh, A. (2010). Impact of child sexual abuse and lifetime diagnosis of psychiatric disorders: Systematic review and meta-analysis. *Mayo Clinical Proceeding, 85*(7), 618–629.

Conte, J. R., & Vaughan-Eden, V. (2018). Child sexual abuse. In J. B. Klika & J. R. Conte (Eds.), *The APSAC handbook on children maltreatment* (4th ed., pp. 95–110). Sage Publication.

Ford, J. D., & Courtois, C. A. (2013). *Treating complex traumatic stress disorders in children and Adolescents: Scientific foundations and therapeutic models.* Guilford Press.

Gil, E. (2011). Children's self-initiated gradual exposure: The wonders of posttraumatic play and behavioral reenactments. In E. Gil (Ed.), *Working with children to heal interpersonal trauma: The power of play* (pp. 44–63). Guilford Press.

Gil, E. (2012). Trauma-focused integrated play therapy (TF-IPT). In P. Goodyear-Brown (Ed.), *Handbook of child sexual abuse: Identification, assessment, and treatment* (pp. 251–278). John Wiley & Sons.

Gil, E. (2017). *Posttraumatic play in children: What clinicians need to know.* Guilford Press.

Kenney-Noziska, S. (2022). Play therapy group work with sexually abused children. In J. Stone, R. J. Grant, & C. Mellenthin (Eds.), *Implementing play therapy with groups: Contemporary issues in practice* (pp.196–207). Routledge.

Lalor, K., & McElvaney, R. (2010). Child sexual abuse, links to later sexual exploitation/high risk sexual behavior, and prevention/treatment programmes. *Trauma, Violence, and Abuse, 11*, 159–177.

Ray, D. C. (2021). *Advanced play therapy: Essential conditions, knowledge, and skills for child practice.* Routledge.

Stewart, A. L., & Echterling, L. G. (2014). Therapeutic relationship. In C. E. Schaefer & A. A. Drewes (Eds.), *The therapeutic powers of play* (pp. 157–170). Wiley.

Terr, L. (1981). Forbidden games: Posttraumatic child's play. *American Academy of Child Psychiatry, 20*, 741–760.

Terr, L. (1992). *Too scared to cry*. Basic Books.

Terr, L. C. (1991). Childhood traumas: An outline and overview. *American Journal of Psychiatry, 148*, 10–19.

Thielemann, J. F. B., Kasparik, B., König, J., Unterhitzenberger, J., & Rosner, R. (2022). A systematic review and meta-analysis of trauma-focused cognitive behavioral therapy for children and adolescents. *Child Abuse & Neglect, 134*. https://doi.org/10.1016/j.chiabu.2022.105899

Trask, E., Walsh, K., & DiLillo, D. (2011). Treatment effects for common outcomes of child sexual abuse: A current meta-analysis. *Aggression and Violent Behavior, 16*, 6–19.

van der Kolk, B. (2015). *The body keeps the score: Brain, mind, and body in the healing of trauma*. Penguin Books.

CHAPTER 18
SANDTRAY INTEGRATION IN PLAY THERAPY WITH SEXUALLY ABUSED CHILDREN AND ADOLESCENTS

Linda E. Homeyer and Marshall Lyles

Sophia skipped into the sandtray room with a spark in her eyes. From the freedom in her movement to the lift in her voice, this seemed like an entirely different child from a few months ago. Playful and unburdened, Sophia moved toward the sand tray and announced there was no time to waste. She had a world to create!

Invitation

We, Linda and Marshall, invite you to this chapter. We invite you to come with curiosity and intent. Written from a cross-theoretical perspective, you may more easily apply your theory or approach as you read. We both have long clinical histories of experience with children, adolescents, and their families and caregivers who have experienced child sexual abuse (CSA). It is a challenge, to be sure. It is also rewarding to see the impact early intervention can have on the trajectory of their lives. As you will soon discover, we share Sophia's case study throughout the chapter. Then, we interject the content as the case progresses, using a format we use when teaching in person. So, let's get started. Welcome Sophia!

Sophia's parents tell the therapist about her recent disclosure of sexual abuse by a male adolescent neighbor. This resulted in calls to child protection, a forensic interview, and legal investigations. The family's collective life had paused while all navigated the intense unknowns of what might unfold. Sophia's parents' initial parent consultation had a certain anxiety within the opening minutes. When caregivers need to seek mental health treatment for their child, it usually indicates

DOI: 10.4324/9781003451549-21

life has brought unexpected grief and struggle into the family. This feeling can have added potency when the reason for seeking profes- sional support has resulted from childhood sexual abuse. No parent plans for these moments, including Sophia's. Aware of this, the thera- pist held the space and allowed for pain and uncertainty.

Before Sophia first disclosed the abuse to her school counselor, her parents had noticed changes in her appearance, mood, and behav- iors. She was described as bubbly and social just months before, but her "light began to dim." Being a tight-knit family, her parents tried to talk with Sophia about these changes and she shared nothing. The parents described the devastation they felt when getting the call from the school counselor, which revealed the likely cause of Sophia's shifts.

The therapist listened to the story with presence and compassion. When the appropriate time presented itself, the therapist spoke to the noticeable shame, guilt, and grief in the room, offering caring reassurance. In digestible bits, the impact of sexual trauma was discussed in a manner that supported the parents' understanding of Sophia's recent changes. Then, the experienced sandtray thera- pist asked if they could share about an approach to healing that they have often found to be safe and effective for children needing empowered space to work through this particular type of traumatic exposure. This began the family's sandtray journey toward healing, patiently allowing Sophia to use created sand worlds as she moved through the phases of trauma recovery

(Gomez & Lyles, 2025).

Overview and Basic Tenets of Sandtray Therapy

Let's pause Sophia's story momentarily and look at the modality she will utilize in her play therapy work. Margaret Lowenfeld (1979), one of the first play therapists, had a sand tray within her playroom as early as 1928. Named the *World Technique* by a child client of Lowenfeld's, various forms of the sand tray and materials have been used for nearly a century (Homeyer & Sweeney, 2023; Lowenfeld, 1979). Today, play therapists may have the sand tray and materials in their playroom or a separate sandtray therapy room.

Sandtray therapy is defined as "an expressive and projective mode of psychotherapy involving the unfolding and processing of intra- and inter-personal issues through the use of specific sandtray materials as a nonverbal medium of communication, led by the client or therapist and facilitated by a trained therapist" (Homeyer & Sweeney, 2023, p. 9). Used by play therapists with various clinical theories and approaches, sandtray therapy can easily be integrated into the play therapist's current way of working with clients. Most play therapists using a sand tray value the additional option of these materials in supporting the client to more fully express themselves nonverbally, using symbolic and metaphorical play, just as the client does in a traditional playroom. Homeyer and Lyles (2022) discuss in detail the value of using sand tray with clients who have experienced trauma, such as sexual abuse. This parallels the client's ability to have emotional and psychological distancing of their work and expression that happens in the play and the tray. Play in both settings utilizes the therapeutic powers of play (TPOP; Schaefer & Drewes, 2014). The play therapist can identify the TPOP the client is activating in their play – whether in the playroom or the sand tray. Homeyer and Lyles (2024) discuss the TPOP, integral to the play therapist's work, and what the person of the sandtray therapist's presence activates and holds, such as therapeutic relationship, empathy, social competence, and attachment.

The materials to provide a sand tray experience include a tray (preferably painted blue inside), sand (natural sand or various colors), water (usually in a spray bottle), and a collection of miniature figures. The miniature figures are typically organized by categories on shelves, just like toys in a traditional playroom. This allows the client to know where to look for specific miniatures – such as people (families, occupational), animals (domestic, wild, prehistoric), buildings (houses, schools, jails), vehicles (cars, police, rescue), vegetation (trees, bushes, flowers), and more. Typical to sand therapy are also categories like spiritual (cross, Star of David, Buddha) and mystical (crystals, gems, angels). As in play therapy, we understand "toys are their words, play is their talk," and so are the miniature figures; offering plenty of "words" is the goal of a miniature collection. When working with sexually abused clients, offer ample potential words and symbols to express fear, victimization, abuse, protection, and rescue. Also, offering miniature figures reminiscent of places where abuse might occur, such as bedroom furniture and bathroom fixtures, is helpful so the client does not have to verbally communicate their experience.

Sophia's Opening Phase of Treatment

Sophia first entered the sandtray treatment room with a blend of hesitation and curiosity in her eyes. The therapist introduced the room and the process with a certain welcoming stillness. Reassured that there were no expectations and no right way to make a sand world, Sophia started exploring the feel of the sand with just her fingertips. She occasionally glanced at the shelves of miniatures with restrained interest.

Sophia's first few sand worlds were created slowly, and the narratives were somewhat disjointed and sparse. Her worlds featured a mix of fleeting whimsy and security with ever encroaching threats. Initially, the threats in the worlds came from imposing dragons and oversized aggressive animal figures like alligators and snakes. They would sneak into towns and upend peace. These narratives would quickly become incoherent and her internally stored chaos was mirrored in the choppy sand and haphazardly placed miniatures. Eventually, the threats in her created worlds transitioned from beasts to human male figures.

The sandtray therapist tracked, reflected, and occasionally asked organizing and orienting questions. Sophia seemed to quickly catch on to the inherent opportunity of externalization through metaphor. Over the first four or five sessions, she made more eye contact with the therapist and moved through the sandtray sessions more fluidly. This relational steadiness and age-appropriate understanding of the process allowed her to reach for some worlds of emerging resources and other worlds that allowed for the possible telling of her painful story. Sophia was ready to begin the internally complex work of integrating fragmented traumatic memories.

Research and Literature Support the Use of Sandtray Therapy

Sophia represents the experience of a sexual abuse victim with a single traumatic event who also has supportive, functioning parents. For others, this wounding occurs within more complicated systems and circumstances, such as family violence, physical abuse, neglect, drug abuse, alcoholism, and homelessness, often resulting in being removed from their parents and placed in foster care, shelters, or long-term residential homes.

The body of research and literature supporting various sand therapies as an intervention for sexual abuse and trauma has become substantive. Kosanke's (2013) content analysis of sexual abuse treatment in the sand therapy literature resulted in a valuable conceptualization for sand therapists. The model begins with two overlapping circles. These represent the client's traumatized part of self and their resourceful part. When within the sand tray, we work with the client's wounded part as well as their healing part. The overlap is where the sand therapy process occurs. These working parts are all contained and held by the tray. Holding the experience within the tray is the sand therapist; holding the sand therapist is their clinical theory. This representation reinforces the importance of several levels of holding within the therapeutic process.

Early research studies by Grubbs (1994) and the writings of Carey (1999) are among the many that identified using sand therapy with CSA. Research around the world and in many settings now reveals the universality of the use of sand therapy: Taiwan/United States (Hong, 2011), Brazil (Matta & Ramos, 2021), Malaysia (Ismail et al., 2020), Nepal (Maharjan, 2019), Italy (Herce et al., 2024), and California (Cunningham et al., 2000) to name a few recent research projects.

Some of these studies report themes in the sand work of participants who had experienced CSA along with other forms of abuse and neglect. Matta and Ramos (2021) noted during the first phase of sandtray intervention, there were scenes of war and violence, expressions of anger and sadness through conflicted, wounded, and dead characters. The second intervention phase included negative scenes of deceased figures and noted a gradual change in behavior with increased control over impulsive acts. The final phase included increased self-awareness and scenes with greater organizational harmony and psychic integration. Cunningham et al. (2000) noted that in the first and only sandtray creation of their participants (boys aged 6–11) who experienced CSA used significantly fewer items in the tray (average of 9.3) than those in other comparison groups. They also displayed the inability to plan, structure, and integrate figures into a single picture. All these first trays were without hope and resolution.

Sophia's Processing Phase of Treatment

Sophia's sand worlds generally became more organized as she found some sense of empowered safety while exploring her complex internal states through externalized metaphors. However, these sand worlds were no less intense. Alternating between some narratives and imagery that referenced coherent resources (such as imaginary safe places and wise guides) and destructive moments of miniatures experiencing victimization, Sophia was allowing herself to pendulate (Gomez, 2013) between the security she needed to restore and the pain she had endured. Some of the more terrifying elements of pain expressed in the tray brought brief moments of dissociation. This sometimes looked like a momentary loss of motor control with the sand and figures (clumsy interaction with the materials), and other times sounded like uncharacteristic drops into silence (followed by slight confusion). Being experienced in working with sexual abuse trauma, Sophia's therapist knew to stay grounded in these moments and to avoid imposing an agenda of overregulation. Sophia deserved a space to explore all of her stored and unfolding reactions to her trauma exposure.

Sophia's sandtray therapist conducted regular parent consultations, with Sophia's knowledge, and obtained her parents' consent to consult with the pediatrician and school professionals who all had already been involved in supporting the family through the process of abuse disclosure. As treatment progressed, Sophia was touching into her abuse trauma and these moments of dissociative self-protection could show up in other settings. Sophia's sandtray therapist briefly described the nature of sandtray work and the process of healing from trauma to each professional, respecting Sophia's story while making sure all near her were prepared to navigate these moments with gentle care.

Sophia's parents needed time to practice holding sacred space for their daughter's emerging responses to her trauma. These new emotional and behavioral expressions challenged her parents in previously unpracticed manners. Sophia's sandtray therapist allowed her parents time to work in the tray during parent consultations in order for them to feel prepared to participate in needed future family sandtray sessions. This allowed them time to experience what Sophia was navigating as she worked in the sand and gave the opportunity to trust the capacity of the sand tray to hold the struggle. Referrals for individual and couples' therapists were also provided to Sophia's parents in the event that their own traumas began to interfere with their daily functioning.

Importance of Parent Consultations

Regular parent consultations are critical. It strengthens parents' perception that they are part of the treatment team (Homeyer & Bennett, 2023). The involvement of caregivers has been shown to be effective in prognosis (Bratton et al., 2005; LeBlanc & Ritchie, 2001). Nonoffending parents, such as Sophia's, often hold feelings of guilt over not having protected their child. They may have issues surrounding how to parent a sexually abused child and how to maneuver legal issues, such as the involvement of child protective services and the potential prosecution of the offender. Parents need a great deal of support and, perhaps, their own individual or couples counseling. Including school personnel and pediatricians expands the treatment team to support the child and caregivers.

Homeyer and Lyles (2024) discuss using sand tray work in parent consultations. These experiences can be used to explore these issues. Additionally, sand tray work can help the sandtray therapist assess the capacity for parental reflective functioning in preparation for family sand therapy sessions. Sand sessions with the parents allow them to experience the power of metaphors and miniatures in the sand and more fully understand the work their child is doing in sessions. The sandtray therapist can discuss the importance of attunement to the child's internal states while monitoring their own (Homeyer & Lyles, 2024).

Sophia's Final Phase of Treatment

As Sophia began to merge her resource-themed sand worlds more seamlessly with her pain-themed worlds, her affect brightened. Sophia's parents were doing their own personal work and their parent consultations showed a return to levels of parental reflective functioning likely present prior to the revelation of sexual abuse. All involved seemed ready to embrace the final section of sandtray treatment that would heavily feature family sandtray sessions.

Sophia had begun to show mastery over holding the painful and empowered parts of her narrative together in individual sandtray sessions. However, her therapist wanted to support this emerging version of self by ensuring her progress was also present when in her family system. As Sophia and her parents settled around the group tray, Sophia took the lead. She confidently created a world and asked her parents to gather specific miniatures with her. The parents demonstrated the applied ability of attunement and co-regulation as practiced during parent consultations. The sandtray therapist stepped in as needed to interrupt small moments of interpretation or potentially intrusive questioning around painful themes, but these moments were rare.

Later family sessions became more collaborative with all creating in harmonious spontaneity. The abuse narrative was no longer prominent. The sand worlds featured dreams for the future alongside acknowledgement of everyday gratitudes. A final session featured a ritual where everyone acknowledged their hard work in the sand and Sophia's efforts were celebrated.

Limitations

Sand therapy needs more research specific to many presenting issues, including, in this case, child sexual abuse. This would include research for various age levels: children, adolescents, and adults. There is a sufficient body of sand therapy research to conduct four meta-analyses (Holliman & Foster, 2023; Koh & Ha, 2022; Lee & Jang, 2015; Wiersman et al., 2022). Three found a large effect size, and one a medium effect size. While these support a broad range of effectiveness, increased study of child sexual abuse is warranted. In addition to research, the need for more dissemination of substantial, theoretically grounded literature for practical application, such as working with clients experiencing dissociation, is also critical. Gomez and Lyles (2025) discuss this topic in detail, articulating an integrative and phase-oriented approach to working with dissociation in sand therapy.

As sandtray therapies become more widely used, the importance of education, training, and supervision cannot be overstated. Even those with some sand therapy experience would be wise to be in consultation when using sand therapy with new clinical populations, such as child sexual abuse. Research-based sand therapist competencies are now identified (Kjellstrand Hartwig et al., 2023). As these competencies become infused into sand therapy training, the field will become increasingly grounded, further establishing robust, research-based experience.

Conclusion

As this case study of Sophia demonstrates, sandtray therapy is an effective treatment intervention for her and her family. Having experienced

CSA, Sophia can express herself within the tray, using miniature figures and their arrangement to communicate about herself and work through the impact of her experience. Sandtray therapy has been used for nearly 100 years and continues to demonstrate its effectiveness. Research and professional literature support its use.

Considerations for Practice: Key Takeaways

- Sand therapies are effective for the treatment of children and adolescents experiencing child sexual abuse.
- The informed sandtray therapist will include miniature figures in their collection to include representations of places where abuse occurs, protectors, and perpetrators.
- The use of sand trays in parent consultations and family therapy are encouraged.

References

Bratton, S., Ray, D., Rhine, T., & Jones, L. (2005). The efficacy of play therapy with children: A Meta-analytic review of the outcome research. *Professional Psychology: Research and Practice, 36*(4), 376–390.

Carey, L. (1999a). *Sandplay therapy with children and families.* Rowman & Littlefield.

Carey, L. (1999b). *Sandplay therapy with children and families.* Aronson.

Cunningham, C., Fill, K., & Al-Jamie, L. (2000). Sandtray play with traumatized children. *Journal of Aggression, Maltreatment & Trauma, 2*(2), 195–205. http://doi.org/10.1300/J146v02n02_09

Gomez, A., & Lyles, M. (2025). An integrative and phase-oriented approach to sandtray therapy. In A. M. Gomez & J. Hosey (Eds.), *Handbook of complex trauma and dissociation in children: Theory, research, and clinical applications.* Routledge.

Gomez, A. M. (2013). *EMDR therapy and adjunct approaches with children: Complex trauma, attachment, and dissociation.* Springer Publishing Company.

Grubbs, G. A. (1994). An abused child's use of sandplay in the healing process. *Clinical Social Work Journal, 22,* 193–209. https://doi.org/10.1007/BF02190474

Herce, S. B., Alda, I. O., & Marrodán, J. L. G. (2024). Sandtray and sandplay in the treatment of trauma with children and adolescents: A systemic review. *World Journal for Sand Therapy Practice®, 2*(1). https://doi.org/10.58997/wjstp.v2i1.74

Holliman, R., & Foster, R. D. (2023). The way we play in the sand: A meta-analytic investigation of sand therapy, its formats, and presenting problems. *Journal of Child and Adolescent Counseling, 2*(9), 205–221. http://doi.org/10.1080/23727810.2023.2232142

Homeyer, L., & Bennett, M. (2023). *The guide to play therapy documentation and parent consultations.* Routledge.

Homeyer, L., & Lyles, M. (2022). *Advanced sandtray therapy: Digger deeper into clinical practice*. Routledge.

Homeyer, L., & Lyles, M. (2024). Safety in sand and symbols: Polyvagal shifts in the sand tray. In P. Goodyear-Brown & L. Yasenik (Eds.), *Polyvagal power in the playroom* (pp. 192–207). Routledge.

Homeyer, L., & Sweeney, D. (2023). *Sandtray therapy: A practical manual* (4th ed.). Routledge.

Hong, G. (2011). *Sandplay therapy: Research and practice*. Routledge.

Ismail, M. R., Amat, S., Johari, K. S. K., & Mahmud, Z. (2020, August). Sandtray therapy for young girls in a shelter home. In *1st Progress in social science, humanities and education research symposium (PSSHERS 2019)* (pp. 666–670). Atlantis Press.

Kjellstrand Hartwig, E., Homeyer, L., & Stone, J. (2023). Sand therapy competencies: A qualitative investigation of competencies for sand therapy practitioners. *World Journal for Sand Therapy Practice®*, *1*(5). https://doi.org/10.58997/wjstp.v1i5.32

Koh, H., & Ha, J. (2022). A meta-analysis on the effectiveness of sand play therapy in adults. *Journal of Symbols & Sandplay Therapy*, *13*(2), 137–156.

Kosanke, G. C. (2013). *The use of sandtray approaches in psycho-therapeutic work with adult trauma survivors: A thematic analysis* [Unpublished master's thesis, Auckland University of Technology]. http://aut.researchgateway.ac.nz/handle/10292/5592.

LeBlanc, M., & Ritchie, M. (2001). A meta-analysis of play therapy outcomes. *Counselling Psychology Quarterly*, *14*(2), 149–163.

Lee, S., & Jang, M. (2015). The effectiveness of sand play treatment meta-analysis. *Korean Journal of child Psychological Therapy*, *10*(1), 1–26.

Lowenfeld, M. (1979). *Understanding children's sandplay: Lowenfeld's World Technique*. Allen & Urwin.

Maharjan, C. L. (2019). *Sandplay therapy for children with trauma living in a residential facility in Nepal: A multiple case study*. Publication No. 27669449 [Doctoral dissertation, California Institute of Integral Studies]. ProQuest Dissertations and Theses Global.

Matta, R. M., & Ramos, D. R. (2021). The effectiveness of Sandplay therapy in children who are victims of maltreatment with internalizing and externalizing behavior problems. *Estudos de Psicologia (Campinas)*, *38*, e200036. https://dio.org/10.1590/1982-0275202138e200036

Schaefer, C. E., & Drewes, A. A. (2014). *The therapeutic powers of play: 20 core agents of change* (2nd ed.). John Wiley & Sons.

Wiersman, J. K., Freedle, L. R., McRoberts, R., & Solberg, K. B. (2022). A meta-analysis of sandplay therapy treatment outcomes. *International Journal of Play Therapy*, *21*(4), 197–215.

CHAPTER 19
TRAUMAPLAY™

A FLEXIBLY SEQUENTIAL APPROACH FOR HEALING SEXUAL TRAUMA

Paris Goodyear-Brown

Childhood sexual abuse (CSA) is an unspeakable betrayal perpetrated by those closest to the child. Sexual abuse is categorized as an adverse childhood experience (ACEs) in large part because of the rippling ruptures this kind of betrayal creates in the developing trust between a caregiver, a child, and the child's internal organization of the self. CSA represents an interruption to the mastery of core developmental tasks, impeding development in multiple areas (Groh et al., 2017). Betrayal trauma can result in coping strategies such as dissociation and even forms of hallucination (Gómez & Freyd, 2017; Katz et al., 2020), as well as coping responses based on sympathetic activations or externalizing behaviors (Langevin et al., 2023; Van Meter et al., 2020).

Overview and Basic Tenets of This Play Therapy Theory

TraumaPlay is an attachment-grounded, evidence-informed, flexibly sequential play therapy model that integrates best practice standards for working with traumatized children and their caregivers (Goodyear-Brown, 2009, 2021). While core components of treatment provide a phase-based continuum of treatment, clinicians are trained to follow the child's need all along the way, moving between components as needed (see Figure 19.1).

Far from protocol driven therapy, TraumaPlay invites clinicians to follow the child's needs flexibly throughout a continuum of treatment. This integrative model draws from Child-Centered Play Therapy (CCPT), Theraplay, Polyvagal theory, and Trauma-Focused Cognitive Behavioral Therapy (TF-CBT) and offers multiple pathways for treatment goals to be

DOI: 10.4324/9781003451549-22

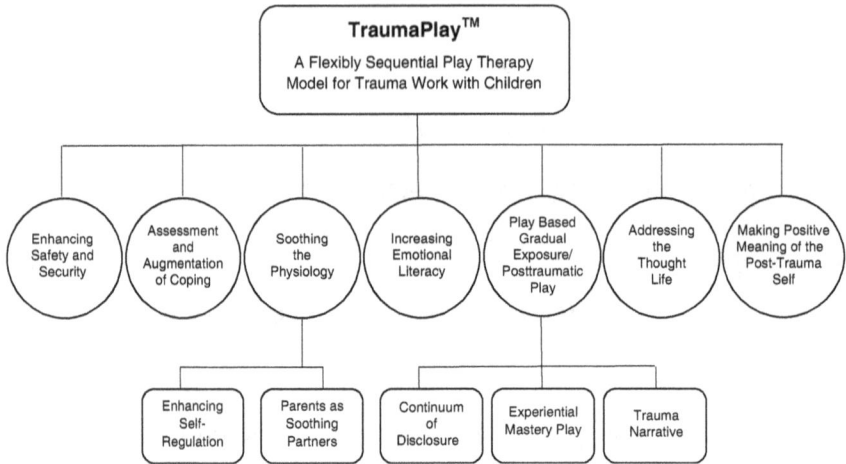

Figure 19.1 *Flowchart of TraumaPlay™ Components.*

achieved. TraumaPlay and EMDR are often implemented together, and all work is scaffolded on the importance of the attachment relationships, both with the therapist and the primary caregivers. TraumaPlay posits that there is no "one size fits all" treatment for CSA survivors, but rather the umbrella framework of best practice guidelines and meaningful components of trauma treatment encourage nuanced case conceptualization.

Application of TraumaPlay With Victims of CSA

The TraumaPlay components represent best practices within the global field of childhood trauma and are especially meaningful for survivors of CSA due to the betrayal trauma that has often compromised a child's ability to trust grown-ups (Hujing & Yalch, 2024). There is a strong focus on enhancing attachments with coregulating caregivers prior to entering trauma narrative work or posttraumatic play. The therapist is always working to embody the three roles that the child may not have had from adults: Safe Boss, Nurturer, and Storykeeper, and to embody these roles for the caregiver as well.

The following explains the core components of TraumaPlay with empirical support of this framework for CSA. Enhancing Safety and Security must be addressed before therapeutic work can occur. The play therapist and therapeutic space must invite a felt sense of safety. This goal is empirically informed by polyvagal theory (Dana, 2018;

Goodyear-Brown & Yasenik, 2024; Porges, 2011, 2015), attachment theory (Bowlby et al., 1992); neurosequential development (Barfield et al., 2012; Gaskill, 2019; Gaskill & Perry, 2012); and Interpersonal Neurobiology (Siegel & Gottman, 2015; Schore, 2022). TraumaPlay therapists begin case conceptualization with a view toward how we will offer *safety with skin on*. The science of the senses leads us to invite interoceptive and exteroceptive experiences (Goodyear-Brown, 2019). Because children often cope with CSA by disconnecting or dissociating from their bodies, we invite child survivors to expand their interception in numerous ways. TraumaPlay therapists greet children and ask them to check in with their bodies, "What is your body telling you? What does your body need?" CSA survivors need support in coming back into their bodies. Explaining body autonomy is an important part of enhancing safety and security. Seeking permission before touching the child or coming too far into the child's physical space can go a long way toward enhancing felt safety. Child-led play approaches, including CCPT, are highly effective in furthering a sense of felt safety for children who have experienced CSA and provide a good starting place for enhancing safety and security (Ray et al., 2022).

The next goal is to assess current coping and augment adaptive coping. Coping choices made by victims of CSA, such as disembodiment or dissociation, may have been genius adaptations for survival (Goodyear-Brown & Kenney-Noziska, 2024). But these may become problematic once the child is safe. It is important to know how a child is likely to cope with distressing feelings, thoughts, and memories before opening trauma narrative work (Goodyear-Brown, 2010, 2021). Avoidant coping leads to worse PTSD outcomes (Fletcher et al., 2021), as does emotion-focused coping (crying and verbal aggression) (VanMeter et al., 2020), while coping strategies utilizing social supports (Gruhn & Compas, 2020), problem-solving (Alix et al., 2020), and mindfulness reduce posttraumatic stress.

Soothing the physiology is aimed at a better understanding of how their bodies have responded to trauma, how to recognize when they are outside their window of tolerance, and chart paths for coming back into their optimal arousal zone. We may approach somatic understandings through the Polyvagal Zoo (Goodyear-Brown, 2021, 2022). TraumaPlay therapists employ playfully framed movement into ventral vagal social engagement, sympathetic activation, or dorsal vagal collapse and death feigning. Death feigning tonic immobility is often employed by survivors of CSA (Katz et al., 2020) and can be reframed as a brilliant response during CSA.

One pathway for soothing the physiology is enhancing self-regulation. Since somatic symptoms are over-represented in survivors of CSA (Chang et al., 2025), playful interventions and concrete strategies for mindfulness and breath work are often needed (Dussault et al., 2024). The second pathway is Parents as Soothing Partners. The earlier trauma occurs in a child's life, the more interpersonal and chronic the adverse experiences are, and the more important it will be for the caregiver to become a co-regulator. Coregulation *always* precedes self-regulation, and caregivers recapitulating early attuned, need-meeting behaviors may be critical in CSA healing.

Caregiver involvement is a central value in TraumaPlay. Parent involvement in intervention targeting CSA is well-documented (Rudolph et al., 2023). Goals for caregivers include facilitating parental paradigm shifts, learning, and practicing specific skill sets, expanding their own window of tolerance for distress, expanding reflective capacity, and engaging in Reflective Attachment Work (RAW) when needed.

Increasing emotional literacy is a necessary component of trauma treatment for children who, when asked how they are feeling, are likely to answer with "bad" or "fine." These children need help expanding their feelings vocabulary and deepening their emotional granularity prior to deeper trauma processing. Trauma narrative work is most helpful when it includes thoughts, feelings, and sensory impressions. Therefore, coherent trauma narrative is amplified when children have a large emotional vocabulary.

Play-based gradual exposure and posttraumatic play describe processes used to approach trauma content, work toward desensitization to trauma reminders, create a coherent narrative, and build a self-image as a survivor. TraumaPlay lays out three separate pathways used in pursuit of this integration. The continuum of disclosure refers to the process by which children give glimpses and snapshots of trauma. They enter the playroom ready to play through the trauma and our primary job is to *be with* them and answer each glimpse with the communication, "I see what you are showing me, and you can show me more." Experiential mastery play is important for children who come in stripped of personal goodness or power and cannot approach trauma content until they have had many competency surges. These experiences of strength or mastery mitigate the approach hard things. Trauma narration is built on the understanding that integrating trauma facilitates trauma recovery (Van der Westhuizen et al., 2023). This path provides structured support for children who have not embraced the previous paths. These children are entrenched in avoidance symptoms and need active alignment from the therapist to get unstuck. The therapist communicates that when we stick together, we can name the trauma. Caregivers are critical Storykeepers in this process (Goodyear-Brown, 2021).

Addressing the Thought Life serves as a broom, coming behind and cleaning up cognitive distortions or false attributions that remain. Clinicians often cannot identify the core distortions until the child or adolescent is working through the play-based gradual exposure process.

Making Positive Meaning of the Posttrauma Self is the final component of the model. This includes celebrating therapeutic growth and learning that they have happened in therapy while also making a meaningful goodbye during the termination phase.

Limitations of This Approach

TraumaPlay is designed to give permission for a "yes, and" approach to treatment. However, after all the core components of the model are addressed, two sets of residual symptoms may remain: child sexual behavior problems (CSPB) and specific anxieties or phobic responses that may require exposure/response prevention treatment.

Child sexual behavior problems may have emerged. These children require additional treatment specific to treating CSBP. Topics like body autonomy, consent, safe and unsafe secrets, private parts and public parts, and the creation and rehearsal of new sexual behavior rules for the family may be necessary (Goodyear-Brown, 2013) and are most effective when nonoffending caregivers are included.

Another limitation of TraumaPlay is that it does not include a structured approach to exposure/response prevention (ERP). CSA victims may have an idiosyncratic anxiety symptom that remains. This trauma residue is typically tied to avoidant coping and may need a very structured ERP program. The Worry Wars curriculum (Goodyear-Brown, 2010) was designed to meet this additional treatment need.

Lastly, parts work may need to be woven into TraumaPlay for extreme dissociation and depersonalization. Splintered parts of self may need intentional support to compassionately welcome all parts of self (Hodgdon et al., 2022; Schore, 2022).

Clinical Case Study

Jessica, who was placed with a foster family, came to therapy due to big behaviors at school and a history of sexual abuse by her brothers. Jessica was constricted in affect and body. In an early session, she entered the playroom and stood in the center of the room for a long time, looking from toy to toy. Her face lit up as she noticed the princess dresses. I stated, "your eyes lit up when you saw those dresses." Jessica shyly asked if she could put one on and I gave my standard response, which is, "you can do whatever you need to do in here." She chose the Sleeping Beauty dress and struggled for several minutes to put it on over her clothes. She did not ask for help, and I reflected her choice to do it by herself. When she was dressed, I offered an amplification of her experience by letting her know a full-length mirror hung inside the wardrobe cabinet. She went over and looked at herself in the mirror. I said, "You put on the princess dress . . . and you are enjoying seeing how it looks on you!" She smiled widely for a moment and then her affect flattened. In an abrupt shift in the play, she moved over to the sand tray, picked up the bottom edge of her princess skirt and began dumping sand into it. Once her skirt was full of sand, she carefully sat down cross-legged on the floor so that the pouch of sand she had created with the top layer of the princess dress was resting between her thighs. She looked up at me and began taking fistfuls of the sand and rubbing it all over the bodice and arms of the princess dress. Her facial expression vacillated between blunted affect (dissociative in nature) and fierce anger as she did this. Her angry face was daring me to stop her. Instead, I said, "The princess dress is getting so dirty!"

JESSICA:	"Soooooooo dirty!"
ME:	"You want me to see how dirty the princess feels."
JESSICA (WITH MORE EMPHASIS):	"Princesses shouldn't get dirty!!"
ME:	"You think the princess is supposed to stay clean . . . but there is dirt all over her. Hmmm." Jessica looked at me for a long moment, then sighed and asked for help in taking the princess dress off.

At the start of the next session, Jessica came into the room and wanted to play "washing dishes." I did not have a sink in the playroom, so I kept a deep Rubbermaid storage bin in the corner that could be filled with fresh water each day. Jessica was sitting on one side of the tub, I was sitting on the other, and we were washing play dishes. About five minutes into this play sequence, Jessica asked, "Miss Paris, could you get me the bowl behind you?" I turned around to get the bowl and when I turned back around, she sat down inside the tub with her knees pulled up to her chest. The water rose up to her kneecaps and her shoulders and she was soaking wet. I sat down in the child's chair I had previously pulled up next to the tub and leaned toward her, saying "You really need for me to see you getting clean." Jessica looked me directly in the eyes and said, "YES!" When she saw that I was going to hold space for her to play in this way, she demanded, "Hand me that sponge" (pointing to the wooden block in the basket next to me). She took the block/sponge and began to scrub herself fiercely over her clothes. I explained to her foster mother what I thought was happening in the play, and she agreed that this important work, the work of experiencing personal cleansing from the shame and humiliation of her sexual abuse, was critical. For the next six weeks, Jessica would arrive with her foster mom and a change of clothes in a plastic bag. We would go play, she would take her fully clothed bath, and then her foster mother would help get her changed into dry clothes. During this six-week interval she also painted pictures during each session and, as she enacted the cleansing rituals, the themes of hopelessness in the paintings were replaced with themes of life, hope, and connection to others.

Conclusion

The vignette above represents the first months of Jessica's TraumaPlay journey. While several core components are represented in Jessica's work (Enhancing Safety and Security, Experiential Mastery Play, Soothing the Physiology, Continuum of Disclosure) we moved next to strengthening her attachment with her foster mother; explored her core cognitive distortions, increased her emotional literacy, and graduated Jessica with a celebration of her growth and resilience. While the healing journey of each client with CSA will be unique, the TraumaPlay umbrella framework provides guidance for the process while encouraging nuanced application through clinical case conceptualization.

Considerations for Practice: Key Takeaways

- The attachment relationship between the TraumaPlay therapist and both the child and the child's caregiver(s) are key to treatment.

- TraumaPlay core components are an umbrella framework that protects the traumatized system from increasing symptomology.
- Flexibly following the child's need is the guiding principle in case conceptualization.
- Play-based gradual exposure and posttraumatic play can take several forms. Clients may use various pathways to integrate their trauma content into a healthy sense of self.

References

Alix, S., Cossette, L., Cyr, M., Frappier, J. Y., Caron, P. O., & Hébert, M. (2020). Self-blame, shame, avoidance, and suicidal ideation in sexually abused adolescent girls: A longitudinal study. *Journal of Child Sexual Abuse, 29*(4), 432–447.

Barfield, S., Dobson, C., Gaskill, R., & Perry, B. D. (2012). Neurosequential model of therapeutics in a therapeutic preschool: Implications for work with children with complex neuropsychiatric problems. *International Journal of Play Therapy, 21*(1), 30.

Bowlby, J., Ainsworth, M., & Bretherton, I. (1992). The origins of attachment theory. *Developmental Psychology, 28*(5), 759–775.

Chang, H. A., Silver, R. C., & Holman, E. A. (2025). Betrayal trauma and somatic symptoms among patients in a medically underserved primary care clinic. *Psychological Trauma: Theory, Research, Practice, and Policy, 17*(1), 97–104.

Dana, D. (2018). *The Polyvagal theory in therapy: Engaging the rhythm of regulation. Norton series on interpersonal neurobiology.* W. W. Norton.

Dussault, É., Fernet, M., Guyon, R., & Godbout, N. (2024). Mindfulness and posttraumatic growth in childhood sexual abuse and psychological maltreatment survivors. *The Canadian Journal of Human Sexuality, 33*(1), 72–85.

Fletcher, S., Elklit, A., Shevlin, M., & Armour, C. (2021). Predictors of PTSD treatment response trajectories in a sample of childhood sexual abuse survivors: The roles of social support, coping, and PTSD symptom clusters. *Journal of Interpersonal Violence, 36*(3–4), 1283–1307.

Gaskill, R. L. (2019). Neuroscience helps play therapists go low so children can aim high. *Play Therapy, 14*(3), 8–10.

Gaskill, R. L., & Perry, B. D. (2012). Child sexual abuse, traumatic experiences, and their impact on the developing brain. In P. Goodyear-Brown (Ed.), *Handbook of child sexual abuse: Identification, assessment, and treatment* (pp. 29–47). Wiley.

Gómez, J. M., & Freyd, J. J. (2017). High betrayal child sexual abuse and hallucinations: A test of an indirect effect of dissociation. *Journal of Child Sexual Abuse, 26*(5), 507–518.

Goodyear-Brown, P. (2009). *Play therapy with traumatized children: A prescriptive approach.* Wiley.

Goodyear-Brown, P. (2010). *The worry wars.* Author.

Goodyear-Brown, P. (2013). *Tackling touchy subjects.* Author.

Goodyear-Brown, P. (2019). *Trauma and play therapy: Helping children heal.* Routledge.

Goodyear-Brown, P. (2021). *Parents as partners in child therapy: A clinician's guide.* Guilford Press.

Goodyear-Brown, P. (2022). *Big behaviors in small containers: 131 trauma-informed play therapy interventions for treating disorders of dysregulation.* PESI.

Goodyear-Brown, P., & Kenney-Noziska, S. (2024). The genius of the disembodied self: Coping with child sexual abuse. In P. Goodyear-Brown & L. Yasenik (Eds.), *Polyvagal power in the playroom: A guide for play therapists* (pp. 42–58). Routledge.

Goodyear-Brown, P., & Yasenik, L. (2024). Listening inside our bodies, outside our bodies, and between bodies: Interoception, exteroception, and setting up a polyvagal informed playroom. In P. Goodyear-Brown & L. Yasenik (Eds.), *Polyvagal power in the playroom: A guide for play therapists* (pp. 14–28). Routledge.

Groh, A. M., Fearon, R. P., van IJzendoorn, M. H., Bakermans-Kranenburg, M. J., & Roisman, G. I. (2017). Attachment in the early life course: Meta-analytic evidence for its role in socioemotional development. *Child Development Perspectives, 11*(1), 70–76.

Gruhn, M. A., & Compas, B. E. (2020). Effects of maltreatment on coping and emotion regulation in childhood and adolescence: A meta-analytic review. *Child Abuse & Neglect, 103,* 104446.

Hodgdon, H. B., Anderson, F. G., Southwell, E., Hrubec, W., & Schwartz, R. (2022). Internal family systems (IFS) therapy for posttraumatic stress disorder (PTSD) among survivors of multiple childhood trauma: A pilot effectiveness study. *Journal of Aggression, Maltreatment & Trauma, 31*(1), 22–43.

Hujing, C., & Yalch, M. M. (2024). The influence of betrayal trauma on complex posttraumatic stress disorder symptoms. *Psychological Trauma: Theory, Research, Practice, and Policy, 16*(8), 1276–1280.

Katz, C., Tsur, N., Nicolet, R., Klebanov, B., & Carmel, N. (2020). No way to run or hide: Children's perceptions of their responses during intrafamilial child sexual abuse. *Child Abuse & Neglect, 106,* 104541.

Langevin, R., Marshall, C., Wallace, A., Gagné, M. E., Kingsland, E., & Temcheff, C. (2023). Disentangling the associations between attention deficit hyperactivity disorder and child sexual abuse: A systematic review. *Trauma, Violence, & Abuse, 24*(2), 369–389.

Porges, S. W. (2011). *The polyvagal theory: Neurophysiological foundations of emotions, attachment, communication, and self-regulation.* Norton series on interpersonal neurobiology. W.W. Norton.

Porges, S. W. (2015). Play as neural exercise: Insights from the polyvagal theory. In *The power of play for mind brain health* (pp. 3–7). Mindgains.org, GAINS.

Ray, D. C., Burgin, E., Gutierrez, D., Ceballos, P., & Lindo, N. (2022). Child-centered play therapy and adverse childhood experiences: A randomized controlled trial. *Journal of Counseling & Development, 100*(2), 134–145.

Rudolph, J. I., van Berkel, S. R., Zimmer-Gembeck, M. J., Walsh, K., Straker, D., & Campbell, T. (2023). Parental involvement in programs to prevent child sexual abuse: A systematic review of four decades of research. *Trauma, Violence, & Abuse, 25*(1), 560–576.

Schore, A. N. (2022). Attachment trauma and the developing right brain: Origins of pathological dissociation and some implications for psychotherapy. In J. O'Neil, M. Dorahy, & S. Gold (Eds.), *Dissociation and the dissociative disorders: Past, present, future* (pp. 177–208). Routledge.

Siegel, D. J., & Gottman, M. (2015). An interpersonal neurobiology approach to developmental trauma. In *Mindfulness-oriented interventions for trauma: Integrating contemplative practices* (pp. 210–226). Gilford Press.

Van der Westhuizen, M., Walker-Williams, H. J., & Fouché, A. (2023). Meaning making mechanisms in women survivors of childhood sexual abuse: A scoping review. *Trauma, Violence, & Abuse, 24*(3), 1363–1386.

VanMeter, F., Handley, E. D., & Cicchetti, D. (2020). The role of coping strategies in the pathway between child maltreatment and internalizing and externalizing behaviors. *Child Abuse & Neglect, 101*, 104323. https://doi.org/10.1016/j.chiabu.2019.104323

Part IV

Additional Considerations When Using Play Therapy With Sexually Abused Children and Adolescents

CHAPTER 20
INCORPORATING A MULTICULTURAL ORIENTATION IN PLAY THERAPY WITH VICTIMS OF CHILDHOOD SEXUAL ABUSE

Kadesha Adelakun and Erica Tatum-Sheade

Childhood sexual abuse (CSA) is a prevalent and persistent problem that reaches all aspects of society. The effects of CSA transcend all cultures and can be seen across all ethnic and racial groups, socioeconomic classes, and religious groups. One barrier to addressing CSA is that many reports of child sexual abuse go unreported, especially in minority communities. Disparities in access to culturally competent mental health care, cultural influences and norms, and cultural biases all contribute to the underreporting of these cases (Fontes & Plummer, 2010). CSA has short- and long-term emotional, physical, and mental consequences that require those treating victims to be aware of how this presents within and across areas of cultural diversity and how to best intervene from a lens that focuses on the unique cultural needs of the victim (Fontes & Plummer, 2010; Shuman, 2022).

This chapter will examine how to utilize a Multicultural Orientation (MCO) lens that can be applied across play therapy theories and modalities to effectively meet the needs of children and adolescents seeking services to address CSA. Play therapy, specifically when addressing CSA, is focused on creating space to build safety and healing for both the victim and their family (Shuman, 2022). We will examine the importance of cultural humility on the part of the practitioner, how to utilize cultural opportunities, and the cultural comfort level of practitioners. When practitioners of play therapy are focused on understanding an MCO when working with diverse populations, they are more likely to recognize cultural opportunities when they present themselves as well as understand which cultural aspects to engage with within treatment.

DOI: 10.4324/9781003451549-24

Defining Culture

In play therapy with victims of CSA, we often hear words such as culture, cultural, multicultural, and similar words, but what do the words mean? Is culture related to race? Ethnicity? Nationality? Religion? Sexual orientation? Socioeconomic status? Gender? All of the above? Culture encompasses all these variables and more.

Culture is the set of knowledge, behaviors, beliefs, values, and symbols shared and implemented by a large group of people. Culture is passed along by communication and learned behavior from one generation to the next and is generally considered to be the tradition of that people. By means of an example, in the culture of Trinidad and Tobago, and similarly in many other cultures of the Caribbean and West Indies, "jet beads" are traditionally given to newborn children to help protect them from evil, violent, or negative energies. In these cultures, one may also see adults wearing them for protection or to represent their cultural heritage. A naming ceremony is another example of culture that is practiced in many countries and religious communities. When a baby is born in Yoruba cultures, no one is told the baby's name until the naming ceremony when the baby is 8 days old. In the United States, families of mixed cultural backgrounds may observe specific cultural practices such as these. However, practitioners must remember that a person's cultural identity may differ, as people are individuals and may choose or not choose to observe ceremonies and traditions specific to their various cultural backgrounds.

Cultural Considerations in Play Therapy

When considering culture in play therapy, practitioners must also remember that culturally and historically, counseling and therapy were primarily developed through a White, Euro-American, Western, middle-class lens (Coleman et al., 1993). In conjunction with this, lack of representation, systemic racism, and a lack of trust in medical and mental health systems has resulted in fewer Black, Indigenous, and People of Color (BIPOC) clients in therapy when compared to White counterparts. Due to these barriers, BIPOC parents and children in therapy may be unfamiliar with the counseling or therapeutic process. They may not approve of or feel comfortable sharing sensitive information, such as CSA, to a stranger (i.e., counselor, therapist). When BIPOC victims of CSA do choose to tell an adult, they often prefer to tell an elder in their family or a religious leader (Coleman et al., 1993).

There are many cultures in which speaking of sexual matters is seen as taboo. This taboo may delay disclosing and reporting CSA. Research has shown that in some Latin, Arab, and East Indian cultures, there is a strong focus on "purity" and a lack of sex education. Thus, there is a delay in disclosure of CSA because survivors fear being disconnected from the larger group if they are seen as "unworthy" or "unclean" (Fontes & Plummer, 2010; Haboush & Alyan, 2013; Rueda et al., 2022). In cultures that hold strong traditional gender roles and strong beliefs about what masculinity and femininity are, it has been found that these beliefs interfere with males coming forward and disclosing sexual abuse, especially when the perpetrator is female. Research has also shown that, in addition to gender roles, especially in young Black males, they are more likely to be seen by their delinquent coping behavior versus being seen as needing therapeutic intervention (Fontes & Plummer, 2010; Josenhans et al., 2020)

In the Black American community, beliefs such as "Superwoman Syndrome" and the trope of the "strong black female" leave Black girls and women unable to disclose CSA because they carry the belief that they are supposed to be able to manage the emotional, physical, and mental toll of the abuse on their own. Other factors such as "adultification bias," where Black children are seen as older and more mature than their non-Black peers, may also come into play as authoritative figures and caregivers often see Black children as older, more sexual, and less in need of protection. This is especially for Black girls (Epstein et al., 2017; Fontes & Plummer, 2010). This can lead to a mistrust of the very systems designed to help these vulnerable clients.

Black, Native American, and Latino children are over-represented in the child welfare system and are more likely to receive care that is adversarial versus helpful (Fontes & Plummer, 2010; Josenhans et al., 2020; Ray et al., 2022). These children are also more likely to receive care from a practitioner who is of a different race than them because the vast majority of play therapists (estimated at over 68%) identify as White (Abrams et al., 2006; Fontes & Plummer, 2010; Hinman, 2003; Zippia, n.d.).

Among clients of minority cultures, reporting CSA is delayed or may not happen at all. While the outcome of how CSA is handled once disclosed may vary by culture, CSA does not discriminate and is found in most cultures, causing long-lasting effects (Fontes & Plummer, 2010). Some research has shown significant differences in disclosure when cultural influences are controlled for cultural while other findings have not. Some studies have shown that CSA victims in Hispanic and Latino cultures may be more likely to live with their perpetrator or have a perpetrator be a family member than non-Hispanic victims (Rueda et al., 2022; Runarsdottir et al., 2019; Shuman, 2022). Other studies have shown that girls from Hispanic and Latino cultures experience more CSA, waited longer to disclose, and were more likely to be abused by their fathers and stepfathers when compared with African American girls (Fontes & Plummer, 2010).

The cost of reporting CSA may also create a barrier or a concern for some victims, especially those who are BIPOC, immigrants, or low socioeconomic status. Being BIPOC and/or an immigrant or the child of an immigrant comes with another set of challenges including systemic racism and/or discrimination, disproportionate poverty, and fear of deportation. The realities of these fears may cause a victim of CSA to not disclose their sexual abuse.

Cultural Competency Versus Cultural Humility

Because of these limitations and the resultant lack of felt safety to disclose CSA, it is important for practitioners to understand cultural humility rather than trying to practice cultural competency. In other words, practicing cultural humility maybe more effective when working with people of marginalized cultures. Cultural competency implies that one has suitable or sufficient skill, knowledge, or experience regarding culture. However, one can never truly be sufficient or knowledgeable in someone else's culture. Cultural humility is the process of self-reflection and discovery to first understand oneself and then to understand others in a manner which builds honest and trustworthy relationships (Tervalon & Murray-Garcia, 1998). Cultural humility is a lifelong process that individuals consciously enter into with clients, colleagues, friends, and themselves.

Culture-Based Assessment and Treatment

When working with children and families impacted by CSA, one of the foundations of the treatment process is to explore culture, personal meanings, acculturation, and how culture plays a part in the client's current life (Gil & Drewes, 2021). This can be reflected by questions in the practitioner's intake forms (e.g., "Do you consider your faith and/or religion meaningful in your life?" "What is your ethnic or racial identity?" "Do you consider your sexual orientation as influential in your life?"). Other ways for the practitioner to explore a client's culture is to ask about special foods, music, family rituals, religious practices, and holidays (Gil & Drewes, 2021). Inquiring how the client and family typically manage challenges (i.e., prayer, meditation, talking to a faith-based leader or elder, music, rituals) is another important consideration in assessment and treatment of victims of CSA.

Clinicians who practice cultural humility and enter the ongoing, life-long practice of learning about different cultures and understanding their own culture and biases become more effective not only with clients of differing cultures but also with clients of similar cultures. Practitioners must always take culture (i.e., race, ethnicity, religion, socioeconomic status, gender) into account when assessing and providing treatment to sexually abused children, adolescents, and their families. In doing so, it is important to carefully select toys, books, and other images that represent diverse cultures, races, ethnicities, nationalities, religions, genders, sexual orientations, etc.

When selecting dolls or people figures for the playroom, it is important for the practitioner to choose items with ethnic features, not simply different skin tones. While having dolls and people of different skin tones is important, there are also certain features (e.g., eye shape and/or color and hair texture) that are more common among specific races. The practitioner must also consider having representation of dolls and people with diverse cultural apparel. When using crayons, markers, and paint, the best practice is to provide clients with colors that reflect different skin tones and shades. This should be taken into consideration with the books the practitioner uses for bibliotherapy as well as the games, toys, and even decorations in the playroom. Having a variety of toys and therapeutic materials in the playroom may allow clients to fully express the diversity of their own individual experiences of CSA.

Cultural Comfort

Those practitioners who move toward expressing cultural comfort are those for whom diversity and openness to multicultural expression have become second nature. Diversity in staff, education, training, supervision, and consultation from an MCO lens is a part of this shift. These things may help children, and their families feel more comfortable in the therapeutic setting, as well as with the therapist, to process CSA and express themselves more meaningfully.

There are also taboos around sexual activity or even speaking about sex, which may contribute to a child not disclosing, delaying disclosure, and processing CSA (Fontes & Plummer, 2010). In some cultures (e.g., religion, nationality, ethnicity, race), sex is not discussed or virginity for females is sacred. Due to the lack of conversations and shame of being "ruined" or no longer being "marriage material," many victims of CSA may not disclose their sexual abuse. Another barrier is the stereotype of being a "strong Black woman" and being able to manage whatever challenges or burdens come your way. This false narrative may cause a Black female to think there is no need to "complain" about their sexual abuse because they can or should be able to handle it or their ancestors experienced worse. While mainstream religion does not condone CSA, some religious communities may believe sexual abuse was their fate or has happened for some reason by God or that God would not allow them to experience something that they could not handle. In some religions, being a child bride is an acceptable practice. The same goes for the oppression of females.

There is not enough research and consistent findings in the research regarding cultural implications and disclosure of CSA. This includes studies on the relationship between economic status and sexual abuse. Some studies have found poverty to be a risk factor for CSA, while others have not (Runarsdottir et al., 2019). Disclosure and the role of the therapist may be dependent on the cultural values and family's position within society as well as fear of judgment, shame, and other responses (Fontes & Plummer, 2010). While no culture is monolithic, it is important to understand that the cultural values held closely by clients and families may create barriers to disclosure and treatment of CSA.

Moving Toward a Multicultural Orientation in Play Therapy

Multicultural Orientation stems from work done by Derald Wing Sue and colleagues in the early 1980s (Sue et al., 1982). These researchers are credited with developing "Multicultural Competencies" focusing on a therapist's self-awareness, knowledge for working with diverse populations, and the ability to develop skills to help clients within the therapeutic space (Hook et al., 2017; Sue et al., 1982). MCO focuses not only on how the practitioner thinks about utilizing diversity and competency in therapy space but also on how they value diversity and taking opportunities to explore a client's culture. This includes the practitioner's comfort level in addressing cultural nuances both in session and out of session. MCO focuses on moving away from a way of *doing* culturally competent or humble therapy into a way of being in the therapy space, focusing on embracing and even celebrating culture (Hook et al., 2017). Over time, the practitioner with an MCO learns to include culture with every client as a part of who that client is in the world, not simply addressing culture only when the client presents an aspect that differs from the dominant culture.

It is also important for the multiculturally oriented practitioner to be aware of their own limitations, communicate these to clients and their families, and refer out when needed. While it is important to learn these things and to know how they play a role in the lives of the children and families that the practitioner is working with, it is even more important for the individual practitioner to seek their own learning (e.g., training, classes, workshops, books, consultation, supervision, attend local events and activities). It is never the client or their family's responsibility to be the "cultural guide," spending time during treatment teaching the practitioner the basics about the client's or family's culture. It is always the practitioner's responsibility to learn, grow, and change in their cultural understanding and awareness, leading to the development of an MCO.

MCO and Childhood Sexual Abuse

Embracing an MCO lens when working with victims of CSA from diverse populations allows play therapists to engage at a deeper level, providing better therapy outcomes (Ogawa et al., 2022). Understanding how cultural influences factor into the disclosure and treatment of CSA for clients and families within underrepresented cultural minority groups not only helps in the assessment process but also gives play therapists the tools needed to aid those impacted by CSA.

Conclusion

We have seen that culture can be difficult to define. Ray et al. (2022) point out that a child may see their culture as one thing, while the parent may have a different view and the play therapist a third. It is important for a play therapist not to assume anything when engaging with clients and families who have experienced CSA. When focusing on cultural diversity to address CSA, the practitioner must understand the underlying cultural influences that enter the room with a child and how the practitioner's own identity comes into play when interacting with clients (Ray et al., 2022). It is important for play therapists working with victims of CSA to pay attention to themes that appear in the playroom, including cultural themes that emerge, which may provide insight for the play therapist. Understanding how culture and ethnic identity show up in the playroom and influence how a child may or may not disclose childhood sexual abuse are key factors for play therapists to consider (Hinman, 2003). This includes not just taking what the therapist has learned from the client directly but also information the therapist has gained from self-awareness and knowledge they have gained from engaging with diverse populations (Hook et al., 2017; Hinman, 2003)

From an MCO lens, understanding the impact of historical trauma, cultural influences, and bias may increase practitioner insight into themes that emerge in the playroom (Hinman, 2003). Incorporating cultural beliefs into the therapeutic process returns power to a client who has experienced CSA, creates a sense of safety, and facilitates rapport. An MCO lens is beneficial when used appropriately by the therapist and is free of stereotyping; meaning the therapist must go beyond basic knowledge and truly incorporate an MCO lens within their practice. Utilizing and recognizing cultural strengths and interweaving those practices into the therapeutic space fosters improved outcomes for those impacted by CSA (Fontes & Plummer, 2010; Hinman, 2003; Shuman, 2022).

Considerations for Practice/Key Takeaways

- Culture encompasses more than race and ethnicity. It includes religious beliefs, sexual orientation, socioeconomic status, and other variables. Each of these factors can influence the disclosure and treatment of CSA. Cultural groups are not monolithic. Even though those who belong to the same group may share a cultural history, issues like acculturation, immigration status, and location may influence how one identifies culturally.
- A practitioner's own cultural identity and perceived cultural identity come into play when addressing cultural issues in the playroom.

- When working with victims of CSA, a practitioner needs to understand cultural influences may interfere with how and when disclosure of CSA occurs.
- Incorporating an MCO lens when working with those impacted by CSA goes beyond just including culturally diverse items in the playroom. It includes understanding the nuances of clients' cultural language in their play and the cultural influences that enter the room with them.

References

Abrams, L., Post, P., Algozzine, B., Miller, T., Ryan, S., Gomory, T., & Cooper, J. B. (2006). Clinical experiences of play therapists: Does race/ethnicity matter? *International Journal of Play Therapy, 15*(2), 11–34. https://doi.org/10.1037/h0088913

Coleman, V. D., Parmer, T., & Barker, S. A. (1993). Play therapy for multicultural populations: Guidelines for mental health professionals. *International Journal of Play Therapy, 2*(1), 63–74.

Epstein, R., Blake, J. J., & González, T. (2017). *Girlhood interrupted: The erasure of Black girls' childhood.* Georgetown Law Center on Poverty and Inequality. https://papers.ssrn.com/sol3/papers.cfm?abstract_id=3000695

Fontes, L. A., & Plummer, C. (2010). Cultural issues in disclosures of child sexual abuse. *Journal of Child Sexual Abuse, 19*(5), 491–518. https://doi.org/10.1080/10538712.2010.512520

Gil, E., & Drewes, A. A. (2021). Redefining and broadening the definition of culture. In E. Gil & A. A. Drewes (Eds.), *Cultural issues in play therapy* (2nd ed., pp. 1–11). The Guilford Press.

Haboush, K. L., & Alyan, H. (2013). "Who can you tell?" Features of Arab culture that influence conceptualization and treatment of childhood sexual abuse. *Journal of Child Sexual Abuse, 22*(5), 499–518. https://doi.org/10.1080/10538712.2013.800935

Hinman, C. (2003). Multicultural considerations in the delivery of play therapy services. *International Journal of Play Therapy, 12*(2), 107–122. https://doi.org/10.1037/h0088881

Hook, J. N., Davis, D., Owen, J., & DeBlaere, C. (2017). *Cultural humility: Engaging diverse identities in therapy.* American Psychological Association. https://doi.org/10.1037/0000037-000

Josenhans, V., Kavenagh, M., Smith, S., & Wekerle, C. (2020). Gender, rights, and responsibilities: The need for a global analysis of the sexual exploitation of boys. *Child Abuse & Neglect, 110*, 104291. https://doi.org/10.1016/j.chiabu.2019.104291

Ogawa, Y., Cheng, Y.-J., & Ray, D. C. (2022). Cultural opportunities and comfort in play therapy. In D. C. Ray, Y. Ogawa, & Y.-J. Cheng (Eds.), *Multicultural play therapy: Making the most of cultural opportunities with children* (pp. 29–43). Routledge.

Ray, D. C., Ogawa, Y., & Cheng, Y.-J. (Eds.). (2022). *Multicultural play therapy: Making the most of cultural opportunities with children*. Routledge.

Rueda, P., Ferragut, M., Cerezo, M. V., & Ortiz-Tallo, M. (2022). Knowledge and myths about child sexual abuse in Mexican women. *Journal of Interpersonal Violence*, *37*(13–14), NP11743–NP11760. https://doi.org/10.1177/0886260521993927

Runarsdottir, E., Smith, E., & Arnarsson, A. (2019). The effects of gender and family wealth on sexual abuse of adolescents. *International Journal of Environmental Research and Public Health*, *16*(10), 1788. https://doi.org/10.3390/ijerph16101788

Shuman, T. (2022). Intervention strategies for promoting recovery and healing from child sexual abuse. In E. Kalfoğlu & S. Kalfoglou (Eds.), *Sexual abuse: An interdisciplinary approach* (pp. 1–11). Intech Open. https://doi.org/10.5772/intechopen.97106

Sue, D. W., Bernier, J. E., Durran, A., Feinberg, L., Pedersen, P., Smith, E. J., & Vasquez-Nuttall, E. (1982). Position paper: Cross-cultural counseling competencies. *The Counseling Psychologist*, *10*(2), 45–52. https://doi.org/10.1177/0011000082102008

Tervalon, M., & Murray-Garcia, J. (1998). Cultural humility versus cultural competence: A critical distinction in defining physician training outcomes in multicultural education. *Journal of Health Care for the Poor and Underserved*, *9*(2), 117–125.

Zippia. (n.d.). *Play therapist demographics and statistics in the US*. Author. https://www.zippia.com/play-therapist-jobs/demographics/

Chapter 21
Ethical Considerations in Play Therapy With Sexually Abused Children and Adolescents

Jeffrey S. Ashby and H.M. Cowart

Play therapy with child and adolescent clients who have experienced childhood sexual abuse (CSA) poses a number of discrete ethical challenges to the practitioner. While all of the primary ethical constructs of mental health practice apply (e.g., informed consent, confidentiality), specific challenges in the area of competence arise in working with clients who have experienced sexual abuse. This chapter is not meant to be an exhaustive account of ethical concerns; however, it will highlight notable challenges and offer some basic guidelines (e.g., "stay in your lane") to assist the play therapist in doing this important work ethically.

Competence Defined: "Can I Even Do This Work?"

Play therapy is considered a secondary profession or a specialized area in one's primary professional identity as a counselor, social worker, psychologist, or marriage and family therapist. As a result, each play therapist has a primary obligation to abide by the ethical codes of their profession. Because play therapy is considered a secondary professional identity, there are no play therapy-specific ethical codes. However, the Association for Play Therapy (APT) has published practice guidelines (2022) that include an extension of traditional ethical codes' tenets to play therapy. Consistent with the ethical codes of primary professions (e.g., American Counseling Association, 2014), the APT practice guidelines state, "Play therapists must only practice within the scope of their competence" (p. 14). Fairburn and Cooper (2011) defined therapist competence as "the extent to which a therapist has the knowledge and skill required to deliver a treatment to the standard needed for it to achieve its expected effects" (p. 375). The APT guidelines state that this knowledge and skill is gained through appropriate training, relevant supervised experience, holding primary credentials (e.g., state licensure), and professional experience.

An important challenge in determining competence is that there are no specific guidelines for knowing when one has achieved sufficient competence. In the United States, practicing therapy without a license is typically a violation of state law (e.g., Practicing Without a License, 2023). As a result, acquiring an appropriate license (e.g., Licensed Professional Counselor) in one's primary profession is an essential component of developing competence. Once licensed, each profession has a scope of practice associated with the license. This scope of practice, which can include treatment, evaluation, consultation, and other roles, establishes parameters for the areas in which a licensed professional can legally practice. However, just because one could legally do the work within the scope of practice of one's license, this does not, in itself, establish competence across the entire scope of practice. In fact, it is highly unlikely that a person would be competent across all areas of their scope of practice and, as a result, the scope of practice simply outlines areas of potential competence.

Within the scope of practice of one's primary credential (e.g., Licensed Clinical Social Worker), competence is generally understood to be established by two components: knowledge and ability to apply skills. Cooper et al. (2017) note that knowledge can be assessed by determining what the therapist knows about the treatment, including specifics about the intervention, the cultural and demographic background of the client, and how and when to use specific strategies and interventions. The second component involves the therapist's ability to apply their knowledge skillfully in practice. Ashby et al. (in press) translate these concepts into the more concrete categories of formal didactic training (e.g., courses in graduate school) and supervised experience (e.g., pre- and post-licensed, supervised experience by someone competent in the area of practice). Ultimately, prior to providing services to children and adolescents who have been sexually abused, all play therapists must assess their knowledge and abilities by considering the primary question: Am I competent to do *this specific work*? That is, do I have the appropriate training and supervision to provide these services independently without supervision or other oversight?

Roles Defined: "Stay in My Lane? What Lane Am I In?"

One relatively unique ethical challenge for play therapists working with children and adolescents who have experienced sexual abuse is the identification of the play therapist's specific role. There are two primary roles a play therapist can serve in working with this population. One is the treating clinician, working with the child or adolescent to address issues, symptoms, and concerns related to the play therapy client's experience. The second role is forensic evaluator, to determine if a child or adolescent has experienced sexual abuse and, if so, in what form, for how long, and by whom. Because these roles have different functions and require different competencies, the identification and delineation of these roles are paramount in determining competence and practicing ethically.

When clearly defined, the play therapist role of forensic evaluator is distinct from the role of treating clinician and involves the elicitation of as much reliable information as possible from the child to determine whether sexual abuse occurred. Practice guidelines (e.g., APSAC Taskforce, 2023) highlight the tensions between eliciting information about specific facts that can be verified by other aspects of an investigation, minimizing any potential trauma to the child or adolescent, and considering all reasonable explanations for any allegations. To this end, the play therapist who is serving as a forensic evaluator may ultimately inform the legal system by collecting data using forensic interviews, psychological testing, and reviews of records. They may also summarize and integrate this material with relevant findings from social science research (Herman, 2005). There is a general consensus that this role requires specialized training and supervision, as a number of reviews have noted the potential errors and forms of bias that may impact this practice (e.g., O'Donohue & Cirlugea, 2021). As Gino et al. (2020) note, "the competence of personnel who come into contact with the abused person in conducting the examination and collecting evidence is of fundamental importance" (p. 2).

Distinct from the role of forensic evaluator, the play therapist may work with a child or adolescent who has experienced childhood sexual abuse, as a treating clinician. This is a role more familiar to most play therapists and an area where they are likely to have a greater degree of competence, as it is more consistent with the general training for the primary professions of play therapists (e.g., counselor and social worker).

Despite its importance, this delineation of roles may be obscured by the nature of work as a play therapist. Most play therapists have not had training in forensic interviewing and evaluation, as it is not a standard part of accredited training in mental health fields (e.g., Council for the Accreditation of Counseling and Related Educational Programs, 2024) or included in the APT practice guidelines (Association of Play Therapy, 2022). As a result, relatively few will intentionally take on the role of forensic evaluator without specialized training. However, because there is no single symptom, syndrome, or diagnosis associated with the experience of child abuse (e.g., van den Heuvel & Seedat, 2013) and because the experience of childhood sexual abuse is often characterized by a lack of eye witnesses, secrets, threats, withdrawals, and other aspects (Schaefer et al., 2018) and limited physical or biological evidence (Joki-Erkkila et al., 2014), play therapists may begin treatment of clients before there is a finding of sexual abuse. Either because of client behaviors consistent with the experience of sexual abuse (e.g., inappropriate sexualized behaviors; Friedrich et al., 2001) or allegations made in the child or adolescent client's life, the play therapist may find themselves in the role of a treating clinician who can also provide information that may be helpful in a forensic evaluation. Because parents, concerned others, and sometimes the court may view the treating play therapist as having insight and expertise that would be helpful in making a determination of sexual abuse, play therapists can find themselves in a conflation of roles that can include aspects of forensic evaluation.

Poorly delineated roles can cause significant conflict due to the roles' competing priorities. The treating clinician's priority is to facilitate the client's well-being, whereas the forensic evaluator's priority is more complex. While the play therapist who is acting as forensic evaluator does not want to undermine the well-being of the client in any way, the primary goal is to gather the appropriate information to determine whether sexual abuse has occurred. This goal could lead to situations in which a forensic evaluator would make ethical and practice decisions that conflict with those that would be made by a treating clinician. The nature of the relationship between the child or adolescent client and the clinician would also necessarily differ as a result of these potentially conflicting priorities.

Once a play therapist clearly identifies their role, they must also make efforts to avoid allowing roles to be obscured by external entities. The most likely scenario is for the treating play therapist to be drawn into a situation where they are asked to give opinions about whether abuse has occurred, the extent of the abuse, the identity of the perpetrator, etc. Despite not identifying as a forensic evaluator nor claiming competence in the area, it is not unusual for play therapists to find themselves being asked questions that go beyond their scope of treatment as a treating clinician and into the domain of forensic evaluation. While legal issues are beyond the scope of this chapter, it is important to acknowledge that it is particularly important to outline in informed consent what one's role is clearly and to "stay in your lane" by fulfilling that role in treatment, assessment, documentation, and any interactions with the legal system.

Determining Competence: "How Much Training and Supervision Is Enough?"

The mandate to practice only within the boundaries of competence is clearly documented in the ethical codes of all mental health professions. For instance, the Code of Ethics for the National Association of Social Workers (NASW) states, "Social workers should provide services and represent themselves as competent only within the boundaries of their education, training, license, certification, consultation received, supervised experience, or other relevant professional experience" (National Association of Social Workers, 2021, Section 1.04). The assessment of competent practice differs considerably across the two potential roles of forensic evaluator and treating play therapist, with different training, supervised experience, and secondary credentialing.

The role of forensic evaluator is recognized as a specialty practice with specialty guidelines from the American Psychological Association (2013) and prominent secondary credentials (e.g., Clinical Mental Health Counseling Specialist in Forensic Evaluation, American Mental Health Counselors Association, 2023) requiring specific training, experience, and supervision. As a result, and because forensic training is outside the scope of traditional training in most play therapists' primary training, the burden is on the play therapist to show that they have developed the competence to do this work ethically. Play therapists serving as forensic evaluators for clients who may have experienced sexual abuse would be best served by abiding by the guidelines offered by their respective fields and maintaining documentation of the steps they have taken to obtain training, experience, and appropriate supervision.

Assessing competence as a treating play therapist is a multilayered process as there are several domains to assess and competence, within the scope of one's license, is generally self-determined (Ashby et al., in press). The first domain to assess is the competence to provide play therapy interventions. Play therapists have most often been trained as generalists and many complete their graduate training with limited focus on children and play interventions. Turner et al. (2020) note that play therapy competence requires "specialized knowledge and skills for effective practice" (p. 177). As a result, at minimum, clinicians practicing as play therapists would need to show a minimum level of academic and professional training and supervised experience in play therapy (Pope et al., 2021). While not a certification of competence, meeting the requirements to be a Registered Play Therapist (Association for Play Therapy, n.d.) is a way clinicians can "demonstrate their play therapy competency to the general public, parents, and other mental health professionals."

The second domain in the assessment of competence in the role of play therapy involves one's multicultural orientation. The National Association of Social Workers (NASW) ethical code indicates, "Social workers should demonstrate knowledge that guides practice with clients of various cultures and be able to demonstrate skills in the provision of culturally informed services that empower marginalized individuals and groups" (National Association of Social Workers, Standard 1.05-B, 2021). Before treating a client who has experienced sexual abuse, the play therapist will need to assess their multicultural orientation and cultural humility (e.g., Watkins et al., 2019) and whether they are competent to make appropriate cultural adaptations to best meet the needs of the client (Sorenson & Harrell, 2021).

The third domain in the assessment of the play therapist's competence in working with clients who have experienced childhood sexual abuse is in their ability to treat the presenting issues effectively. A number of studies have found that child and adolescent clients who have experienced sexual abuse may present with attention problems, posttraumatic stress disorder (PTSD), and depression (e.g., Strathearn et al., 2020). The play therapist treating clients who have experienced sexual abuse will need to assess whether they have the appropriate level of training and supervised experience to treat the presenting issues at their level of severity. In addition, it is important for the play therapist to assess whether they are competent to treat these issues in the complex context of sexual abuse with the related disruptions in attachment and violations of trust inherent in these experiences (Ensink et al., 2020).

Emotional Competence: "How Do I Know If I Can Continue This Hard Work?"

This chapter thus far has focused primarily on establishing the intellectual competence to ethically provide services to children and adolescents who have experienced childhood sexual abuse. However, Koocher and Keith-Spiegel (2016) highlight the interdependent nature of intellectual competence and emotional competence. They note that most of our ethical discussions and decision making are based on the construct of intellectual competence, involving training and knowledge acquisition, along with supervision of clinical practice applying that knowledge. As a compliment to intellectual competence, the authors define emotional competence as a therapist's "ability to emotionally contain and tolerate the clinical material that emerges in treatment . . . and their capacity for self-care in the context of the difficult work of psychotherapy" (p. 2016).

While there is a growing awareness of the value and importance of self-care for therapists across areas of practice (e.g., Posluns & Gall, 2020), given the often difficult clinical material that arises when play therapists treat clients who have experienced CSA, there is likely to be a greater threat to emotional competence for play therapists in this setting. This is consistent with a number of studies that have documented the development of stress-related conditions, including burnout, secondary traumatic stress, vicarious traumatization, and compassion fatigue in clinicians working with clients who have experienced traumas like sexual abuse (e.g., Shepherd & Newell, 2020). For play therapists to ethically treat clients who have experienced child abuse, they will need to consistently monitor their emotional competence and take ongoing steps to engage in self-care as well as ongoing professional consultation and support.

Conclusion

Play therapy has been shown to be an effective treatment for children and adolescents who have experienced childhood sexual abuse (Reyes & Asbrand, 2005). Working with this population requires attention to ethical challenges as well as intellectual and emotional competence over and above that required by one's primary credential. With no specific guidelines for these requirements, each play therapist is responsible for assessing their own appropriateness for this important work. It is our hope that this chapter will further enable play therapists to ethically prepare for, and engage in, work with this population.

Considerations for Practice: Key Takeaways

- Play therapy competence in working with children and adolescents who have been sexually abused is best supported through formal didactic training and supervised experience.

- It is important to distinguish between the roles of forensic evaluator and treating clinicians when a play therapist is working with children and adolescents who have been sexually abused.
- Working with clients who have experienced sexual abuse may put an inordinate strain on the emotional competence of the play therapist given the difficult clinical material that may arise.

References

American Counseling Association. (2014). *2014 ACA code of ethics.* https://www.counseling.org/docs/default-source/default-document-library/2014-code-of-ethics-finaladdress.pdf

American Mental Health Counselors Association. (2023). *Certification – clinical mental health counseling specialist in forensic evaluation.* https://www.amhca.org/members/career/credential/apply/forensicevalutation

American Psychological Association. (2013). Specialty guidelines for forensic psychology. *American Psychologist, 68*(1), 7–19. https://doi.org/10.1037/a0029889.

APSAC Taskforce. (2023). *Forensic interviewing of children.* The American Professional Society on the Abuse of Children. https://www.apsac.org/guidelines

Ashby, J. S., McKinney-Clark, K., & van Nuenen, M. (in press). Ethics in play therapy. In D. Crenshaw, D. Ray, & A. Stewart (Eds.), *Play therapy: A comprehensive guide to theory and practice* (2nd ed., pp. 32–47). Guilford Press.

Association for Play Therapy. (2022). *Play therapy best practices.* https://cdn.ymaws.com/www.a4pt.org/resource/resmgr/publications/best_practices.pdf

Association for Play Therapy. (n.d.). *Play therapy credentials.* Retrieved January 25, 2025, from https://www.a4pt.org/page/CredentialsInfo

Cooper, Z., Doll, H., Bailey-Straebler, S., Bohn, K., de Vries, D., Murphy, R., O'Connor, M. E., & Fairburn, C. G. (2017). Assessing therapist competence: Development of a performance-based measure and its comparison with a web-based measure. *JMIR Mental Health, 4*(4), e51. https://doi.org/10.2196/mental.7704

Council for Accreditation of Counseling and Related Educational Programs. (2024). *2024 CACREP standards.* https://www.cacrep.org/wp-content/uploads/2023/06/2024-Standards-Combined-Version-6.27.23.pdf

Ensink, K., Borelli, J. L., Normandin, L., Target, M., & Fonagy, P. (2020). Childhood sexual abuse and attachment insecurity: Associations with child psychological difficulties. *American Journal of Orthopsychiatry, 90*(1), 115–124.

Fairburn, C. G., & Cooper, Z. (2011). Therapist competence, therapy quality, and therapist training. *Behaviour Research and Therapy, 49*(6–7), 373–378. https://doi.org/10.1016/j.brat.2011.03.005

Friedrich, W. N., Fisher, J. L., Dittner, C. A., Acton, R., Berliner, L., Butler, J., & Wright, J. (2001). Child sexual behavior inventory: Normative, psychiatric, and sexual abuse comparisons. *Child Maltreatment, 6*(1), 37–49. https://doi.org/10.1177/1077559501006001004

Gino, S., Bo, M., Ricciardelli, R., Alu, M., Boschi, I., Carnevali, E., Fabbri, M., Fattorini, P., Piccinini, A., Previdere, C., Verzeletti, A., Tozzo, P., & Caenazzo, L. (2020).

Evaluation of critical aspects in clinical and forensic management of sexual violence: A multicentre GeF.I. project. *Forensic Science International, 314*, 1–7. https://doi.org/10.1016/j.forsciint.2020.110387

Herman, S. (2005). Improving decision making in forensic child sexual abuse evaluations. *Law and Human Behavior, 29*(1), 87–120. https://doi.org/10.1007/s10979-005-1400-8

Joki-Erkkila, M., Niemi, J., & Ellonen, N. (2014). Child sexual abuse – Medical statement conclusions in criminal legal process. *Forensic Science International, 239*, 31–36. https://doi.org/10.1016/j.forsciint.2014.03.006

Koocher, G. P., & Keith-Spiegel, P. (2016). *Ethics in psychology and the mental health professions* (4th ed.). Oxford University Press.

National Association of Social Workers. (NASW). (2021). *Code of ethics*. https://www.socialworkers.org/About/Ethics/Code-of-Ethics/Code-of-Ethics-English

O'Donohue, W., & Cirlugea, O. (2021). Controlling for confirmation bias in child sexual abuse interviews. *The Journal of the American Academy of Psychiatry and the Law, 49*(3), 371–380.

Pope, K. S., Vasquez, M. J. T., Chavez-Dueñas, N. Y., & Adames, H. Y. (2021). *Ethics in psychotherapy and counseling: A practical guide* (6th ed.). Wiley.

Posluns, K., & Gall, T. L. (2020). Dear mental health practitioners, take care of yourselves: A literature review on self-care. *International Journal for the Advancement of Counseling, 42*(1), 1–20.

Practicing without a License, GA Code § 43-39-7 (2023). https://law.justia.com/codes/georgia/title-43/chapter-39/article-1/section-43-39-7/

Reyes, C. J., & Asbrand, J. P. (2005). A longitudinal study assessing trauma symptoms in sexually abused children engaged in play therapy. *International Journal of Play Therapy, 14*(2), 25–47.

Schaefer, L. S., Brunnet, A. E., Lobo, B. D. O. M., Carvalho, J. C. N., & Kristensen, C. H. (2018). Psychological and behavioral indicators in the forensic assessment of child sexual abuse. *Trends in Psychology, 26*, 1467–1482.

Shepherd, M. A., & Newell, J. M. (2020). Stress and health in social workers: Implications for self-care practice. *Best Practices in Mental Health, 16*(1), 46–65.

Sorenson, C., & Harrell, S. P. (2021). Development and testing of the 4-domain cultural adaptation model (CAM4). *Professional Psychology: Research and Practice, 52*(3), 250–259.

Strathearn, L., Giannotti, M., Mills, R., Kisely, S., Najman, J., & Abajobir, A. (2020). Long-term cognitive, psychological, and health outcomes associated with child abuse and neglect. *Pediatrics, 146*(4), 1–15.

Turner, R., Schoeneberg, C., Ray, D., & Lin, Y. W. (2020). Establishing play therapy competencies: A Delphi study. *International Journal of Play Therapy, 29*(4), 177–190.

van den Heuvel, L., & Seedat, S. (2013). Screening and diagnostic considerations in childhood posttraumatic stress disorder. *Neuropsychiatry, 3*(5), 497–511. https://doi.org/10.2217/npy.13.61

Watkins, C. E., Hook, J. N., Owen, J., DeBlaere, C., Davis, D. E., & Van Tongeren, D. R. (2019). Multicultural orientation in psychotherapy supervision: Cultural humility, cultural comfort, and cultural opportunities. *American Journal of Psychotherapy, 72*, 38–46. https://doi.org/10.1176/appi.psychotherapy.20180040

Chapter 22
Secondary Traumatic Stress Stewardship
The Practice of Bearing Light

Janine Shelby

Child-focused therapists often describe their work as enormously gratifying. This sense of fulfillment is derived not only from positive treatment outcomes and enjoyment of interacting with children, but also from the deep sense of purpose and meaning many child-focused therapists associate with their work. Paradoxically, the intensely rewarding work of helping children heal and grow can also be the source of therapists' own suffering. Children's innocence and vulnerability can evoke poignant reactions among helping professionals, particularly when therapists learn of appalling events that befall some children. This includes childhood sexual abuse (CSA). Also, therapists' great empathy for their young clients may lead to rumination about the children's suffering long after the sessions have ended, and therapists may develop distorted views about safety and benevolence in the world. Further, therapists' unprocessed emotions related to their families of origin can be rekindled when working with families who have unhealthy – but familiar – interpersonal dynamics. It can be particularly upsetting for therapists with personal histories of child maltreatment to have their own dormant memories roused when working with maltreated youth. At times, some therapists find themselves inflicted with posttraumatic symptoms based on the experiences of their young clients. All of these experiences can constrain therapists' clinical effectiveness, enjoyment of life, and connection to others, though they also create opportunities for positive growth.

To reduce the risk of unwanted outcomes from secondary trauma exposure, it is essential for child-focused therapists to develop sound *trauma stewardship* (van Dernoot Lipsky, 2009), which involves the acknowledgment that "both joy and pain are realities of life, and that suffering can be transformed into meaningful growth and healing when a quality of

DOI: 10.4324/9781003451549-26

presence is cultivated and maintained, even in the face of great suffering" (p. 11). This chapter is written to support the work of child-focused therapists. In the chapter, secondary traumatic stress (STS) and related concepts are summarized, the phenomenon called posttraumatic growth (PTG) is described, STS intervention research is presented, and eight field-tested, practical methods to enhance secondary trauma stewardship are rendered.

Secondary Traumatic Stress (STS)

Across the last three decades, there has been increasing recognition that occupational exposure to suffering individuals may lead to adverse reactions among helping professionals (Elwood et al., 2011; Figley, 1995; Mitchell, 1983; Pearlman & Saakvitne, 1995). Although there is widespread agreement that such adverse reactions may occur, these reactions have been variously described in the literature with overlapping terms such as compassion fatigue, vicarious traumatization, and STS. The term STS has been used to denote distress/impairment and PTSD symptoms as a result of exposure to the suffering of others. STS may occur either abruptly or across time. A different term, burnout, has been used to describe a somewhat related phenomenon, but burnout is generally considered to be a cumulative reaction to occupational stressors and is not necessarily the result of indirect trauma exposure.

Prevalence/Incidence Rates and Risk Factors

Prevalence and incidence studies have yielded varied STS rates, from single digit percentages (e.g., [8%] Kintzle et al., 2013) to a majority of respondents (e.g., [92%]; Bride et al., 2007). According to the National Child Traumatic Stress Network (2011) 6% to 26% of therapists working with traumatized populations and up to 50% of child welfare workers are at high risk for STS, PTSD, or vicarious trauma. It is important to note that not all STS reactions constitute PTSD. Many STS reactions are expected, transient, and normative (i.e., part of the ebb and flow of therapists' lives). In fact, distress or subthreshold PTSD symptoms are more common than the development of full PTSD (Bride et al., 2007; Whitt-Woosley & Sprang, 2018).

Risk factors for STS remain poorly understood, and findings are sometimes contradictory (e.g., personal history of trauma exposure has been found to be both highly related and unrelated to STS; and years of

professional experience have been correlated both positively and negatively with STS). Although research in this area is in its infancy, commonly cited risk factors include the following: (a) *organizational factors:*
organizational culture or perceived lack of organizational support; (*b*)
work-related contributors: frequency or ratio (i.e., the proportion of
trauma-related to non-trauma-focused work) of trauma-related exposure, years of experience, or caseloads involving high acuity, complexity,
or dangerousness; (c) *training and supervision variables:* lack of formal
trauma training, absence of trauma-informed supervision, underutiliza-
tion of evidence-based treatments; and (d) *individual variables:* personal
trauma history or use of maladaptive coping skills.

Overview of STS Research and Guidelines

Review articles of STS-related interventions have yielded scant conclusions, both due to the absence of a uniform conceptual definition and the
paucity of rigorously conducted research. A large review of STS interventions based on over 4,000 citations, 159 full-text reports, and two studies
resulted in *no* studies meeting the research eligibility criteria (Bercier &
Maynard, 2015). In a later review, 27 studies of the 1,315 citations found
in the literature met study inclusion criteria (Kim et al., 2022). They were
categorized as follows: (a) psychoeducation; (b) mindfulness; (c) art and
recreational programs; and (d) alternative medicine practices (e.g., acu-
puncture or Reiki). All of these interventions showed promising results,
including a reduction in STS and related phenomena, but the authors
noted methodological shortcomings in much of the STS intervention
literature. A third review resulted in nine of 127 reviewed studies meeting the methodological criteria (Potocky & Guskovict, 2020). Findings
included both organizational and individual interventions. Organizational
best practices were identified as follows: (a) improved work schedules; (b)
lower caseloads; (c) more diverse caseloads; (d) job rotation; (e) organizational support; (f) improved work environment; (g) collegial support;
and (h) teambuilding. Individual best practice interventions included
the following: (a) psychoeducation about stress, trauma, and STS; (b)
stress management training; (c) debriefing and communication skills; (d)
relaxation and mindfulness; (e) coping strategies; (f) social support; (g)
counseling; and (h) resiliency training. Based on subsequent interviews
with managers, six overarching themes believed to be helpful in addressing STS within organizations were identified as follows: (a) leadership; (b)

TABLE 22.1 STS Intervention Guidelines

Individual Principles	Organizational Principles
Awareness of STS risks and knowledge about mitigation strategies	Provides evidence-based, culturally responsive STS training
Development and maintenance of a well-being ideology related to the helping role	Nurtures a culture of psychological safety, team support, and respect for personal boundaries
Awareness of personal strengths and vulnerabilities to STS	Design workloads to mitigate secondary trauma exposure
Use of strategies to promote well-being	Demonstrates commitment to workforce's well-being, through policies and practices
Use of strategies to remain within a zone of tolerance during exposure and recovery	Offer trauma-informed supervision
Discussion of thoughts and feelings related to secondary trauma exposure with a collaborative workplace team	Model secondary trauma-responsive leadership behaviors
Responsibility for recognizing the need for and accessing counseling or other external support services	Prioritize workforce wellness

Note: Adapted from "Principles for secondary traumatic stress-responsive practice: An expert consensus approach," by B.E. Bride, G. Sprang, A. Hendricks, C.R. Walsh, F. Mathieu, K. Hangartner, L.A. Ross, P. Fisher, & B.C. Miller, 2024, *Psychological trauma: Theory, research, practice, and policy, 16(8)*, 1301–1308 (*https://doi.org/10.1037/tra0001575*). Copyright 2024 by the American Psychological Association.

workload; (c) physical space; (d) proactive supervision; (e) peer support; and (f) individualized approaches (e.g., developing specific coping plans based on individual needs).

Although not derived from a research study, recent expert consensus research led to a set of principles for best practice STS interventions (Bride et al., 2024). The seven principles outlined in this article include both individual and associated organizational issues, as depicted in Table 22.1.

Posttraumatic Growth

For decades, clinicians and authors have noticed that individuals who experience adversity (e.g., surviving crimes, natural disaster, life-threatening illness, or having seriously ill children) often describe emotional growth as a positive outcome of dealing with their difficulties. This phenomenon, *Posttraumatic Growth* (PTG), was explored in the development of a questionnaire to measure PTG (Tedeschi & Calhoun, 1996). Tedeschi and Calhoun (2004) defined the five domains of PTF as follows: (a) increased appreciation for life (e.g., greater appreciation for existence, changes in priorities, or an increased sense of living life to the fullest); (b) more meaningful interpersonal relationships (e.g., development of closer relationships, realization of how important one's relationships are, self-protection from unhealthy relationships, or greater use of social support); (c) increased sense of personal strength (e.g., greater self-reliance, appreciation of one's inner strength, and acceptance); (d) changed priorities (e.g., making needed changes, developing new interests, or shifting one's life in a more positive direction); and (e) a richer existential or spiritual life (e.g., strengthening of religious beliefs or developing realizations about the meaning of life).

In addition to several other studies that have found a relationship between STS and PTG, my colleagues and I (Tominaga et al., 2019), published a study of 230 mental health clinicians who participated in a disaster relief mission following the Tohoku earthquake and tsunami disaster in Japan. We found that one-fifth of clinicians reported clinically significant PTSD symptoms immediately following their deployment, but 97% of these interventionists no longer met criteria for PTSD two months later. Remarkably, the severity of intrusive reexperiencing immediately following the relief mission was associated with *greater* levels of PTG. That is, the therapists who had the most frequent rumination about their disaster relief work also experienced the greatest level of psychological growth. We concluded that both adaptive and maladaptive cognitive rumination processes may co-exist following secondary exposure, and not all ruminative thoughts related to secondary exposure are inherently maladaptive. This is not a unique finding in the literature, but adds weight to the notion that there can be an adaptive element to at least some experiences currently regarded as secondary trauma symptoms. Another finding of the study was that the therapists' knowledge and skill predicted compassion satisfaction (i.e., sense of gratification from one's work) and negatively predicted (i.e., reduced the likelihood of) burnout.

Lessons Learned and Time-Tested STS Management Strategies

In the absence of compelling empirical guidance for STS management, this segment of the chapter is filled with suggestions based on the author's long, gratifying, trauma-focused career. These strategies are presented as areas for therapists to ponder, or *check-ins*, to encourage therapists' self-reflection and robust secondary trauma stewardship:

Check-in 1. Assess organizational fit. Although STS interventions often emphasize the therapist's coping and self-care strategies, a less pronounced – but equally important – research finding is that burnout is a strong predictor of STS (Shoji et al., 2015). That is, organizational stressors seem to play a key role in the development of STS. Ironically, some trauma-focused organizations lack a trauma-responsive approach with respect to their internal operations, management practices, leadership styles, and workplace culture. Child-focused therapists sometimes erroneously conflate their commitment to children with their commitment to the specific position of employment they hold. Therapists are encouraged to remember that they are responsible for choosing a workplace where staff members use trauma-informed practices not only with clients, but also in their interactions with each other.

Check-in 2. Monitor STS and seek therapy when needed. It can be helpful to use an assessment tool, such as the Professional Quality of Life Scale, Version 5 (ProQOL, Version 5; Stamm, 2009), to monitor STS levels across time. The ProQOL is available online at no cost. Therapists who experience prolonged or intense reactions are encouraged to seek professional support (e.g., mental health services or consultation).

Check-in 3. Engage in self-compassion. Although helping professionals often regard themselves as extremely compassionate toward others, they may have surprisingly little self-compassion. As Jack Kornfield (1994) wisely wrote, "If compassion does not include yourself, it is incomplete" (p. 196). While at work many therapists postpone or forego their own basic needs to eat, hydrate, take bathroom breaks, or rest at work. Too often, trauma-focused professionals move at a frenzied pace during much of their workday, as if in a pressure-filled race toward exhaustion. When therapists slow the pace of their thoughts and movements, pause to breathe, and notice the world around them, they create increased opportunities to reconnect to themselves, value their basic needs, practice greater self-compassion, and sustain the important work of helping others.

Check-in 4. Disentangle from those you help. During sessions it is important for therapists to share a deep empathic connection with the children and caregivers they serve. Afterward, it is equally important to mindfully disengage from clients' experiences to reclaim the therapists' own lives. Without separating from clients' experiences, therapists tend to become saturated with the suffering of others. Too many unprocessed, unsettling, second-hand experiences of anguish are beneficial to neither the client nor the therapist. STS stewardship means refocusing on and reclaiming one's own emotions, thoughts, hardships, aspirations, and loved ones. For therapists who are experiencing this form of saturation, it can be helpful to ritualistically remind themselves at the end of a workday that the clients' experiences do not belong to them, and it is time to re-immerse into their own lives.

Check-in 5. Create a life that balances suffering and joy. If therapists do not inject extremely pleasant or joyous activities into their lives, the balance of experience is likely to tilt heavily toward trauma or suffering. This imbalance is a prescription for psychological fatigue. Therapists are encouraged to assess and monitor the amount of time they spend experiencing joy versus secondary trauma exposure. Therapists who regard scheduling weekly joyful experiences as essential rather than optional remain anchored in a world that involves delight, wonder, and hope. This is critical in maintaining a balanced worldview, given the skewed nature of child-focused therapists' work.

Check-in 6. Create an individualized coping plan. The worst time to decide how to cope with STS is after a therapist is already suffering from it. Therapists can prevent this situation by engaging in anticipatory planning for STS. Therapists should speculate about what situations might be most likely to result in STS (e.g., working with upset caregivers, an abused child, a client who reminds the therapist of a loved one or a personal experience, or suspicion of child abuse) and proactively develop an individualized coping plan so the therapist is prepared to react quickly and effectively to potentially distressing clinical situations. The content of a coping plan usually involves the use of cognitive, behavioral, and social support-based strategies, as well as mindfulness practices.

In cognitive behavior therapy (CBT), clients are encouraged to replace untrue and/or unhelpful thoughts with true and helpful cognitions. Although many therapists are familiar with these tenets of CBT, untrue and unhelpful thoughts persist in the minds of many child-focused therapists. For example, the skewed thought, "almost all children are abused," could be replaced with a cognition recognizing that the therapist's greater awareness of child abuse does not mean that most children are abused. Behavioral activation is a widely used CBT technique that involves scheduling pleasant activities and monitoring whether and/or the extent to which employing the activity is helpful to elevate mood. Noticing and replacing maladaptive behaviors (e.g., alcohol consumption to tune out difficult session content) is also an important behavioral coping strategy. Strengthening work-related and personal social support networks is essential. Mindfulness practices have been positively associated in research with a variety of psychological health indicators, including elevated mood, life satisfaction, improved emotion regulation skills, reduced reactivity to emotional stimuli, and improvements in a range of other symptoms (Keng et al., 2011). Mindfulness skills allow therapists to increase distress tolerance while remaining present.

Check-in 7. Transform the suffering of others into positive growth. Therapists are encouraged to employ strategies to help transform indirect trauma exposure into positive, meaningful, or helpful experiences. To do this, therapists can complete the Posttraumatic Growth Inventory (Tedeschi & Calhoun, 1996) to identify ways in which their work has been enriching to them and continue to consider how their work has led to positive changes (i.e., increased appreciation for life, more meaningful interpersonal relationships, increased sense of personal strength, changed priorities, and a richer existential and spiritual life). Additionally, it is helpful to develop therapist-oriented termination rituals (i.e., outside the clients' or families' awareness) to reconfigure experiences with a child/family into lessons learned or a positive experience shared. For example, after the termination session, the therapist might mentally review the child's treatment, identify the therapist's own regrets or concerns about the child, the treatment, or factors beyond the therapist's control. After identifying these areas, therapists can explore whether the pinpointed concerns reveal insights about the therapist's own history or unresolved issues. Next, the therapist acknowledges ways in which the therapist is enriched because of experiences with the child. Then, the therapist acknowledges how the child's life is better because the therapist was part of it. Finally, the therapist vows to leave behind what cannot be changed or controlled, in order to embrace a lesson learned, new insight, or a positive experience shared with the child or family.

Check-in 8. Maintain hope. Therapists often see clients who are either in or depicting the worst moments of their [the clients'] lives. Exposure to so much suffering can result in moments when therapists struggle to maintain their own hopefulness. One strategy to assist with this issue is to remember that your session with the child or family is only one moment or phase of their life, not the totality of their lives or futures. Surviving trauma does not sentence children to unfulfilling or unproductive lives. The world is full of remarkable survivors, including many public figures, authors, and mental health professionals, who have transformed their traumatic experiences in amazing ways. It is essential to have fervent, unwavering faith that trauma victims can recover, trauma can be transformed, and traumatized individuals can move forward to lead gratifying lives.

Conclusion

Entwined with the enormous gratification of providing child-focused therapy is the toll that therapists pay for caring in the unique way they do. This chapter is written in support of the mental health professionals who courageously march – or sometimes tromp – forward in their work despite its challenges. Although indirect trauma exposure characterizes the work of many child-focused therapists, a variety of research-based strategies have shown promise in helping prevent or ameliorate STS, and additional principles for trauma stewardship have been suggested in the literature. As detailed in this chapter, therapists are encouraged to assess the degree of fitness between their work organization and their own needs, monitor their STS level, show self-compassion, disengage from clients after clinical responsibilities have been completed, develop an individualized coping strategy, balance suffering and joy, transform suffering into growth, and maintain hopefulness. By focusing on STS management and sound trauma stewardship practices, child-focused therapists can both endure the challenges they face and remain torchbearers of hope for the youth they serve.

References

Bercier, M. L., & Maynard, B. R. (2015). Interventions for secondary traumatic stress with mental health workers: A systematic review. *Research on Social Work Practice*, *25*(1), 81–89. https://doi.org/10.1177/1049731513517142

Bride, B. E., Jones, J. L., & Macmaster, S. A. (2007). Correlates of secondary traumatic stress in child protective services workers. *Journal of Evidence-Based Social Work, 4,* 69–80. https://doi.org/10.1300/J394v04n03_05

Bride, B. E., Sprang, G., Hendricks, A., Walsh, C. R., Mathieu, F., Hangartner, K., Ross, L. A., Fisher, P., & Miller, B. C. (2024). Principles for secondary traumatic stress-responsive practice: An expert consensus approach. *Psychological Trauma: Theory, Research, Practice, and Policy, 16*(8), 1301–1308. https://doi.org/10.1037/tra0001575

Elwood, L. S., Mott, J., Lohr, J. M., & Galovski, T. E. (2011). Secondary trauma symptoms in clinicians: A critical review of the construct, specificity, and implications for trauma-focused treatment. *Clinical Psychology Review, 31*(1), 25–36. https://doi.org/10.1016/j.cpr.2010.09.004

Figley, C. R. (1995). *Compassion fatigue: Coping with secondary traumatic stress disorder in those who treat the traumatized.* Brunner Mazel.

Keng, S. L., Smoski, M. J., & Robins, C. J. (2011). Effects of mindfulness on psychological health: A review of empirical studies. *Clinical Psychology Review, 31*(6), 1041–1056. https://doi.org/10.1016/j.cpr.2011.04.006

Kim, J., Chesworth, B., Franchino-Olsen, H., & Macy, R. J. (2022). A scoping review of vicarious trauma interventions for service providers working with people who have experienced traumatic events. *Trauma, Violence & Abuse, 23*(5), 1437–1460. https://doi.org/10.1177/1524838021991310

Kintzle, S., Yarvis, J. S., & Bride, B. E. (2013). Secondary traumatic stress in military primary and mental health care providers. *Military Medicine, 178,* 1310–1315. https://doi.org/10.7205/MILMED-D-13-00087

Kornfield, J. (1994). *Buddha's little instruction book.* Bantam Books.

Mitchell, J. T. (1983). When disaster strikes . . . The critical incident stress debriefing process. *Journal of Emergency Medical Services, 13*(11), 49–52.

National Child Traumatic Stress Network, Secondary Traumatic Stress Committee. (2011). *Secondary traumatic stress: A fact sheet for child-serving professionals.* National Center for Child Traumatic Stress. https://www.nctsn.org/sites/default/files/resources/fact-sheet/secondary_traumatic_stress_child_serving_professionals.pdf

Pearlman, L. A., & Saakvitne, K. W. (1995). *Trauma and the therapist: Countertransference and vicarious traumatization in psychotherapy with incest survivors.* W.W. Norton.

Potocky, M., & Guskovict, K. L. (2020). *Addressing secondary traumatic stress: Models and promising practices.* Grantmakers Concerned with Immigrants and Refugees. https://www.gcir.org/sites/default/files/resources/final_Addressing%20Secondary%20Traumatic%20Stress%20Final%20Report%20%28Sept%202020%29.pdf

Shoji, K., Lesnierowska, M., Smoktunowicz, E., Bock, J., Luszczynska, A., Benight, C. C., & Cieslak, R. (2015). What comes first, job burnout or secondary traumatic stress? Findings from two longitudinal studies from the U.S. and Poland. *PLoS One, 10*(8), e0136730. https://doi.org/10.1371/journal.pone.0136730

Stamm, B. H. (2009). *Professional quality of life: Compassion satisfaction and fatigue version 5 (ProQOL).* www.proqol.org.

Tedeschi, R. G., & Calhoun, L. G. (1996). The posttraumatic growth inventory: Measuring the positive legacy of trauma. *Journal of Traumatic Stress, 9*(3), 455–471.

Tedeschi, R. G., & Calhoun, L. G. (2004). Target article: "Posttraumatic growth: Conceptual foundations and empirical evidence." *Psychological Inquiry, 15*(1), 1–18. https://doi.org/10.1207/s15327965pli1501_01

Tominaga, Y., Goto, T., Shelby, J., Oshio, A., Nishi, D., & Takahashi, S. (2019, August). Secondary trauma and posttraumatic growth among mental health clinicians involved in disaster relief activities following the 2011 Tohoku earthquake and tsunami in Japan. *Counselling Psychology Quarterly.* https://doi.org/10.1080/09515 070.2019.1639493

van Dernoot Lipsky, L. (2009). *Trauma stewardship: An everyday guide to caring for self while caring for others.* Berrett-Koehler Publishers.

Whitt-Woosley, A., & Sprang, G. (2018). Secondary traumatic stress in social science researchers of trauma-exposed populations. *Journal of Aggression, Maltreatment & Trauma, 27*(5), 475–486.

CHAPTER 23
WORKING WITH CHILDHOOD SEXUAL ABUSE
CONSIDERATIONS FOR PROFESSIONAL DEVELOPMENT FOR PLAY THERAPISTS

Anne Stewart and Hannah Pellegrino Jarrett

Childhood and adolescence are times of rapid physical and mental growth characterized by dependence, vulnerability, and resilience. Unfortunately, statistics show it is a time too often characterized by interpersonal violence and harm. Given the number of children who experience childhood sexual abuse (CSA) and the significant compounding mental and physical health implications related to trauma experiences, mental health providers must receive adequate training to support child survivors and their families. The literature demonstrates that mental health professionals, including social workers, school counselors, counselors, and psychologists, report feeling underprepared to address the complex needs of survivors (Kenny & Abreu, 2015).

Research shows that most graduate programs for counseling professionals lack specific training focused on working with children who have experienced trauma, such as sexual abuse, or include training via optional elective courses (Kenny & Abreu, 2015; Mathew et al., 2023). Despite the recognition of trauma as a public health crisis, only 20% of doctoral training programs offered a trauma psychology course or practicum experience working with traumatized clients (Cook et al., 2017). While accrediting bodies have endorsed the importance of training students in trauma-informed practices, programs note significant challenges in adding new courses due to accreditation standards and in attempting to integrate the information into existing classes (Adams, 2019; Cook et al., 2019).

Given the scarcity of graduate coursework, it is not surprising that 78% of practitioners stated they were not trained in evidence-based treatment (EBT) approaches for CSA (Czincz & Romano, 2013). Some practitioners acknowledge their preference for using other non-EBT approaches

DOI: 10.4324/9781003451549-27

and cite inadequate time and resources for training and supervision or consultation in EBT as barriers to acquiring pertinent knowledge and skills (Cook et al., 2017). These findings highlight the need for increased education and training focused on working with child and adolescent CSA survivors through formal graduate education and continuing professional development. While not all play therapists are expected to have specialized CSA or complex trauma training, there is a need for basic competencies in CSA. Hence, children and adolescents receive appropriate treatment from competent providers.

Underlying Assumptions to Keep in Heart and Mind

As we examine considerations for professional development related to CSA for play therapists, we first invite you to reflect on your knowledge, clinical skills, and attitudes regarding trauma-informed principles and CSA. It is important to acknowledge that identifying, responding to, and supporting child and adolescent survivors of CSA can be profoundly gratifying and also clinically complex and emotionally distressing for providers. We encourage you to be generous in extending compassion to yourself as you continue reading the remainder of this chapter and work to support the healing and well-being of children and adolescents.

Reframe Self-Compassion as an Ethical Imperative

Recognizing that working with CSA survivors will understandably result in emotional distress necessitates that play therapists consistently and compassionately attend to their well-being. Research has shown that, over time, mental health providers may experience reduced empathy and less compassion toward their clients. Professional development can help grow and build the ability to maintain an empathic connection and strengthen clinical competencies (Butler et al., 2017). Obtaining education and training to prevent secondary traumatic stress (STS) is a crucial component of professional development. Strategies such as incorporating effective self-care routines, knowing the signs of STS and burnout, and having supervisory and collegial support can help mitigate possible negative impacts.

As discussed, the prevalence of trauma in our culture is high, and studies have demonstrated that CSA among mental health providers is common, with studies noting prevalence rates ranging from 10% to 20% (Leung et al., 2022). Opportunities to process a clinician's possible history of maltreatment can be addressed through personal counseling, and participating in supervision and professional development can enhance personal well-being and professional efficacy.

Practice With Cultural Humility

Practicing cultural humility is vital in all our work and particularly salient in working with survivors of CSA. Cultural humility is defined as "a life-long process of self-reflection and self-critique whereby the individual not only learns about another's culture, but one starts with an examination of her/his own beliefs and cultural identities" (Tervalon & Murray-Garcia, 1998, p. 1) The definition also includes the importance of "redressing power imbalances" and creating clinical and advocacy relationships with clients and communities. These elements are all relevant activities in cases of CSA (Tervalon & Murray-Garcia, 1998, p. 1). Vulnerable or oppressed youth (e.g., LGBTQAI+, disabled, and unhoused) are at disproportionate risk for CSA and would benefit most from systems-level actions and personalized interventions that address the negative impact of policies and institutional biases.

Adopt a Trauma-Informed Care Approach

Many mental health and educational organizations and community agencies incorporate trauma-informed care (TIC) tenets at individual and organizational levels. Adopting a TIC viewpoint in delivering CSA services acknowledges that culture will influence the meaning of traumatic events, the understanding of symptoms, and the appropriateness of seeking professional assistance. Successfully implemented, we believe that applying the principles of TIC helps ensure services are conducted in ways that honor the relevant cultural context for the child and family and help reduce institutional harm by addressing the four R's of TIC. First, the persons in the organization and mission of the organization *realize* the broad impact of trauma and acknowledge multiple pathways for recovery; secondly, they *recognize* the signs and symptoms of trauma for anyone involved in the system (clients, families, staff); thirdly, they *respond* proactively by integrating knowledge about trauma into policies, procedures, and practices; and, lastly, they seek to actively resist *retraumatization* in the provision of services (Substance Abuse and Mental Health Services Administration, 2014).

Play therapists can also promote resilience by closely monitoring the client's physical and psychological safety using a strengths-based approach, shifting from "What is wrong with you?" to "What happened to you?" "What has worked for you?" and "Are you safe now?" (Perry & Winfrey, 2021).

As you continue your professional development, we encourage you to adopt and deepen your knowledge of trauma-informed care principles and conduct your work with the presumption that your child and adolescent clients (as well as their family members and your colleagues) may have experienced trauma, including the possibility of CSA (Knight, 2021).

Foundational Knowledge and Basic Competencies

All mental health practitioners working with children and adolescents need foundational knowledge and clinical competencies to screen for and respond to disclosures of CSA routinely. Efforts to increase competent trauma treatment have recognized several challenges and generated recommendations for training for working with CSA victims (Cook et al., 2019; Kenny & Abreu, 2015). The following topics reflect these findings and recommendations for CSA and trauma training.

Obtain a Trauma History

One unfortunate impediment to effective CSA care is the failure of clinicians to routinely inquire about the client's trauma exposure (Hepworth & McGowan, 2013). This may be due to not wishing to upset the client, prioritizing other client concerns, or avoidance due to the therapist's discomfort or perceived competence, such as not knowing how to inquire and respond if the client confirms child sexual abuse or trauma (Cook et al., 2019). Since trauma survivors are more likely to disclose this information when explicitly asked (Briere & Zaidi, 1989), it is vital to engage in conversations with caregivers and children in your intake process and throughout treatment.

Consult Your Professional Code of Ethics

Play therapists are expected to be familiar with and act by the code of ethics and standards of practice associated with their discipline-specific license or certification (counseling, social work, marriage and family,

psychology, school counseling, school psychology, etc.) and state stat-
utes and regulations related to sexual abuse and mandated reporting
procedures. If you work in an organization, you should follow the policies and guidelines for founded or suspected CSA cases. In addition, we
want to encourage you to consult the Association for Play Therapy (APT
at https://www.a4pt.org/) and the National Child Traumatic Stress
Network (NCTSN at https://www.nctsn.org/) websites for information about training and resources.

Know CSA Symptoms and Mandatory Reporting

Our understanding of child sexual abuse continues to evolve and now
encompasses a wide range of sexual victimization experiences, including trafficking, obscene text messages, and interactions on various social
media platforms. The use of social media to target and sexually exploit
youth is growing, and research indicates that one in three children who
use social media can expect unwelcome sexual interactions online before
they turn 18 (Setter et al., 2022). While child sexual abuse definitions
vary, every state and territory has adopted definitions and approved stat-
utes related to child maltreatment.

Recognizing when children are reenacting or communicating about
a traumatic experience is another essential part of the assessment and
screening process. For play therapists, it is important to be familiar with
the presentation of a child engaged in posttraumatic play or expression.
For children who have experienced CSA, examples of posttraumatic play
or self-expression could include repetition of themes of threat and danger, poor interpersonal boundaries, or reenacting specific aspects of their
sexual abuse (Gil, 2017).

Offer Attuned Responses to Disclosures and Conduct Ongoing Assessments for Abuse

Disclosure of CSA is now understood as a process and not a discrete
event with clear evidence that many children are reluctant to disclose.
Therefore, assessment for possible abuse is an ongoing endeavor. Play
therapists are uniquely positioned to hear a verbal disclosure or witness
play depicting scenarios or themes of harm or threat. It is critical to
respond in ways that are supportive and congruent with your role, which
is most frequently as the client's therapist. CSA survivors are at increased

risk for revictimization, and receiving training can help ensure we engage in ways that convey our belief in the client, develop comfort in directly inquiring about trauma and abuse, explore the impact of intersecting identities as it relates to systems of oppression, and resist assumptions, such as sexual abuse not occurring with males.

Subsequently, when reporting your concern about the possibility of CSA, it is essential to have the relevant information for the caregivers and maintain clear boundaries with collateral contacts, especially with colleagues from child protective services, law enforcement, and the legal system. Establishing boundaries and clarifying roles will enhance achieving helpful outcomes for the survivor (Kenney-Noziska, 2025).

We encourage you to seek consultation with a supervisor, even if you believe you know the appropriate course of action. CSA cases are often complex and psychologically taxing. Of course, it is critical to document the information and processes you engaged in promptly and accurately.

Professional Development Considerations in the Treatment of CSA Survivors

Adopting a contextual, culturally-attuned, and holistic approach when working with children who have experienced CSA was emphasized by Saunders (2011), who stated, "Best practice is for treatment to be responsive to the individual psychological needs of each victim and not be based primarily on the nature of the emergent abuse report" (p. 176).

Multidisciplinary Team Work and Role Clarification

Responses to CSA allow play therapists to engage with many systems, including child protective services, medical teams, law enforcement, the legal system, the educational system, child welfare agencies, and foster care. Research demonstrates that a multidisciplinary approach can enhance the number of successful prosecutions and improve mental health outcomes (Herbert & Bromfield, 2019) and is regarded as the standard of care for CSA (Murray et al., 2014). Because play therapists can expect to be asked to participate in legal proceedings, including the possibility of testifying in court, it is important to reflect on and establish your scope of practice (and continue to monitor your involvement). This will help roles remain clear with child protection and legal system representatives. Child Advocacy Centers (CAC) were created to offer integrated responses to CSA and are typically strong treatment team partners for play therapists working with CSA survivors.

Vulnerable and Oppressed Children and Adolescents and CSA

It is recommended that play therapists and mental health providers routinely review emerging research related to CSA, including populations that experience higher rates of CSA and treatment considerations for populations that are at increased vulnerability to such trauma exposure. Research indicates that children and adolescents do not experience exposure to trauma and sexual abuse equally. Youth who are marginalized are disproportionately exposed to adverse events with higher rates of childhood sexual abuse for children with LGBTQIA+ identities (Georges, 2023), children with disabilities (Brendli et al., 2022), and children who are experiencing homelessness or unstable housing (Bender et al., 2015)., including refugees and unaccompanied minors (van Os et al., 2016).

Treatment of CSA

As previously noted, a trauma-informed framework is strongly recommended when working with survivors of CSA. The depth of research support for CSA and trauma treatments is growing and varies widely, so it is essential to think critically about your scope of practice. Available research suggests that providing intervention from a trauma-informed framework involves sensitively considering brain development and functioning. Foundational principles of brain development and functioning have been innovatively translated into therapeutic approaches and can be used to inform conceptualization and integrated into play therapy practice. Play therapists are also encouraged to consider polyvictimization (exposure to multiple forms of maltreatment, including different types of abuse, crime, and violence) in their work with clients to develop comprehensive interventions (Finkelhor et al., 2009).

They Are Integrating Neurobiologically Informed Findings

Some consistent components of neurobiologically informed therapeutic approaches are particularly relevant for work with survivors of (CSA: 1) Acknowledging that the developmental age and state of regulation impact neurological capacity and functioning. By attending to a child's developmental age and state of regulation, play therapists can attune their presence and therapeutic support to appropriately and effectively respond. 2) Exposure to adverse experiences can negatively impact brain development and functioning. Play therapists must gather a thorough developmental history and routinely assess for risk and safety. 3) The brain maintains its ability to create new neural pathways and rewire existing pathways through repeated experiences. Lastly, and importantly for our work across all theoretical orientations, 4) Relationships and interpersonal interactions can potentially support neurological healing. Neuroscience-informed resources continue to develop, and you are encouraged to integrate these principles into your existing theoretical framework.

Generating Your Treatment Framework

In addition to working from a trauma-informed framework and integrating principles from neurologically informed approaches, play therapists should be informed by their theoretical orientation, professional knowledge, relevant clinical competencies, and an examination of research support for treatments for CSA as they create their professional development plan related to interventions. We refer the reader to the other chapters for in-depth discussions of the treatment of CSA for children and adolescents to inform and guide their process.

In addition to filial approaches, Trauma-Focused Cognitive Behavioral Therapy (TF-CBT), Eye Movement Desensitization and Reprocessing (EMDR), and Trauma-Focused Integrated Play Therapy are commonly used with children and adolescents who have experienced CSA (Kenny & Abreu, 2015; Shelby, 2025). TF-CBT and EMDR have empirical support for use with survivors of CSA, and these approaches have also been integrated into play-based approaches.

Ending the Chapter With the Beginning of Your Journey: Professional Development Personalized for You

Your professional development journey is likely under construction, and you are invited to use this book to create a personalized road map. You might find it is relevant to begin by solidifying your foundational knowledge of the treatment needs of CSA survivors or determine that exploration into your theoretical orientation will help consolidate your conceptual framework in relationship to your work with CSA survivors.

You may be curious to investigate an emerging approach with a client who has experienced CSA as the first "point of interest" for you or is ready to examine one of the many cogent topics aligned with CSA treatment. Whatever step you decide to take, we wish you well as you embark on your adventure in learning and healing.

Considerations for Practice: Key Takeaways

The key takeaways listed below include information relevant to the prevalence and impact of childhood sexual abuse (CSA), as well as reminders for the play therapists engaged in this important work.

- Mental health professionals report feeling underprepared to support children and adolescents who have experienced CSA. Before and during work with this population, play therapists must reflect on their personal experiences, education, and clinical training.
- Working with victims of CSA can be emotionally taxing and clinically complex, and potentially lead to secondary traumatic stress (STS) among practitioners. It is crucial for play therapists to prioritize self-care and seek supervision or consultation to mitigate these effects.
- Practicing with cultural humility and implementing principles of trauma-informed care is foundational in responding to the needs of children and adolescents who have experienced CSA.
- Play therapists working with victims of CSA must be prepared to actively collaborate with multidisciplinary teams, review research on evidence-based interventions, and integrate of principles of neurobiology.

We wish you well as you create your plan to enhance your CSA competencies by through practicing self-compassion, working with cultural humility, participating in education, training, and supervision, and adopting a trauma-informed approach.

References

Adams, C. (2019). *Teaching trauma theory and practice to master's level counselors-in-training: A multiple case study* [Doctoral dissertation, University of Tennessee]. Tennessee Research and Creative Exchange. https://trace.utk.edu/utk_graddiss/5594/

Bender, K., Brown, S. M., Thompson, S. J., Ferguson, K. M., & Langenderfer, L. (2015). Multiple victimizations before and after leaving home are associated with PTSD, depression, and substance use disorder among homeless youth. *Child Maltreatment*, *20*(2), 115–124. https://doi.org/10.1177/1077559514562859

Brendli, K. R., Broda, M. D., & Brown, R. (2022). Children with intellectual disability and victimization: A logistic regression analysis. *Child Maltreatment*, *27*(3), 320–324. https://doi.org/10.1177/1077559521994177

Briere, J., & Zaidi, L. Y. (1989). Sexual abuse histories and sequelae in female psychiatric emergency room patients. *The American Journal of Psychiatry*, *146*(12), 1602–1606. http://dx.doi.org/10.1176/ajp.146.12.1602

Butler, L. D., Carello, J., & Maguin, E. (2017). Trauma, stress, and self-care in clinical training: Predictors of burnout, decline in health status, secondary traumatic stress symptoms, and compassion satisfaction. *Psychological Trauma: Theory, Research, Practice, and Policy*, *9*(4), 416–424. https://doi.org/10.1037/tra0000187

Cook, J. M., Newman, E., & Simiola, V. (2019). Trauma training: Competencies, initiatives, and resources. *Psychotherapy*, *56*(3), 409–421. https://doi.org/10.1037/pst0000233

Cook, J. M., Simiola, V., Ellis, A. E., & Thompson, R. (2017). Training in trauma psychology: A national survey of doctoral graduate programs. *Training and Education in Professional Psychology*, *11*(2), 108–114. https://doi.org/10.1037/tep0000150

Czincz, J., & Romano, E. (2013). Childhood sexual abuse: Community-based treatment practices and predictors of use of evidence-based practices. *Child and Adolescent Mental Health*, *18*(4), 240–246. https://doi.org/10.1111/camh.12011

Finkelhor, D., Turner, H., Ormrod, R., & Hamby, S. L. (2009). Violence, abuse, and crime exposure in a national sample of children and youth. *Pediatrics*, *124*(5), 1411–1423. https://doi.org/10.1542/peds.2009-0467

Georges, E. (2023). Review of the literature on the intersection of LGBTQ youth and CSEC: More than a monolith. *Current Pediatrics Reports*, *11*(4), 105–115.

Gil, E. (2017). *Posttraumatic play in children: What clinicians need to know.* Guilford Press.

Hepworth, I., & McGowan, L. (2013). Do mental health professionals enquire about childhood sexual abuse during routine mental health assessment in acute mental health settings? A substantive literature review. *Journal of Psychiatric and Mental Health Nursing*, *20*(6), 473–483. http://dx.doi.org/10.1111/j.1365-2850.2012.01939.x

Herbert, J. L., & Bromfield, L. (2019). Better together? A review of evidence for multidisciplinary teams responding to physical and sexual child abuse. *Trauma, Violence, & Abuse*, *20*(2), 214–228. https://doi.org/10.1177/1524838017697268

Kenney-Noziska, S. (2025). Systemic applications: The play therapist, child protection, and the legal system. In D. A. Crenshaw, A. L. Stewart, & D. Ray (Eds.), *Play therapy: A comprehensive guide to theory and practice.* Guilford Press.

Kenny, M. C., & Abreu, R. L. (2015). Training mental health professionals in child sexual abuse: Curricular guidelines. *Journal of Child Sexual Abuse*, *24*(5), 572–591. https://doi.org/10.1080/10538712.2015.1042185

Knight, C. (2021). Trauma-informed supervision. In K. O'Donoghue & L. Engelbrecht (Eds.), *The Routledge international handbook of social work supervision* (1st ed.). Routledge. https://doi.org/10.4324/9780429285943

Leung, T., Schmidt, F., & Mushquash, C. (2022). A personal history of trauma and experience of secondary traumatic stress, vicarious trauma, and burnout in mental health workers: A systematic literature review. *Psychological Trauma: Theory, Research, Practice, and Policy, 15*(2), 213–221.

Mathew, S., Qiao, B., & Kaszynski, E. (2023). Training counselors to vide trauma informed care: CACREP-accredited program survey. *International Journal for Multidisciplinary Research, 5*(4). https://doi.org/10.36948/ijfmr.2023.v05i04.4510

Murray, L. K., Nguyen, A., & Cohen, J. A. (2014). Child sexual abuse. *Child and Adolescent Psychiatric Clinics of North America, 23*(2), 321–337. https://doi.org/10.1016/j.chc.2014.01.003

Perry, B. D., & Winfrey, O. (2021). *What happened to you?: Conversations on trauma resilience and healing* (1st ed.). Flatiron Books.

Saunders, B. E. (2011). Determining best practice for treating sexually victimized children. In P. Goodyear-Brown (Ed.), *Handbook of child sexual abuse* (pp. 171–197). Wiley and Sons. https://doi.org/10.1002/9781118094822.ch8

Setter, C., Green, N., Newman, N., & Perry, J. (2022). *Against child sexual exploitation and abuse online.* WeProtect Global Alliance.

Shelby, J. (2025). Treatment of child sexual abuse: A practical guide for play therapists. In D. A. Crenshaw, A. L. Stewart, & D. Ray (Eds.), *Play therapy: A comprehensive guide to theory and practice.* Guilford Press.

Substance Abuse and Mental Health Services Administration. (2014). *SAMHSA's concept of trauma and guidance for trauma-informed approach.* https://store.samhsa.gov/product/samhsas-concept-trauma-and-guidance-trauma-informed-approach/sma14-4884-

Tervalon, M., & Murray-Garcia, J. (1998). Cultural humility versus cultural competence: A critical distinction in defining physician training outcomes in multicultural education. *Journal of Health Care for the Poor and Underserved, 9*(2), 117–125. https://doi.org/10.1353/hpu.2010.0233

van Os, E. C. C., Kalverboer, M. E., Zijlstra, A. E., Post, W. J., & Knorth, E. J. (2016). Knowledge of the unknown child: A systematic review of the elements of the best interests of the child assessment for recently arrived refugee children. *Clinical Child Family Psychology Review, 19*(3), 185–203. https://doi.org/10.1007/s10567-016-0209-y

INDEX

Note: Page numbers in *italics* indicate figures, and page numbers in **bold** indicate tables in the text.

For Product Safety Concerns and Information please contact our EU
representative GPSR@taylorandfrancis.com
Taylor & Francis Verlag GmbH, Kaufingerstraße 24, 80331 München, Germany

www.ingramcontent.com/pod-product-compliance
Lightning Source LLC
Chambersburg PA
CBHW050340270326
41926CB00016B/3534